AF560173

Literature's Children

Bloomsbury Perspectives on Children's Literature

Bloomsbury Perspectives on Children's Literature seeks to expand the range and quality of research in children's literature through publishing innovative monographs by leading and rising scholars in the field. With an emphasis on cross and interdisciplinary studies, this series takes literary approaches as a starting point, drawing on the particular capacity for children's literature to open out into other disciplines.

Titles in the Series:

Adulthood in Children's Literature, Vanessa Joosen

The Courage to Imagine: The Child Hero in Children's Literature, Roni Natov

Ethics in British Children's Literature: Unexamined Life, Lisa Sainsbury

Fashioning Alice: The Career of Lewis Carroll's Icon, 1860–1901, Kiera Vaclavik

From Tongue to Text: A New Reading of Children's Poetry, Debbie Pullinger

Literature's Children: The Critical Child and the Art of Idealization, Louise Joy

Rereading Childhood Books: A Poetics, Alison Waller

Forthcoming Titles:

Metaphysics of Children's Literature: Climbing Fuzzy Mountains, Lisa Sainsbury

The Styles of Children's Literature: A Century of Change, Peter Hunt

Literature's Children

The Critical Child and the Art of Idealization

Louise Joy

B L O O M S B U R Y
NEW DELHI • LONDON • OXFORD • NEW YORK • SYDNEY

BLOOMSBURY INDIA
Bloomsbury Publishing India Pvt. Ltd
Second Floor, LSC Building No. 4, DDA Complex, Pocket C–6&7,
Vasant Kunj, New Delhi 110070

BLOOMSBURY, BLOOMSBURY ACADEMIC INDIA and the Diana logo are trademarks of Bloomsbury Publishing Plc

First published in India 2024
First published in Great Britain 2019

Cover design: Eleanor Rose
Cover image © Artists Estate / Bridgeman Images

This edition published with permission from Bloomsbury Publishing Plc, 50 Bedford Square, London, WC1B3DP, UK

A catalogue record for this book is available from the British Library.
A catalogue record for this book is available from the Library of Congress.

ISBN: 978-93-61311-33-8

Series: Bloomsbury Perspectives on Children's Literature

Typeset by Newgen KnowledgeWorks Pvt. Ltd., Chennai, India
Printed and bound in India by Replika Press Pvt. Ltd.

Contents

Acknowledgements

Work for this book was made possible by support from the Cambridge Centre for Research in the Arts, Social Sciences and Humanities; from Homerton College, University of Cambridge; and from the Friends of the Princeton University Library.

I am immensely fortunate to have so many people at Homerton College and in the Cambridge English Faculty on whom I can count for support, both practical and moral, and for stimulating intellectual exchange. For their advice, encouragement and collegiality over the years, I would like to thank Penny Barton, Pete de Bolla, David Clifford, Bill Foster, Pam Hirsch, Mary Jacobus, Matthew Moss, Kate Pretty, Corinna Russell, Geoff Ward and Steve Watts. I would especially like to thank David Whitley, who has been a source of exceptional kindness and wisdom, and who has quietly emboldened and motivated me from the sidelines. She may not know it, but Philippa Hunt kick-started my adult return to children's literature and indelibly shaped my thinking about children, literature and education. As this interest became more scholarly, it was fanned and given clearer direction and definition by Morag Styles and Maria Nikolajeva. I am enormously grateful to all three formidable women for their encouragement, their mentorship and for the example of their own professionalism.

Working with such passionate, driven and intellectually curious undergraduate and graduate students is a source of constant pleasure and inspiration. Notable among these are Clémentine Beauvais, Jessica Lim, Debbie Pullinger and Kate Wakely-Mulroney, in dialogue with whom I have tested out and developed my own ideas and interests and from whom I have learned, and continue to learn, so much.

The team at Bloomsbury have steered this project through with efficiency and good humour. I should like in particular to thank Lisa Sainsbury, the series editor, for her enthusiasm and for her generous and incisive remarks at every stage. She has been a critical reader in the best possible sense, and I have valued her input greatly. David Avital, Clara Herberg and Mark Richardson have been gracious and easy to work with throughout the process, and I am very grateful to them for being so patient and so helpful. Thank you, too, to Alka Kulkarni for her scrupulous copy-editing and to Angelique Neumann for steering the project through its final stages.

Earlier versions of Chapters 2 and 3 appeared in *Literary Cultures of the Child* (2018), edited by Andrew O'Malley, and *The Aesthetics of Children's Poetry: A Study of Children's Verse in English* (2017), edited by Kate Wakely-Mulroney and Louise Joy. I am grateful to Routledge and Palgrave, respectively, for permission to reproduce portions of these. An earlier version of Chapter 4 appeared in Tim Webb's *Towards a Lachrymology: Tears in Literature & Cultural History* (2012). Thank you to *Litteraria Pragenzia* for permission to adapt this. Parts of Chapter 6 appeared in Peter Hunt's collection of essays, *J. R. R. Tolkien: The Hobbit and The Lord of the Rings* (2013) and Chapter 7 in *Children's Literature Association Quarterly* 14.1 (Spring 2016). I am grateful to Palgrave and Johns Hopkins University Press for permission to reproduce these. I am also grateful to Andrew O'Malley, Peter Hunt and Tim Webb for invaluable comments on draft chapters during these early stages.

Conversations with friends have sustained me through the project. Thank you to Ruth Abbott, Ellie Birne, Georgina Evans, Sarah Haggarty, Zoe Jaques, Jane Partner, Sophie Read, Marcus Waithe, Alice Wilson and Jane Wright.

Above all, thanks to my parents, Hilary Joy and Martin Joy, from whose love and nurture it all originally stems, and my children, Zachary and Tobias Williams, whose existence puts it all in perspective. My greatest debt of gratitude is to my husband, Richard Williams, who makes it all possible. I dedicate this book to him, with love.

Introduction

As Matthew Lipman has observed, 'children are not easily prevented from thinking' (Lipman, 2003, p. 1). The existence of children's literature testifies to the child's need to imagine and to wonder, to question and to doubt. The very diversity of such literature evidences children's eagerness to reach beyond the same familiar mental horizons. And yet literary scholarship which concerns itself with the child reader (invariably envisaged as a monolithic category) is repeatedly drawn back to an idea that the child reader is inert: at one extreme, a passive receptacle for the adult to fill, and at the other, an impossibility. The discursive conceit of the *tabula rasa* – the child as that which the adult desires it to be – continues to loom large in children's literature scholarship, even though the empirical validity of the idea has long been disproven. As Clémentine Beauvais has recently observed, its continued dominance is expressed most vividly in the readiness with which critics invoke Jacqueline Rose's totemic thesis, even as they purportedly seek to distance themselves from it (Beauvais, 2015). The idea that the literary text manipulates the child reader to serve adult ends remains firmly entrenched, whether those ends are seen to be dictated by the desires of the author (Jackie Wullschlager), the agenda of the narrator (Barbara Wall), the aesthetic demands of the text (Perry Nodelman) or the ideologies embedded in discourse (Stephens) – be they patriarchal (Lissa Paul), heteronormative (Kenneth Kidd) or occidental (Roderick McGillis). This hermeneutics of suspicion reaches its acme in oft-cited works by Jacqueline Rose and James Kincaid which identify the power dynamics at operation in children's literature as mechanisms for the subjugation of the child, but it is also present in more dilute form in a notion such as Peter Hunt's, that 'the realisation of a text, and especially of a text for children, is closely involved with questions of control, and of the techniques through which power is exercised over, or shared with, the reader' (Hunt 1988, p. 163), and discernible too in notions such as Jack Zipes's Marxist conviction that '[a]t the same time as the child reads and views signs, he or she is being configured by the material conditions of a particular social class, ethnic group, region, and genetic background within a particular field of children's literature production' (Zipes, 2009, p. 6).

A number of critics have recently begun to challenge this metanarrative which has held such sway over children's literature criticism since the 1980s, and to attempt to shift the terms of the debate. For example, David Rudd's 2013 book, *Reading the Child in Children's Literature*, concludes with the wish that 'instead of claiming that we can only *text*, or *page*, or, indeed, simply *read* the child in a self-indulgent, nostalgic way, there is now the opportunity . . . to take cognizance of the child who might text back' (Rudd, p. 191). This acknowledgement of the child's resistance to being positioned by the text is central to Clémentine Beauvais's 2015 study, *The Mighty Child: Time and Power in Children's Literature*, which complicates the nature of the power structures at work in children's literature, seeking to move debates away from the belief that the adult is always an 'omnipotent, manipulative, authoritarian, repressive, oppressive entity', and instead proposing that at the heart of 'the didactic discourse of contemporary children's literature, even at its most didactic, lies a tension of powers – of time-bound powers – between the authoritative adult and its desired addressee, the mighty child' (p. 3). Beauvais's category of the 'mighty child' – who is 'not just a subject but also a project' (p. 205) – provides us with a much-needed way of identifying the audience of children's literature as one defined more by its *potential* – emphasizing the implicit unpredictability of the process of didacticism at work in the exchanges which take place in and through literature, exchanges which play out what she characterizes as 'the paradoxical adult desire to *ask the child didactically for an unpredictable future*' (p. 4) – than by its impotence. However, each of these counterarguments which have sought to provide a non-suspicious account of the unique dynamics at work in children's literature has stayed faithful to the idea, even as this idea is problematized, which critics including Jacqueline Rose and Peter Hunt placed firmly at the heart of the debate in the 1980s: that what is centrally at stake is *power*. So firmly established is the belief that children's literature is fundamentally concerned with *power* that it has even been identified as that which provides its quintessential definition. Maria Nikolajeva, for example, has argued that 'the particular characteristic of children's literature is its focus on child/adult power hierarchy, just as the specifics of feminist literature is the gender-related power structures, and the specifics of postcolonial literature the ethnic-related power structures' (2010, p. 8).[1]

Literature's Children proposes that one of the reasons why, despite repeated attempts to do so, we have found it so difficult to kick into the long grass this unsavoury conviction that the child reader is necessarily a victim of adult machination is that it is intertwined with another totemic belief which cuts through children's literature criticism, and which we have not yet been prepared to relinquish: the belief that what children's literature texts essentially do is to *idealize* the worlds they represent. As Peter Hunt has put it, literary texts for children, '[p]erhaps more than any other texts . . . reflect society as it wishes to be, as it wishes to be seen, and as it unconsciously reveals itself to be' (p. 2). This is a belief which is played out again and again in critical discussion of literary works for children, and it is a belief which has taken various different forms. One of its manifestations is the observation made by critics including James Holt McGavran (1999) and Anne Higonnet (1998) that much children's literature since the middle of the nineteenth century channels or redirects versions of the *romantic* child. These accounts tend to place an emphasis on the importance of the concept of 'innocence' (Natov, 2003; Thacker and Webb, 2002, p. 4) in their efforts to determine the status of works of children's literature as such. Given the pre-eminence in Western thought of the belief so forcefully articulated by Michel Foucault not merely that knowledge is a form of, but moreover that knowledge *is*, power, the concept of innocence, etymologically intertwined with ideas of ignorance, immediately introduces – or takes us back to – questions of domination and subordination, and the presumed affiliation of these with knowledge, on the one hand, and absence of knowledge on the other. Continual recourse to the concept of the romantic child as a means of accounting for the idealizing tendencies in children's literature thus tethers the idea of idealization to a discussion of the power play between experience and inexperience, the fallen and the unfallen. A different variant of a similar theme is the critical argument that children's works (especially those of the second half of the nineteenth century) manifest a 'cult of the child', taking up the phrase coined in 1889 by Ernest Dowson, in which authors for children represent worlds in which the child is protected from routine pain and hardship. Such accounts, for example, those by James Kincaid and U. C. Knoepflmacher, have emphasized the importance of 'delight', both that of the protagonists' carefree existence evoked *in* the text and that of the audience's aesthetic pleasure evoked *by* it. As discussions of aesthetic pleasure have transmuted inexorably into discussions of idealized 'erotic bliss', the matrices involved in the act of reading have become configured as interchangeable with the matrices involved in the act of desiring, once again bringing to the fore issues of domination (gazing, wanting, appropriating, consuming). A further manifestation of the same critical tendency can be seen in the application of the label 'golden age' to certain works of, or indeed whole eras of, children's literature. As its name documents, to ascribe this label is in part to identify such works by way of their perceived pastoralism.[2] But moreover it is to confer on them a kind of canonical, *idealized* status – to imply that in such texts we see an epitomized realization of those values which we aspire to see upheld in children's literature. The insistence of critics including Humphrey Carpenter, Fred Inglis and Jerry Griswold that works written in the decades succeeding the publication of Lewis Carroll's *Alice's Adventures in Wonderland* are a manifestation of a 'golden age' tethers the discussion of children's literature to questions of a different kind of power, the power of literary value: the notion that certain works, especially those produced along certain discernible lines (lines which invariably reach back to *Alice*), have an enduring cultural potency not seen in works which are merely popular. The very notion of what children's literature is, at its best – what it *ideally* is – rests on a set of ideas about cultural capital in which prestige derives from, and is therefore allied to, the power to influence the terms of the debate.

Such critical labels – 'romantic', 'cult of the child', 'golden age' – serve a useful practical function in that they enable us to group together alike works and to perceive connections between the literary texts produced at given historical moments and the wider cultural movements in which they might be seen to participate. However, too often these critical labels have been taken up in uncritical ways. For example, general introductions to children's literature routinely use such terms as descriptors to demarcate (and hence reduce) whole periods of children's literature history. In the relative infancy of the scholarly field of children's literature studies, such introductory overviews have been a mainstay.[3] But as the field has become more established, and as scholars, taking up the gauntlet thrown down by Kimberley Reynolds, begin to specialize in more localized subsets of the field, we need to reconsider the usefulness of labels that derive from an impulse towards generalization and summarization, and which threaten to simplify and falsify.[4] One regrettable consequence of our continued reliance on a label such as 'golden age' is that those works which best reflect the particular attributes of the critical category in question are treated as emblematic or typical of the age itself. This in turn creates a distorted sense that children's literature which does not readily fit into the category, which in practice comprises much children's literature from prior to the late nineteenth century, is homogeneous, readily knowable and of interest to us only in as much as it enables us to formulate with greater confidence our sense of what children's literature since the golden age, by contrast, *is*. As a result of their treatment in this way, certain children's literature texts which have come to be seen as exemplars of the literary categories that are used to characterize them have acquired a kind of normative status against which other (both later and earlier) kinds of children's literature are seen as departures. This has led to the oft-asserted claim, made, for example, by Patricia Demers, that the 'legacy of the best Golden Age books is still evident in outstanding literature for children today' (1983, p. xiv). Where Demers's teleological narrative rests on suppositions about qualities intrinsic to the texts themselves, the same narrative has been plotted in relation to the conditions in which works for children have been produced. Shelia Egoff, for example, has documented the ways in which, unlike that of adult literature, 'the history of children's literature is still very much a part of the present-day character of publishing for children' (McGillis, 2003, p. 4). In part, of course, a certain degree of linear, direct influence is inevitable, particularly since, as Jane Tompkins has shown, a literary work succeeds or fails in terms of its reception in the immediate context 'on the degree to which it provokes the desired response' (Tompkins, 1985, p. xviii). That is to say that a text becomes established – canonized – not on account of its peculiarities, but on account of the ways in which it upholds values which are already accepted. And, as Perry Nodelman has demonstrated, certain works become 'touchstones' when they encourage imitators, providing new benchmarks in relation to which subsequent works of children's literature are judged.[5] By the same token, when we use a critical term such as 'urchin verse'[6], which has been used to characterize some contemporary British children's poetry, we do so to encapsulate the ways in which such poetry spurns convention, thereby reaffirming the status of those values which have been rejected as exemplary or ideal. And yet, intriguingly, this kind of linear narrativizing does not merely consist of a nostalgic reaching back. It also takes the form of a kind of Whiggist march forwards which has led critics to hasten past children's works from the sixteenth, seventeenth, eighteenth and much of the nineteenth centuries until we emerge in the safe territory of the 'golden age', where we can saunter leisurely among the riches. As Mitzi Myers, in her robust critique of Geoffrey Summerfield's *Fantasy and Reason*, observed, there is an unpalatable presentism involved in the denouncement of children's writers, especially female writers, of the late eighteenth and early nineteenth centuries who espoused what Summerfield dismisses as 'grown-up values associated with mature reflection' instead of those values associated with the imagination – values which, as Myers rightly points out, only came to be seen as conventionally (and therefore ideally) childish in a subsequent age (Myers, 1987, p. 109).

On the surface, it may appear that the two critical premises which I have briefly outlined above – first, that the child reader is a powerless victim, and second, that children's literature presents idealized versions of the world – do not obviously have much connection with one another. However, in this book I propose that they do. Specifically, I seek to highlight the ways in which both are predicated on a mutual supposition: the supposition that children's literature is inherently, but regrettably, didactic. That is to say, both premises rest on a belief that children's literature aspires, whether consciously or not, overtly or not, successfully or not, to instruct the reader; and furthermore, they rest on a belief that to aspire to instruct the reader is necessarily objectionable. Since at least the publication of *Alice's Adventures in Wonderland* (1865), in which Lewis Carroll famously and mercilessly parodied a particular mode of moralistic writing most notably associated with Isaac Watts, the idea that children's literature might assume a didactic function has often been viewed with disdain. The critical label *didactic* has sometimes been used not merely to characterize, but moreover to denigrate, the works to which it is attached. It has become a means of casting outside our sphere of interest types of writing which are not seen to be predicated on an aestheticist valuation of art for art's sake. Consequently, swathes of children's literature from prior to the late nineteenth century, which often call attention to their educational pretexts, remain largely unread, certainly rarely *closely* read, by children's literature scholars. By the same token, works which apparently *do* foreground the child's delight by purportedly offering idealized versions of the world for the child's delectation, particularly those works which are perceived to be wrought in the mould of *Alice*, have often been prized largely on account of their apparent reluctance to instruct. While the term 'wonderland' has entered our collective vocabulary as a term to denote the surreal,[7] we seem sometimes to have accepted as real the mischievous presentation of children's literary history which is spun in Carroll's fictional realm.

The primary objective of this book is not to probe the critical accuracy of Carroll's portrayal of children's works in the Wattsian tradition, though a reassessment of such works is indeed long overdue.[8] My aim here is to consider what is at stake at a theoretical level in the crafting of a teleological narrative wherein a move towards aestheticism entails a rejection of didacticism. This is the narrative which critics such as Ulrich Knoepflmacher have entrenched when they claim that the publication of *Alice's Adventures in Wonderland* in 1865 'completed the erosion of a didactic and empirical tradition of children's literature' (p. xi). Such a teleology, epitomized by the title of Patricia Demers's anthology, *From Instruction to Delight*, casts didacticism and aestheticism as oppositional in character. It places the pedagogical function of children's literature in tension with the aesthetic demand for entertainment, envisaging the two as mutually exclusive aims. Hence, the extent to which a work fulfils the former is presumed to compromise its capacity to fulfil the latter, and vice versa. The oppositional character of these two positions is enshrined in the interrogative subtitle of Torben Weinreich's 2000 book, *Children's Literature: Art or Pedagogy?* Peter Hunt reifies the same binary when, echoing the famous inscription to John Newbery's *A Little Pretty Pocket-Book* (based on the Horatian premise which was a foundational principle of Western literary aesthetics long before John Newbery perceived its peculiar aptness for the children's text), he asks: 'Should children's books be for instruction or delight?' (Hunt in Maybin and Watson, 2009, p. 13). It is not a rhetorical question; the answer which critics in our own age have resolutely reached is that children's books should be for delight. In our eagerness to laugh with and not be laughed at by Carroll, we have inherited his contempt for the custom of using literature as a vehicle for instilling rote learning and the parroting of accepted truth, and nurtured full-blown embarrassment towards the notion that children's literature might be educational.

And yet, despite the fact that the notion of didacticism has sometimes provoked uneasiness, claims have repeatedly been made that children's literature has a unique association with it. It has variously been observed that children's literature has its roots in the didactic tradition (Seth Lerer); that all children's literature from prior to the mid-nineteenth century is didactic (Ulrich Knooepflmacher); that all children's literature is *used* didactically (Peter Hollindale); and even that children's literature is *necessarily* didactic – that it is 'inextricably tied to a *prescriptive* role' (Lesnik-Obserstein, 1994, p. 3). Debates about the nature of the education which children's literature offers – or, more particularly, debates about the nature of education which children's literature *should* offer – continue to determine the parameters, and shape the questions we ask, of the field. Just as Sarah Trimmer in the late eighteenth century expressed her nervousness that fairy tales would corrupt the young, so too do cultural commentators today regularly pose anxious questions such as Megan Creasey's 'Does Violence Have a Place in Children's Literature?' (2010), belying a fretting about what impressionable young readers will pick up from the potent reading matter put into their hands.

Didacticism

The incommensurability of this apparent contempt for didacticism with an inability to stop worrying about the corruptive potential of children's literature points towards something unresolved lying at the heart of children's literature studies. It points towards a discomfort which far exceeds the prevalent anti-Leavisite feeling which cuts through literary culture more generally. The view that reading good books might make us better people now firmly belongs to a quaint and receding past. Our peculiar discomfort with the business of didacticism, one which pervades literary studies more generally but which is even more acutely felt in the arena of children's literature studies, derives,

I propose, from the lack of an adequate account of what it might mean for a literary text to be didactic. Specifically, it highlights that we need better to understand what it might mean for a literary text which is written by a knowledgeable party (usually an adult) to educate a reader who is comparatively less knowledgeable (often a child). It indicates that we need to do more further to probe the assumption, as recent scholars including Clémentine Beauvais and Lisa Sainsbury have done, that education entails a one-way, linear transaction – a form of transmission – wherein values which originally reside in the author are straightforwardly passed on to, even imposed on, the reader. Such a notion is tied to a concomitant belief that the delivery of knowledge is bound up with power: it entails an act of giving (or abuse) on behalf of the powerful (the knowledgeable) to the powerless (the ignorant).

But such a model of education is not the only one available to us. In fact, the belief that education comprises a process of indoctrination or inculcation wherein the older generation transmits to the younger generation a heritage the value of which the adult has preordained is now a decidedly outmoded one. It is one, indeed, which philosophers of education have come to distance themselves from to such an extent that it is invariably characterized as *traditional* in contradistinction to the supposedly more modern models that have been influential in the last century or so. Traditional education presupposes a formal, authoritarian educational context, wherein the teacher is conceived as a repository of knowledge which is passed on, intact, to the pupil. The pupil, it is imagined, passively ingests what is provided, complicit in (or forced to submit to) the belief that such knowledge is necessary for initiation into the adult world. With roots in ancient practices, traditional educational practices were popular among Medieval pedagogues, and remained effectively dominant in Europe until the twentieth century, when Anglo-American policymakers first began on a widespread scale to take seriously some of the claims made by proponents of so-called *progressive* education. Although progressive education has a long history, one in which ideas articulated by John Locke, Jean-Jacques Rousseau and Richard and Maria Edgeworth, among many others, play a vital role, it was given coherent formulation in the work of the late nineteenth- and early twentieth-century American philosopher, John Dewey. Consequently, Dewey is often regarded as its progenitor, although in the 1930s Dewey in fact denounced many of the educational experiments carried out in the name of progressive education, and sought to distance himself from the movement. In America and Britain in the first decades of the twentieth century, Dewey popularized a set of educational premises which have been characterized as *child-centred*. Dewey's theories of education, influenced by thinkers as diverse as Gottfried Wilhelm Leibniz, Georg Wilhelm Friedrich Hegel and Charles Darwin, carry into the realm of the philosophy of education a nineteenth-century commitment to the belief that scientific enquiry, as opposed to deference to the classics, was necessary to secure intellectual, and hence political, freedom.[9] Dewey's writings on education emphasize the child as an active learner, a questioner – an experimenter who learns through doing things first-hand, often through play, and not merely through being told what to think. He envisages the teacher as a partner in or facilitator, and not the author, of the learning process. This process is thus one in which the teacher participates, but which he or she does not seek to, indeed recognizes that he or she cannot, dictate. Crucially, then, for Dewey, education originates in, and is driven on by, the activity of the child.[10]

Dewey's theories have been much debated in the century or so since their first articulation, and he is only one among many philosophers of education to propose a model of educational exchange which poses an alternative to those associated with more traditional modes of education.[11] Nonetheless, his influence looms large over contemporary discussions of education, not merely owing to his material importance – his ideas were taken up and tested both by fellow theorists and by practitioners such that he dramatically altered the educational landscape in both Britain and America, as well as in other parts of the world – but also his symbolic importance. By challenging in the mainstream the dominance of traditional ideas about education, he mobilized renewed commitment to the belief that how and what we educate our citizens is vitally important to the social contract. While theorists and practitioners since Dewey have contested, modified or repudiated many of his ideas, his legacy is felt in our continued questioning of educational traditions. And yet, curiously, often when literary scholars employ the term *didactic*, they appear not to take into account the many questions which one might ask of education, and indeed, the many questions which philosophers of education since Dewey habitually *do* ask of education, and often continue to operate on the largely unexamined basis that education entails formal, traditional instruction.[12]

In fact, for all that the term *didactic* has a familiar place in the repertoire of critical terms available to literary scholars, it is a term which has rarely been subject to sustained enquiry or theorization, whether specifically in relation to children's literature or whether in relation to literature more broadly conceived. Certainly, literary critics have rarely looked to the philosophy of education as a field which might have something to offer to such discussions.[13] Perhaps the business of education has seemed self-evident, or, like the literature which the label *didactic* has been used to describe, perhaps the study of literature's alliances with education is deemed embarrassingly retrograde, hence beneath critical notice. Perhaps scholars have been put off by a concern that to study didacticism is tantamount to signing up to the notion that literature *should* be didactic. Whatever the reasons that have caused scholars to skirt around the issue, the result is that there is a surprising dearth of scholarly enquiry into what we might mean or do when we identify a work as didactic. To be sure, a number of recent studies have probed the discursive intersections between theories and practices in the domain of literature and theories and practices within the domain of education. For example, Richard Barney's *Plots of Enlightenment* (1999) and Alan Richardson's *Literature, Education and Romanticism* (1994) consider interrelations between literary and educational thought in the eighteenth century and romantic period respectively. Dinah Birch's *Our Victorian Education* (2007) focusses on concerns that have been dominant since the nineteenth century, while Michael Bell's *Open Secrets* (2007) is a more trans-historical sweep from Rousseau to J. M. Coetzee. Such studies indicate that a scholarly interest in the relevance of ideas about education – particularly as they pertain in and to particular historical periods – is already well established. None of these studies, though, takes head on the question of what it might mean for a literary text to operate didactically. In the field of children's literature study, where it has long been familiar to apply the characterization 'didactic' to certain kinds of literary text, some recent scholars have started to provide revisionist accounts of what the didactic exchange inherent in children's literature might consist. Lisa Sainsbury, for example, in her examination of the ways in which contemporary children's literature fosters philosophical engagement, has argued that the 'didactic impulse' which is 'common to ethical discourse and moralizing' can be viewed as 'liberating' and not just as 'enslaving'. The kind of impulse which can be viewed as 'liberating' can be envisaged, she proposes, as a 'positive didactic drive' (Sainsbury, 2013, p. 7). Sainsbury's welcome re-evaluation of the ethics of didacticism fruitfully moves on the discussion from the centuries-old impulse to pronounce on the moral value of specific systems of thought promoted in and through children's literature, and to shift it instead towards an analysis of how literary works might facilitate moral enquiry. Sainsbury's nuanced account of the didacticism at work in children's literary texts nonetheless continues to adhere to a supposition that the child is invariably in *receipt* of that which the adult *offers*. As a consequence, she finds that what the child gains through moral enquiry is a form of *power* – or, in her own terminology, 'liberty': the freedom not to be overpowered.

My own study is motivated by a conviction that for as long as *power* dominates discussions about children's literature, then the idea that child readers are simply passive consumers of that which the adult provides for them will continue to rear its head. In this book, I therefore deliberately place questions of power to one side, not because I consider them to be unimportant (I do not) nor to deny that power dynamics are at play in the complex encounters that literary texts enable between multiple different human parties. I confess, though, that I frequently find myself losing a grip on any sense of what the term 'power' might mean when it is used in a literary theoretical context, and I observe that its signification is often taken for granted when it is not, in fact, always self-evident. Indeed, when reading about the power dynamics at work in literary texts, I often find myself wondering what, if anything, the term 'power' means when it is used in this context.[14] My desire to place questions of power to one side instead marks an attempt to explore whether the introduction of a different conceptual vocabulary, a vocabulary which places the emphasis on the reader as an active agent in the educational process, might enable us to identify aspects of the nature of didactic transactions which have become obscured by our readiness to read such exchanges as exercises in subjugation.

The account offered in this book explores the ways in which we might reanimate discussions of literary didacticism by considering the relevance for literature of non-traditional ideas about education, specifically those so-called 'progressive', child-centred ideas about education so comprehensively articulated by John Dewey at the turn of the twentieth century. If we turn to an account of education which emphasizes what the child *does*, and not what is done *to* the child, I contend, then we can arrive at a new and less discomfiting way of thinking about the educational character of children's literature. In providing an account of the child reader, following Dewey's account of the child as thinker, as an inquirer – as an active, not a passive, agent of interpretation – I probe the ways in which the child might resist the processes of idealization apparently at work in children's literary texts. In so doing, I add a further voice to the growing call that we need decisively to move away from the too-long-established view that the child reader is a passive, powerless victim of adult machination, as well as the equally outmoded notion that children's literature – any the more than any other kind of literature – ever *could* idealize the world it represents. By thinking our way outside of these positions which have for so long and in so many embedded ways dictated what we see and how we look at reading matter produced for children, we can arrive at a way of approaching children's literature, both at a theoretical level and in practice, which acknowledges the child's capacity to read against the grain: that is to say, an approach towards children's literature which acknowledges the child as *critic*.

The child as critic

In a prolific and astonishingly wide-ranging career, John Dewey played a seminal role in securing public and political interest in child-centred education, particularly through the influence of his major works of education philosophy, *School and Society* (1899), *Child and Curriculum* (1902), *How We Think* (1910), *Democracy and Education* (1916), *Art as Experience* (1934), *Experience and Education* (1938) and *Knowing and the Known* (1949). One of Dewey's most enduring contributions to the philosophy of education, and one of the ideas that has become most closely associated with his name, is his insistence that the primary aim of education ought to be the fostering of critical thinking.[15] Criticism, or critical thinking, for Dewey, is the exercise of 'discriminating judgment' and 'careful appraisal' in an effort to minimize our dependence on 'dispensations of fortune or providence' (LW 1:298). His 1910 study, *How We Think*, outlines in full his understanding of what critical activity entails and why it matters, and he further elaborates on its political role in his seminal work, *Democracy and Education* (1916). For Dewey, critical thinking provides a means of comprehending 'the causes of ideas – the conditions under which they are thought', which enables us, as Lipman puts it, 'to liberate ourselves from intellectual rigidity and to bestow upon ourselves that power of choosing among and acting upon alternatives that is the source of intellectual freedom.' This kind of thinking is *critical* because it is 'aware of its own assumptions and implications as well as being conscious of the reasons and evidence that support this or that conclusion' (Lipman, 2003, p. 35; p. 26). In this way, critical thinking involves interrogation of the very processes involved in thinking even as that thinking is being carried out. It is a form of watching oneself think – a form of consciously and deliberately managing the processes of discovery.

A central proposition of *Literature's Children* is that Dewey's concept of critical thinking provides children's literature scholarship with a valuable means of accounting for the didactic nature of the exchange at work in the reading of children's literature without requiring us to cast the child in the position of a passive victim of adult oppression. The conceptual vocabulary which underpins Dewey's account of education provides us with a means of shifting the discussion about the educative character of children's literature away from discussions of power (predicated on a model of delivery and receipt), and instead towards discussions of *activity*, in which the education experienced by the child reader can be characterized by verbs such as enquire, choose, consider, deliberate, think, experiment, question, seek evidence for and try out. Such an account of the education entailed in the reading of literature enables us more satisfactorily to acknowledge and accept the implications for children's literature of the ways in which poststructuralist literary theory, in the wake of the work of Roland Barthes and Michel Foucault, among others, has destabilized any easy alignment between authorship with authority, and invited us to reconceive the reader as an active agent in the production of meaning. Theorists of children's literature, in their repeated insistence on the peculiar passivity of the child reader, have sometimes shown an apparent reluctance to assimilate into their critical practice poststructuralist ideas about the constitutive role played by the reader, even while mainstream literary critical culture has long ago absorbed this notion as one of its central tenets. Through consideration of John Dewey's account of critical thinking, then, *Literature's*

Children seeks to move the discussion away from what literary texts *do* to children and, building on foundations laid most notably by Margaret Meek in *How Texts Teach What Readers Learn* (1988) and Peter Hollindale in *Signs of Childness* (1997), shift the focus instead towards a reflection on what children might *do* to literary texts.

The central contention of *Literature's Children* is that the child reader can best be understood as a kind of *critic*. That is to say, child readers are active, curious, independent, questioning thinkers who operate in disciplined, inventive, risky ways to arrive at individual, potentially liberated, responsible judgements. By analyzing the sophisticated critical work which the child reader undertakes – that is to say, by acknowledging the questions which a child reader might ask and the inferences which they might draw as they attempt to make sense of the words in front of them – we can, I contend, arrive at a conceptualization of the child reader which shifts the emphasis away from power (bound up with ideology) and towards activity (bound up with *ideas*). We can reconceive the child reader as a mobile, proactive, inventive, experimental, sceptical, artful agent – a doer, a worker, a thinker, a discoverer – and not an inert *tabula rasa*, awaiting the imprint (whether benign or otherwise) of the adult. This is not merely to identify the child as a kind of naïve swain, in the way that William Empson has famously done; nor is it to recapitulate the Wordsworthian conceit that the child knows something of which grown-ups remain ignorant. In fact, it is precisely to avoid viewing the role of the child reader as defined via a binary opposition with the adult reader, an opposition which sets up a perverse trap wherein if we wish to deem that the child's insight is not lesser than the adult's, then we must deem it to be greater. My own, perhaps sceptical, premise – the idea which this book tests out – is that the activity which the child carries out when invited to read a literary text might surely, indeed, *must* surely, unless and until we can prove otherwise, be similar in kind to that carried out by the adult. That is to say that, just like the adult reader, the child reader too is interrogative, deliberate, suspicious, resistant – in short, *critical*.

To assert that the child reader is a kind of critic might appear to be a peculiarly audacious claim when one bears in mind how entrenched is the supposition that critics are not merely adults, but moreover, especially *wise* adults at that. Over the centuries, the critic has variously been conceived as a genius (William Wordsworth, 1974), a moral authority (Matthew Arnold, 1960-77), an aesthete (Oscar Wilde, 1909), a custodian of tradition (T. S. Eliot, 1951), an arbiter of cultural value (F. R. Leavis, 1962), and a virtuoso performer (Derek Attridge, 2015), to cite just a selective handful of theoretical positions. The tendency to view the critic as a figure of prestige in possession of exceptional skill runs hand in hand with, and no doubt derives from, that long-standing tendency to view the author (the point of origin) as possessed of a unique kind of knowledge – as having access to that which eludes the ordinary reader. This belief, which reaches back at least to Plato, can be traced through influential accounts of the function of criticism by poets and authors including Philip Sidney, John Dryden, William Wordsworth, Percy Bysshe Shelley, Oscar Wilde, and T. S. Eliot, and has continued well into the twenty-first century, seen alive and well, for example, in tributes made on the death of Seamus Heaney.[16]

Of course, plenty of alternative ways of understanding the relations between authorship and authority, maturity and wisdom, are available to us. Certain commentators, particularly those who have attended to the literary treatment of childhood in the wake of Rousseau, have turned the customary view on its head, and considered the ways in which it is during *childhood*, and not adulthood, that knowledge is privileged. This Rousseauvian – or in the British tradition, more often Wordsworthian – notion is present, as has been well documented, in autobiographical accounts of childhood from the early nineteenth century by Thomas de Quincey and Hartley Coleridge, and has been reframed, albeit to enable a sceptical view, in our own age by scholarship on romantic childhood by scholars including Judith Plotz (2001), Peter de Bolla (2003) and Sally Shuttleworth (2010).[17] Pursuing a rather different tack, Andrew Bennett (2009) has offered a beguiling counterposition to the customary alliance between authorship and authority which draws attention to the peculiar relationships which subsist between poetry, poets and ignorance. From another angle again, the particular fertility of childhood as the domain of play has been exploited as a means of identifying the kind of aesthetic anarchy witnessed in the works of writers such as Algernon Charles Swinburne and James Joyce, for example.[18] At a more theoretical level, the idea, attributed to Pablo Picasso, that every child is an artist, a reorientation of the Renaissance idea seen in the work of Francis Bacon, popularized anew in the nineteenth century by John Stuart Mill, that every child is a scientist, has already accustomed us to the notion that the untrained child might be capable of excelling in skills which the drudgery of training serves to remove.[19] But the notion that the child might be a kind of *critic* – that the critical faculty might be commensurate with childishness, with that which is originary – the notion, even, that critical reading might constitute a default kind of reading available especially to the young, has not previously been explored.[20] It presents a new challenge to the established view that the capacity to read critically is one that is acquired rather than given, one that is exceptional rather than mainstream, one that is schooled rather than native.[21]

For John Dewey, playfulness – the capacity to try out imaginary scenarios motivated by the sheer pleasure involved in so doing as opposed to for a particular end (the hallmark of *work*) – is fundamental for criticism, since critical activity involves a collapse between the distinction of work and play. For Dewey, the child is peculiarly well positioned to undertake critical experimentation, since the distinction between work and play does not make sense in the realm of childhood; the child has not yet learned to distinguish between the two. The child, therefore, is accustomed to entering into a kind of activity which is purposeful and yet intrinsically motivated. For Dewey, this is what makes the child a kind of artist, that is to say, an exemplary kind of experimenter. If we accept the contours of Dewey's argument, then we might even want to test out the idea that the critical faculty is a *peculiarly* childish faculty; that the child reader might be *peculiarly* suited to critical reading; that is to say, that the child reader is not merely a critic, but an *ideal* kind of critic. Might it be the case that the child, by virtue of her ignorance, could have peculiar access to the kind of 'disinterestedness' which Matthew Arnold extolled, and which, since Arnold's era, in many quarters has become entrenched as a gold standard for literary criticism.[22] Since the child is not (usually) in the pay of interested parties, nor signed up to particular political or economic or any other kinds of positions in the way that the adult can later elect to be, the child is peculiarly able to read the text without prejudging what position she will adopt in response. Karín Lesnik-Obserstein suggested in 1994 (and we might wonder whether much has materially changed since) that the adult critic of children's literature has 'not yet always settled into an academic discourse characterized by what could be loosely described as liberal disinterestedness'

(p. 2). Might it be the case that literature's children have access to precisely that form of liberal disinterestedness which their adult counterparts have found so hard to achieve?

Critical thinking

As Dewey outlines it, critical or reflective thinking is an 'operation in which present facts suggest other facts (or truths) in such a way as to induce belief in the latter upon the ground or warrant of the former' (*How We Think* (hereafter *HWT*), pp. 8–9). Critical thinking, then, is not something which occurs instantaneously or automatically; it arises as a result of a mental *process*. This process entails *interpretation*, that is to say, the reading of *signs*. It involves an attempt to arrive at a rational conclusion about what is unknown by inducing and deducing from that which is known. The end point of critical thinking – *judgement* – may be provisional and uncertain, but it can be supported by justificatory *evidence*, since it results from careful *testing*.

The salient attributes of critical thinking are encapsulated by this key excerpt from *How We Think*:

> Long brooding over conditions, intimate contact associated with keen interest, thorough absorption in a multiplicity of allied experiences, tend to bring about those judgments which we then call intuitive; but they are true judgments because they are based on intelligent selection and estimation, with the solution of a problem as the controlling standard. Possession of this capacity makes the difference between the artist and the intellectual bungler. (*HWT*, p. 105)

Importantly, then, though it may masquerade as something which occurs instinctively or easily, critical thinking takes *time* and *effort*; it requires *proximity* to the available information; it requires undivided *attention*; and it requires personal *interest* in the matter under consideration. It is motivated by a desire to solve a *problem*. In its adherence to these principles, critical thinking, for Dewey, does not merely satisfy intellectual curiosity; it fulfils aesthetic standards of beauty, truth, and excellence. While it may follow scientific procedures, fundamentally it is an *artistic* virtue, demonstrating the pinnacle of human mental achievement, and, like a work of art, is itself to be subjected to critical scrutiny, wonder and judgement. The end point of critical thinking is not a definite answer; it is further critical thinking. The process, then, is *ongoing*, *self-perpetuating*, and *infinite* – a kind of Derridean process of endless deferral wherein the signified of a signifier turns out to yield yet another signifier, *ad infinitum*. For Dewey, through the perpetual dynamism of critical thinking, wherein what we thought we knew is questioned and found wanting, and, therefore, through further testing, is modified and developed, the human race renews itself.

The relevance for literary study of Dewey's ideas about critical thinking is immediately apparent in his insistence that the 'function by which one thing signifies or indicates another, and thereby leads us to consider how far one may be regarded as warrant for belief in the other, is . . . the central factor in all reflective or distinctively intellectual thinking' (*HWT*, p. 8). Like reading, then, thinking is a 'process of reaching the absent from the present' (*HWT*, p. 26) – or to put it another way, it involves extrapolating signifieds from signifiers. As is well known, the process of meaning-making is essentially one which entails the navigation of signs; this is an established tenet of literary criticism, certainly in the wake of structuralist and poststructuralist literary theory. The relevance of Dewey's ideas about signification for the reading of literary texts will be explored in greater detail below; what is interesting to observe at the outset, though, is the way in which Dewey envisages the processes of signification involved in critical thought as ones which are inherently literary – that is to say, linguistic processes which are contrived as opposed to natural, whose ends are beauty, truth and pleasure, and, moreover, which appeal to us on account of their suggestiveness: 'Civilized man deliberately *makes* such signs . . . All forms of artificial apparatus are intentionally designed modifications of natural things in order that they may serve better than in their natural estate to indicate the hidden, the absent, and the remote' (p. 16). Key here is the idea of design: signs are deliberately wrought to communicate efficiently and effectively, whereas that which they signify is not. That which they signify is given, and is therefore of lesser interest to us. Dewey's privileging of the sign is almost directly contrary to Rousseau's romantic prioritization of the natural over the artificial[23]: reappropriating markedly similar vocabulary, but inverting the logic, Dewey aligns the 'artificial' with connotations of artfulness and artistry to hint at the skilfulness required in the making of signs, and the achievement it reflects. To denote such achievement as 'civilized' invests it not merely with artistic, as well as scientific, technological and political sophistication, but it also implies that there is something peculiarly mature, even adult, about such achievement: that the sign-maker is already conversant with codes which the decoder has yet to learn, a paradigm peculiarly apposite for the scenario of children's literature, in which the initiated (adult) writes for the uninitiated (child). Since meaningfulness is not an inherent quality in signs themselves, and is generated by the quality of the thought which is brought to bear on them, those who are not yet familiar with the precedents for their use will be unable to extrapolate sense through mere guesswork: 'words are mere scratches, curious variations of light and shade, to one to whom they are not linguistic signs. To him for whom they are signs of other things, each has a definite individuality of its own, according to the meaning that it is used to convey' (*HWT*, pp. 16–17). Dewey here anticipates an idea which later becomes familiar to literary theorists through the influence of thinkers such as Roland Barthes and Jacques Derrida: that meaning only comes into being through the constitutive presence of the reader, making it inherently 'individual', owing not merely to the distinctiveness of the sign but also to the distinctiveness of the reader, or, here, thinker.[24]

Just as literary criticism takes as its subject matter what Aristotle in *Poetics* characterizes as an *agon* (1970), Wordsworth calls 'the burthen of the mystery' ('Tintern Abbey', 1974, l. 39), and William Empson terms 'ambiguity' (1991), critical thinking arises in the wake of a problem. 'The origin of thinking,' writes Dewey, 'is some perplexity, confusion, or doubt' (*HWT*, p. 12). It emerges when something is not understood, irrespective of whether the particular mental obstacle poses difficulty at large; what is relevant is not whether the issue is generally understood, but whether the particular thinker – the thinking subject (although Dewey himself rejected the term 'subject' for use in this context in favour of the term 'enquirer' – has overcome his or her own difficulty in comprehension. The predicament of the enquirer – the subjective perspective which he or she brings to bear on the problem – is thus vital in determining the extent to which critical thinking can occur. Dewey characterizes this predicament as:

> a *forked-road* situation, a situation which is ambiguous, which presents a dilemma, which proposes alternatives . . . Difficulty or obstruction in the

> way of reaching a belief brings us, however, to a pause. In the suspense of uncertainty, we metaphorically climb a tree; we try to find some standpoint from which we may survey additional facts and, getting a more commanding view of the situation, may decide how the facts stand related to one another. (*HWT*, p. 11)

Dewey's recourse to the metaphors of a physical journey vividly portrays the difficulty as one which derives from a surfeit of options. In order to arrive at understanding, one particular route needs to be selected, but until it can be ascertained which one is optimal, no forward progress can occur. The 'pause' in the journey thus mirrors a type of mental stasis. However, this stasis is not an impasse – a cessation of movement; it involves a different kind of movement, here figuratively denoted as upwards movement (up a tree), such that the perspective is enhanced. The ultimate selection of the route, then, is not random but considered; the hesitation is not paralysis, but deliberation. Dewey's account stresses the effort entailed in critical thinking, and by extension, the stamina required to carry it out; it is prompted by something troubling, but is itself troublesome, since it 'involves overcoming the inertia that inclines one to accept suggestions at their face value; it involves willingness to endure a condition of mental unrest and disturbance. Reflective thinking, in short, means judgment suspended during further inquiring; and suspense is likely to be somewhat painful' (*HWT*, p. 13). Critical thinking, then, does not come easily, even when this may appear to be the case; and the degree of curiosity and intensity of desire to overcome the given obstacle must be strong indeed if they are to outweigh the frustrations posed by the process.

There is of course an element of perversity in the wilful undertaking of that which is laborious and 'painful', a perversity which is also manifest in the practice of literary criticism, itself, at one level, so egregious and pedantic – somehow excessive to that which is required. This perversity, indeed, characterizes the very enterprise of deliberately attempting to impose order on that which presents itself as disorderly – or as Dewey puts it, introducing 'i) *definiteness* and *distinction* and ii) *consistency* or *stability* of meaning into what is otherwise vague and wavering' (*HWT*, p. 122). Indeed, the emphasis Dewey places on the need for 'systematic' methods (p. 13) indicates the extent to which the process strains against itself, and can be controlled only by resolute measures. In a very fundamental way, then, the meaning reached at the end of the process of critical thinking, as in literary criticism, is contrived; it is constituted by that which the critical thinker does to the material, and is not latent in the material itself.

So what is it that the critical thinker *does*? Dewey proposes that the activity entailed in critical thinking is a kind of *experimentation*, specifically, one which is hands-on, that is to say, *practical*. By this, he means that the testing is conducted first-hand, such that the critical thinker collects *evidence* by his own methods and interprets it for himself. By evidence, Dewey has in mind 'something . . . which stands as witness, . . . proof, coucher, warrant; that is, as *ground of belief*' (*HWT*, p. 8). The critical thinker, then, needs to be able to justify the eventual conclusions reached by being able to point to specific reasons which corroborate the findings. There is a clear parallel here with the kind of activity undertaken by the literary critic, who, to support the readings which she wishes to advance, also seeks out evidence, a form of proof which we tend to call textual evidence (or, following Wimsatt and Beardsley, 'internal evidence' (1954, p. 10)) – evidence which takes the form of scriptural signs. For Dewey, the evidence which is sought out in critical thinking also takes the form of signs: the thinker 'wants something in the nature of a signboard or a map, and his reflection is aimed at the discovery of facts that will serve this purpose' (*HWT*, p. 11). If the identification and analysis of such signs does not take place first-hand, then its reliability is not to be taken for granted: 'the material supplied from the experience of others is *testimony*: that is to say, *evidence* submitted by others to be employed by one's own judgment in reaching a conclusion' (*HWT*, p. 197). Such testimonial may facilitate the thinker's critical thinking, but it cannot substitute it. In educational terms, as has been well documented,[25] Dewey's insistence on the necessity for evidence to be collected empirically has major implications, since it constitutes a rejection of traditional modes of passing on knowledge which has been collected by others (by previous generations, or by the teacher), and an embrace instead of a form of so-called 'discovery' learning whereby children arrive at knowledge based on the insights they have gleaned from practical experiments they have conducted for themselves.[26] The language that Dewey uses in relation to this collection of evidence tends to relate to sight – 'observation' – implying a prolonged, sustained and alert kind of scrutiny. That is to say, it involves a form of doing, a form of work – or play – actively applying oneself and not merely passively receiving information. It involves screening localized, 'raw' details, unmediated, uncleansed, as it were – getting one's hands dirty at the coalface rather than being handed an already tidy, polished and validated finished product.

This shift away from knowledge inherited from others (deferring to authority which resides elsewhere) towards knowledge ascertained for oneself (positioning oneself as the authority) is directly paralleled in that major shift which occurred in twentieth-century literary theory, most notably, in the British tradition, at least, associated with I. A. Richards and his famous advocacy of 'practical criticism', wherein the reader is invited to rely not on knowledge which he or she has learned prior to encountering the text, but on what they make of the words on the page that they find in front of them. That is to say, the reader prioritizes their *own* experience of the text over the documented reading experiences of those who have encountered the text before them. Here, too, we tend to have recourse to metaphors of sight; we speak of looking for textual evidence; of observation; of insight. This shift in the perceived location of authority, and the concomitant shift in emphasis in an account of experience which rests on that which is obtained through first-hand experimentation, rather than that which is obtained through the accumulation of knowledge, has particular consequences for the reading of children's literature, dependent as it is on a reading subject whose knowledge is limited. If we reduce the views of others – that is to say, any interpretations of a text proffered by those adults who seek to influence the child (e.g. parent, teacher or even implied author) – to mere *testimony*, to be weighed up alongside, but not to take the place of, other forms of evidence which the child collects first-hand, then it makes it unlikely that the child will wholesale inherit that view of a text which is anticipated or promoted by such adult figures. To accept that this might be the case necessarily has implications for how we consider that a literary text might function didactically, since it makes it impossible any longer to assume that testimony offered by the adult will be taken into account at all, should the child choose to ignore it.

So, having collected evidence through processes of careful observation, what kind of testing does Dewey have in mind to which to subject such evidence? What does Dewey mean when he declares that 'every inference shall be a tested inference' (*HWT*, p. 27)? The nature of the testing which Dewey has in mind is a twofold process which comprises of induction (the movement 'from fragmentary details (or particulars) to a connected view of a situation (universal)') and deduction ('which begins with the latter and works back again to particulars, connecting them and binding them together'). It is in 'so far as we conduct each of these processes in the light of the other,' he asserts, that 'we get valid discovery or verified critical thinking' (*HWT*, pp. 81–2). The process is thus a *dynamic* one, one which emphasizes continuous 'movement' back and forth between induction and deduction such that it is possible to draw an inference.[27] Importantly, though, the experiment which the critical thinker carries out is one that is directed and controlled: Dewey's verbs are active, emphasizing the ways in which 'we' are in charge of the process. The movement inherent in an active thought process, however, is supplied not by the evidence itself, which, naturally, is static; instead, it is supplied by the activity of the enquirer (the scientist or experimenter) who carries out the tasks; the mind which puts the various ingredients together decides upon the order in which to do so, and presses them into the shape of his or her own choosing. To be able to balance induction and deduction in order to arrive at a reasonable conclusion thus requires 'invention and initiative' (*Democracy and Education* (hereafter *DE*), pp. 75–8). In this way, the activity which the critical thinker carries out is practical in the colloquial sense that it entails being adaptable; it requires being capable of thinking on one's feet and being self-sufficient. But the critical thinker is also practical in the alternative sense of being capable of lateral and not merely rectilinear mental activity: a critical thinker must be capable of making believe, of using his or her imagination, of being creative – capable of plotting an unchartered course which is devised spontaneously, rather than adhering to preordained rules.

The instruments which the critical thinker uses to carry out these tests are *ideas*:

> We stop and think, we *de-fer* conclusion in order to *in-fer* more thoroughly. In this process of being only conditionally accepted, accepted only for examination, *meanings become ideas. That is to say, an idea is a meaning that is tentatively entertained, formed, and used with reference to its fitness to decide a perplexing situation, – a meaning used as a tool of judgment.* (*HWT*, p. 108)

An idea, then, for Dewey, is a provisional judgement – one which is mobile rather than static, still under consideration rather than fixed. As Dewey puts it, a 'true conception is a *moving* idea' (*HWT*, p. 213). The concept of motion is thus inscribed in Dewey's understanding of what ideas are: 'tools in a reflective examination' (*HWT*, p. 109). As such, they are not the end in themselves, but a means of arriving at an end: an idea is a 'method of evading, circumventing, or surmounting through reflection obstacles that otherwise would have to be attacked by brute force' (p. 110). This means that ideas must be particular; they must derive from specific circumstances rather than vague, approximate generalities. '"Glittering generalities"', Dewey remarks, 'are inert because they are spurious' (*HWT*, p. 213). This is what Dewey seeks to emphasize in his repeated use of the term *practical* (the term also emphasized, for much the same reasons, by I. A. Richards): that critical thought handles the specific, localized, real details immediately in front of us (*ideas*), and not the abstract and insubstantial generalities which one might imagine, hope or dream to be the case (*ideals*).[28] Equally, the term 'practical' emphasizes that it is not 'the target but *hitting* the target' which is 'the end in view' (*DE*, p. 112). While Dewey repeatedly insists throughout his work that the overriding end of all intellectual inquiry is 'a delight in thinking for the sake of thinking' (*HWT*, p. 141), he also recognizes that the 'need of thinking to accomplish something beyond thinking is more potent than thinking for its own sake' (*HWT*, p. 40). That is to say, we are likely to be galvanized to set ourselves the task of getting to the bottom of a mystery by an immediate and perhaps utilitarian incentive, even though the gain in abstract terms may, ultimately, outweigh the localized gain which motivates the thought process in the first place. It is for this reason that Dewey proposes that if critical thought is to participate in progress, be its contribution to individual understanding or to the understanding of society at large (and central to Dewey's political philosophy is the notion that it achieves the latter through the former), it must be harnessed and concertedly pressed into service. The critical thinker must be not merely active, but moreover, purposeful: 'the ground or basis for a belief is deliberately sought and its adequacy to support the belief examined' (*HWT*, pp. 1–2). The critical thinker is one who is in charge of the direction of his or her thoughts. That is to say, raw data is considered not in a haphazard fashion, but in an orderly manner which is dictated by a conscious end. 'To foresee a terminus of an act is to have a basis upon which to observe, to select, and to order objects and our own capacities. To do these things means to have a mind – for mind is precisely intentional purposeful activity controlled by perception of facts and their relationships to one another' (*DE*, p. 109). As well as being inventive, then, the critical thinker must be methodical: capable of shaping ideas not merely into a sequence, but into 'a *con*sequence' (*HWT*, p. 2).

Critical thinking is therefore not something which can just occur spontaneously and effortlessly. To acquire the capacity for mental orderliness which Dewey's philosophy seeks to place at the heart of education, careful preparation is necessary: 'only systematic regulation of the conditions under which observations are made and severe discipline of the habits of entertaining suggestions can secure a decision that one type of belief is vicious and the other sound' (*HWT*, p. 21). This is not to say that 'routine' is required; in fact, routine 'marks an arrest of growth' (*DE*, p. 57). What is instead required is a kind of *training* which fosters stamina and perseverance, even in the face of difficulties. The key thing is not to give up, but to have the resolve to keep attempting alternative ways forward, aspiring for ever greater familiarity with the material at hand. In his essay 'The School and the Life of the Child', Dewey identifies the key behavioural traits which the critical thinker must acquire, through continual and deliberate practice, as: 'ingenuity, patience, persistence [and] alertness' (*School and the Life of the Child* (hereafter *SLC*), p. 37). There is thus an irony here; in order to secure the necessary conditions for the free play of ideas, concerted effort and controlled work is required. To ensure the liberation which critical thinking brings, the conditions under which that thinking is carried out must be carefully restricted. This brings out another important dimension of Dewey's notion of the practical as that which is *practised*: as that which has been fine-tuned and developed through deliberate, repeated and accumulative exercise. In this far from haphazard way, the thinker makes him- or herself a skilled expert.

Critical thinking, then, has a temporal dimension. Not only does the honing of the practical skills requisite for critical thinking take time, but, since critical thinking itself is a *process*, it is an activity which takes place over time. Dewey repeatedly stresses the need for deceleration – for stretching out the time taken to factor in plenty of room for consideration and reconsideration. Where the process of critical thinking takes place hastily, Dewey proposes that we ought to be suspicious of its outcome: 'If the suggestion that occurs is at once accepted,' he suggests, 'we have uncritical thinking' (*HWT*, p. 13). The implication here is that a reflex answer is necessarily an untested one. Critical thinking involves scepticism towards any initial proposed solution, a process which entails retracing one's steps and examining their validity. Carrying out this process will inevitably delay the conclusion. For this reason, 'slowness and depth of response are intimately connected. Time is required in order to digest impressions, and translate them into substantial ideas' (*HWT*, p. 37). The critical thinker must therefore be capable of arresting the pursuit of meaning in what Dewey calls *suspense*, which implies a kind of temporal protraction 'pending examination and inquiry' (*HWT*, p. 108). The very notion of 'suspense,' as Gérard Genette has shown, is fundamental to narrative construction.[29] In this way, it is a fundamentally literary idea, since our understanding of it is contingent on its deployment in narrative form. Put more simply, we are accustomed to viewing suspense as a *literary* device. In his attempt to articulate the processes at work in critical thinking, Dewey thus draws on an idea which carries with it strong literary associations, implicitly inviting us to reflect on the ways in which we might draw on understanding of how we navigate suspense in the literary realm in order to better understand how we might navigate the suspense entailed in critical thinking.

In Aristotle's account of this phenomenon in *Poetics*, suspense involves not merely the condition of not knowing, but more specifically, a form of readerly anxiety or tension which derives from the condition of not knowing. In Dewey's account, suspense is also allied to notions of danger, the imagined harm, ultimately, being *misunderstanding*. The anxiety posed by this fear of getting it wrong is compounded by the fact that the likelihood of getting it right is diminished by a raft of factors, many of which are beyond the thinker's immediate control:

> The process of reaching the absent from the present is peculiarly exposed to error; it is liable to be influenced by almost any number of unseen and unconsidered causes, – past experience, received dogmas, the stirring of self-interest, the arousing of passion, sheer mental laziness, a social environment steeped in biased traditions or animated by false expectations, and so on. The exercise of thought is, in the literal sense of that word, *inference*; by it one thing *carries us over* to the idea of, and belief in, another thing. It

> involves a jump, a leap, a going beyond what is surely known to something else accepted on its warrant. (*HWT*, p. 26)

The sheer list of perceived impediments to critical thought emphasizes the precariousness of the process; the thinker must strain both against 'the natural tendency [of thought] to go astray' and 'social influences' (*HWT*, p. 29). Furthermore, at a certain basic level, thinking, as the Latin etymology of the word 'inference' encodes, is fundamentally a passive experience – one not altogether under our direct control. In *How We Think*, as elsewhere in his work, Dewey designates the type of thought which impacts on us without our deliberate choice 'unconscious', a term which acknowledges the influence of Freudian ideas on contemporary theories of mind.[30] Dewey does not elaborate on what he has in mind by that which he designates as 'unconscious', but, like Sigmund Freud, he recognizes the prevalence and significance of mental impulses which appear to originate outside of our sphere of direct influence. For Dewey, as for Freud, while such impulses, in their unpredictability, complicate the process of critical thinking, it is in their very inevitability that they are also valuable. Furthermore, Dewey suggests that the ideas which arrive in our conscious minds, seemingly from nowhere, may in fact already have been subject to unconscious testing, and that therefore we ought to allow time for such testing to take place. Prematurely to impose conscious order on a mental process which is being worked out unconsciously will result in contrived results. For Dewey, the optimum scenario is one in which first an idea is explored 'by more unconscious and tentative methods', and then it is more consciously reviewed and tested, such that it can be conceived in precise and definite terms (*HWT*, p. 113). The process of critical thinking is thus fundamentally *risky*, given that it involves temporarily being prepared to surrender control to unconscious and seemingly undirected impulses. However, the risks of attempting to solve the problem far outweigh the risks of not doing so. Indeed, such is Dewey's contempt for persisting in erroneous beliefs – uncritical thinking – that he suggests that ignorance is preferable: 'a being that cannot understand at all is at least protected from *mis*-understandings' (*HWT*, p. 129). For Dewey, misunderstanding invariably derives from 'vagueness' (p. 129) and 'ambiguity' (p. 130), since 'vague meanings are too gelatinous to offer matter for analysis, and too pulpy to afford support to other beliefs. They evade testing and responsibility.' Indeed, 'vagueness disguises the unconscious mixing together of different meanings, and facilitates the substitution of one meaning for another, and covers up the failure to have any precise meaning at all' (*HWT*, p. 130). It is important to note that the kind of 'ambiguity' which Dewey has in mind here is qualitatively different from the kind of uncertainty or doubt – problem – which gives rise to critical thinking, particularly if we seek to pursue the potential literary parallels which can be drawn out here. Both critical thinking and literary criticism are generated, as has been observed already, by a variety of curiosity which derives from uncertainty. Uncertainty as to how to interpret the patterns which emerge from the different signifiers in play is different, however, from uncertainty deriving from clumsy or inaccurate reading of the signifiers in the first place. Here, as in the practice of literary criticism, even where one might suggest, as Dewey does, that there is no end to the process of critical thinking, since critical thinking simply generates further critical thinking, it is still possible to *mis*read by failing to pay sufficient care to the available signifiers.

The riskiness of critical thinking is thrown into even greater relief when one appreciates that genuine critical thought is always *original*; that is to say, it involves creating, and not following precedent – exploring intellectual territory that is as yet unchartered by oneself, irrespective of whether others might have been there before. Dewey writes:

> All thinking whatsoever – so be it *is* thinking – contains a phase of originality. This originality does not imply that the student's conclusion varies from the conclusions of others, much less that it is a radically novel conclusion. This originality is not incompatible with large use of materials and suggestions contributed by others. Originality means personal interest in the question, personal initiative in turning over the suggestions furnished by others, and sincerity in following them out to a tested conclusion. Literally, the phrase "Think for yourself" is tautological; any thinking is thinking for one's self. (*HWT*, p. 198)

The preoccupation here with 'personal interest' has a direct analogue in literary theories which foreground the reader's interest (often, following Richards, envisaged as an *emotional* interest) as a central driver in determining what he or she finds in the literary text. Similarly, literary criticism has, throughout the centuries, been highly concerned with debates about originality, and the question of whether a critical reading must be innovative, or whether it may, as Alexander Pope so memorably put it, convey 'what oft was thought but ne'r so well expressed' in *his* 'Essay on Criticism' (1711), has recurred throughout the history of literary theory. Specifically, however, Dewey implies that it is precisely 'personal interest' which makes critical thinking 'original', and this idea has a very particular resonance with the kind of practical criticism advocated by I. A. Richards, whose own evidence collected in his book of that name demonstrates the unique perspectives which different readers bring to bear on a text, and gives weight to the idea that a reading is inevitably original by virtue of its origination in a different reader. Since the judgement reached is arrived at independently, it entails *taking responsibility*, with all the political, moral and social implications which such a notion brings into play. Or, to give the same idea slightly different emphasis, since as Dewey envisages it, any judgement reached is necessarily an original one, it involves taking ownership of it – figuratively patenting it. 'Reflection is the acceptance of responsibility', he writes in *Democracy and Education* (p. 153), by which he means that the thinker must cultivate 'the disposition to consider in advance the probable consequences of any projected step and deliberately to accept them: to accept them in the sense of taking them into account, acknowledging them in action, not yielding a mere verbal assent' (*DE*, p. 185). This is a key point since it encapsulates why critical thinking matters for Dewey. At stake is not merely the intellectual development of the individual, but de facto the intellectual enrichment (or otherwise) of the community at large. Critical thinking is thus an active process not merely in the senses already outlined above, but also in the sense of impacting on the environment. Since critical thinking affects others, and therefore alters the community in which it takes place, it must be carried out with due care, and the critical thinker must take pains to foresee and take charge of the consequences of his or her judgements. Dewey's views on the political necessity of fostering critical thinking skills in a nation's citizens have been well documented.[31] At stake, ultimately, is democratic freedom – 'emancipat[ion] from the leading strings of others' (*HWT*, p. 64). Through the process of questioning and scrutinising empirical evidence outlined above, an individual is able, at least in part, to overthrow the limitations of his or her bodily instincts and appetites, the claims and demands of other people, prejudice, tradition and custom, and even, conceivably, the propensities of the natural world. For Dewey, therein lies not merely the ever-changing nature of intellectual thought, but, more specifically, its evolution or its progress. Fostering a critical spirit, then, not only entails the taking of responsibility, but moreover, taking responsibility entails being critical, since it is only through individuals exercising ongoing critical vigilance that the freedoms of all are safeguarded. This is a theme which educational philosophers such as Paulo Freire and bel hooks have, in the decades since Dewey, taken up and pushed towards more politically radical ends than those conceived by Dewey, but the indebtedness of these thinkers to the work of John Dewey is everywhere apparent.[32] It is for this reason that to train the child to think sceptically is, for Dewey, the central objective of education. The aim of education, he writes, 'is precisely to develop intelligence of this independent and effective type' (*HWT*, p. 63).[33] The *discipline* of critical thinking, however counterintuitive the notion may seem, secures the independence, the intellectual freedom of the individual from inaccuracy and bigotry, and ultimately holds to account those who wield material power over others.

John Dewey's theories about critical thinking might thus be summarized as follows:

- Critical thinking is an active process which results in judgement.
- It involves signification, a process in which meaning is generated by the nature and quality of the thought involved in reading signs, and not inherent in the sign itself.
- It entails solving a problem, imposing order on that which is apparently disorderly.
- It entails carrying out practical experimentation, for which first-hand evidence must be collected and analyzed via back-and-forth processes of induction and deduction.
- Critical thinking handles mobile ideas, and not fixed ideals.
- It is deliberate and purposeful.
- It involves the conscious testing of ideas which might have already been tested unconsciously.
- It follows orderly, systematic steps in restricted conditions.

- Disciplined habits are required, and for these to be acquired, training is necessary.
- The critical thinker must be creative and playful.
- Critical thinking takes time.
- Critical thinking entails the taking of risks.
- It is motivated by personal interest.
- It entails originality.
- It entails the taking of responsibility.
- Critical thinking secures freedom.

The child in thought

The child is a central site of interest in much of Dewey's work, both in works which expressly address education and in works which do so more tangentially. Dewey was fundamentally interested in the capacities of the child for thought. He was passionately committed to the importance of developing good habits of critical thinking in childhood, and throughout his career championed methods of education which placed this goal at their heart. His stress on the importance of critical thinking, and his theories about how the child thinks, has exerted a strong influence over educationalists since the early twentieth century.[34] Although Dewey is often cited as a key progenitor of the interest in critical thinking which has characterized recent education theory, interest in the child's capacity to think has a long history, and Dewey's ideas show indebtedness to those of John Locke (2007), Maria and Richard Lovell Edgeworth (1798), Jean-Jacques Rousseau (1991) and Friedrich Froebel (2001), with whom he engages directly in his work. Dewey is particularly important in this tradition, however, not only because he lays out his ideas so systematically and thoroughly, particularly in the landmark work, *How We Think*, but also because in doing so, he effected a sea change in educational thinking. To do so was in fact his conscious aim. In *How We Think*, it is his stated objective to debunk what he sees as the 'present' (early twentieth-century) 'notion . . . that childhood is almost entirely unreflective – a period of mere sensory, motor, and memory development, while adolescence suddenly brings the manifestation of thought and reason' (*HWT*, p. 65). He proposes instead that thinking, even in childhood, remains 'just what it has been all the time: a matter of following up and testing the conclusions suggested by the facts and events of life' (*HWT*, p. 66):

> Thinking begins as soon as the baby who has lost the ball that he is playing with begins to foresee the possibility of something not yet existing – its recovery; and begins to forecast steps towards the realization of this possibility, and, by experimentation, to guide his acts by his ideas and thereby also test the ideas. (*HWT*, p. 66)

For Dewey, the hallmarks of thinking – anticipation of that which is absent, generation of ideas, controlled experimentation – are in place from the earliest stages of human development. Indeed, however counterintuitive it may sound, Dewey even suggests that what a baby builds towards through thinking is *judgement*: if he 'takes one thing as *evidence* of something else, and so recognizes a relationship', it is, 'in however simple a fashion, judging' (*DE*, p. 152). So, even though the child's 'traits of carefulness, thoroughness, and continuity' (*HWT*, p. 66) may not be as fully honed as the adult's, we should not be misled by this into assuming that the child cannot exert conscious control over this thoughts, or that he is unable to do so in discriminating and discerning ways to reach deliberate conclusions.

But Dewey in fact goes further than this. For Dewey, the child is not merely capable of critical thought; the child is moreover peculiarly suited to it. This is because there are certain traits which are especially fertile for critical thinking and which are particularly manifest in childhood. This section will briefly outline these traits, and consider their implications for the kinds of critical thinking which might take place during childhood.

Curiosity, for Dewey, is a generative factor which 'suppl[ies] the primary material whence suggestion may issue' (*HWT*, p. 30). What curiosity generates is *problems*. The child observes the world around, and when another person cannot answer the question that arises, he or she 'continues to entertain it in his own head and to be alert for whatever will help answer it' (*HWT*, p. 33). We have seen earlier that critical thinking feeds off problems. Following this logic, the child is peculiarly prone to critical thought since the child is peculiarly exposed to uncertainties, puzzles and enigmas, by virtue of his or her comparative ignorance. Additionally, as Dewey observes, children are also peculiarly determined and self-reliant. Instead of giving up in the face of difficulty, or turning straight away to someone else to solve the mystery, children, simply in order to get through daily life, by necessity persevere, independently and repeatedly trying out alternative solutions to problems until a successful one emerges. In *How We Think*, Dewey recalls Francis Bacon's oft-quoted mantra that 'we must become as little children in order to enter the kingdom of science' (p. 33), gesturing to the history of the belief that the urge to ask questions is somehow less bounded in children than it is in adults. This idea of the child as a questioner par excellence – the idea of the child who persistently asks why – is so familiar that it is almost a cultural cliché. Michael Rosen has pastiched this idea in his poem 'I'm Just Going Out', in which repeated statements are followed by the question 'why?', culminating in the dénouement:

Why don't you stop saying why?
Why?
Tea-time why.
High-time-you-stopped-saying-why-time.
What?'[35]

For Dewey, as for Bacon, the child's approach is exemplary not just because the child is perpetually asking questions, but because the child is also impelled to test out the answers to such questions. Far from taking wisdom on authority, the child is inclined to satisfy him- or herself first-hand that the proffered answer is correct. The child, then, is experimental in ways in which the adult is not. Indeed, Dewey asserts that the 'desire to test' is a 'natural tendenc[y]' (*HWT*, p. 65), implying that, rather than being acquired by children from adults, this tendency is innate in children, perhaps even *typically* childish – or, to acknowledge the ways in which Peter Hollindale has so productively called into question the efficacy of the term *childish*, we might propose instead that the propensity for experimentation is a salient feature of *childness*.[36] By conceiving of it in this way, Dewey figures curiosity as a capacity that can be lost, not gained, over the course of maturation. Indeed, by figuring curiosity as a desire, if we follow Lacanian logic, he points to its origins in lack: the child's hunger for experience (knowledge) is great because that which he has experienced (known) is so minimal. Given how crucial the questioning reflex is for critical thinking, the extension of Dewey's position, then, is that childhood is more fertile for critical thought than adulthood; indeed, that over time the child is in danger of losing his or her capacity for curiosity. Dewey's uncharacteristically romanticized language when he refers to 'the open-minded and flexible wonder of childhood' (*HWT*, p. 33) tacitly registers the fact that the idea of childhood as greater than adulthood in this respect bears hallmarks of a Wordsworthian or Blakean narrative of maturation as loss rather than accumulation (itself an incarnation of Platonic anamnesis) wherein childhood is to be viewed with awe rather than contempt as a state of intellectual richness rather than poverty. Hence, he writes later in *Democracy and Education* that with 'respect to sympathetic curiosity, unbiased responsiveness, and openness of mind, we may say that the adult should be growing in childlikeness' (p. 148). Consequently, the teacher's role cannot be one of bestowal (since the teacher lacks that which the child possesses), and the model of instruction cannot be mimicry; instead, the teacher's task is to 'keep alive the sacred spark of wonder and to fan the flame that already glows. His problem is to protect the spirit of inquiry, to keep it from becoming *blasé* from overexcitement, wooden from routine, fossilized through dogmatic instruction, or dissipated by random exercise upon trivial things' (*HWT*, p. 34). The way in which Dewey casts this as a dramatic battle emphasizes the instability of the outcome and the fragility of the commodity: it is liable to be damaged, indeed *will* be damaged, without the right kind of adult intervention. Of course, we might want to bear in mind here the irony that this romantic view of childhood has itself often been characterized as an ideal.[37] Dewey re-enacts, both in the texture of his prose as well as conceptually, an idealizing tendency even as he equips us with the conceptual vocabulary with which to articulate a model of childhood which redeems the child from views which position it as trapped by adult ideals, and capable of mastering ideas for themselves. The irony is not a logical impossibility; the one, in fact, follows from the other; for what is at stake is the power of authorship: authorship of ideals (the maximum ideas possible). Rather than these being made for the child, the child makes them for him- or herself (and hence becomes an object of admiration – idealization – for the adult).

Just as curiosity is seen as innate, so too are 'the instincts of construction and production' (*The School and* Society (hereafter *SS*), p. 23), 'our impulses and tendencies to make, to do, to create, to produce, whether in the form of utility or of art' (*SS*, p. 26). The terms 'impulse' and 'instinct' underscore the primal motivation behind this tendency: a search for pleasure: 'Children simply like to do things and watch to see what will happen' (*SLC*, p. 43). The implication is that the child has a straightforward relationship with physical activity, wherein to be occupied is gratifying (implicitly contrasted with a more complicated adult relationship with physical activity, wherein apathy, aversion, anticipated boredom prompt deferral). For Dewey, there is a natural evolution from construction to artistry: 'The child's impulse to do finds expression first in play, in movement, gesture, and make-believe, becomes more definite, and seeks outlet in shaping materials into tangible forms and permanent embodiment' (*SLC*, p. 44). The child, then, for Dewey, is intrinsically on the move, gaining pleasure from being on the move, on a trajectory which makes use of movement for creative and utilitarian ends. Dewey asserts that the child 'has not much instinct for abstract inquiry', which renders their relationship with activity more direct and uncomplicated (while the adult will dither, held back from engagement in the immediate task by abstract intellectual ideas). On the one hand, then, the child's preference for the concrete over the abstract makes them peculiarly susceptible to critical engagement. However, it ought to be pointed out that Dewey insists that '*intrinsic* interest in the material', resulting in 'direct or spontaneous attention' does not 'merely of itself' result in critical thinking (*DE*, p. 148). What Dewey terms 'reflective attention proper' (*DE*, p. 146) must entail deliberation and control. Thus, while the child may possess bountiful natural capacities for critical thought, these must be harnessed by concerted application; mere absorption in a task is not in itself critical thought. What is necessary, then, is consciousness that there is a problem to be solved, such that the child poses him- or herself 'an intellectual question' and not merely 'a practical difficulty'. It is not that Dewey perceives the child to lack this capacity to derive an intellectual question from a practical difficulty so much as that he sees it to derive from experience – practice. That is to say, the child becomes a critical thinker through honing a skill and exerting control over his or her evolving capacities, not through losing those capacities and becoming an adult. Dewey's emphasis of the child's appetite for physical activity as a form of experimentation (so integral to his philosophy of progressive education) provides us with a valuable way of casting the child not as a passive recipient of experience (though, as he recognizes, experience necessarily entails an element of '*undergoing*' (*DE*, p. 146)) but as an active essayer, since, Dewey insists, experience is '*trying*' (p. 146). Experience is thus both active and passive: when we experience something, 'we act upon it, we do something with it; then we suffer or undergo the consequences' (p. 146). Children, in this process, are no more passive than their adult counterparts. To plot the one as active (adult) and the other as passive (child), in a false binary, misconstrues the nature of experience itself. By the same token, Dewey insists that while 'Capacity may denote mere receptivity, . . . [and] potentiality a merely dormant or quiescent state – a capacity to become something different under external influences', he also means by capacity 'an ability, a power; and by potentiality potency, force . . . a force positively present – the *ability* to develop' (*DE*, p. 46). If we view childhood in this way, then we can view 'growth' not as 'something done to [children]; it is something they do' (*DE*, p. 47). That is to say, we can reclaim some autonomy for children over the very narratives of maturation that they enact. In children's literature criticism, we have become accustomed to drawing on models of childhood which position the child as deactivated, subjected to adult desire or control or power – as objects not subjects. But if we make use of Dewey's vocabulary of capacity to shift the debate away from 'power' (Stephens) and 'desire' (Rose) and instead towards *activity*, then we can think more creatively and more critically about the kinds of *literary* experiences of which the child subject is capable.

'The attitude of childhood', Dewey writes, 'is naïve, wondering, experimental; the world of man and nature is news' (*DE*, p. 156). While, compared to the adult, the child may have greater desire to understand the world, the child understands less of it. Since critical thinking derives from incomprehension, and the child is full of incomprehension, the child's paucity of understanding thus promotes critical thinking since the child cannot fall back on a repository of familiar ideas but must constantly forge such ideas for the first time. 'Accordingly, mental progress will involve analysis' (*HWT*, p. 115), since the child must continually work out how to connect impressions newly made with impressions formed earlier. The work that this entails is, for Dewey, an 'intimate interaction between selective emphasis and interpretation of what is selected'. That is to say, 'analysis leads to synthesis; while synthesis perfects analysis'. The child constantly draws on his local environment 'to help clarify and enlarge his conceptions of the larger geographical scene to which they belong', but at the same time, 'not till he has grasped the larger scene will many of even the commonest features of his environment become intelligible' (p. 115). This constant back and forth from particular to general, and from general to particular (induction and deduction) is precisely a form of critical thinking. Indeed, we might go so far as to say that the child cannot *but* think critically: far from being an adult faculty, the propensity to question, to derive evidence, to test out that evidence and to form conclusions for oneself, conclusions which are constantly modified in light of new evidence, is precisely what children do all the time. Our propensity to declare that children *know* less than adults might make it easy to assume that children *think* less than adults; but of course, not only does the one not follow from the other, but in fact, the former makes it less likely that the latter is true, since the most effective way in which the child can make up for his or her lack of knowledge is by engaging, 'unconstrainedly and continually, in reflective inspection and testing' (*HWT*, p. 141). Children, then, by *necessity*, must quickly and inevitably become practised thinkers.

For a child, everything is original, since it is always happening for the first time. The child does not have to struggle to think for him- or herself, since the child is accustomed to doing nothing else. Just because the thought may have been had by someone else (indeed, in the case of a child, is likely to have been had by someone else), it does not make that thought any the less groundbreaking for that child. In nature, then, the child's thought is pioneering, even if its contribution to the world of knowledge is not.

Since critical thinking involves continuous testing in the here and now, and not falling back either on comfortable conclusions (dogmas) from the past or on untested beliefs postulated in the future or conditional modes, it is clearly an advantage to be well versed in living in the present. Thus Dewey views the 'proverbial' capacity of children to 'live in the present' not only as 'a fact not to be evaded', but moreover as 'an excellence' (*DE*, p. 59). Children, he declares, are peculiarly well suited to giving their full attention to the world in front of them, aided, presumably, by the comparative paucity of memory and of capacity to design elaborate artificial futures. Indeed, Dewey suggests that for a child, the 'future lacks urgency and body' (*DE*, p. 59), implying that the child does not experience the future as a pressure in the way an adult does, perhaps, we might speculate, because the child has the luxury of being less conscious than the adult of the speed and inevitability with which the future becomes the past.

These differently tuned attitudes towards time correlate with altered relationships with the present: for a child, time is filled with play, whereas for an adult, it is consumed by work. This is not, for Dewey, primarily a difference bound up with financial gain or with professional identity, so much as one dependent on whether one locates the value inherent in one's activities in the process or the product. 'In play,' he suggests, 'interest centers in activity, without much reference to its outcome. The sequence of deeds, images, emotions, suffices on its own account. In work, the end holds attention and controls the notice given to means' (*HWT*, p. 217). For Dewey, as has been explored earlier, the optimum attitude for critical thinking is one which blends work and play, such that play does not degenerate into 'fooling' (p. 217) and work does not become 'drudgery' (p. 217). The child is uniquely well placed to achieve this balance, tempering work with play, since the child cannot but play: play 'designates his mental attitude in its entirety and in its unity' (*SS*, p. 118). The extent to which this is viewed as emancipatory is registered in the name given to this – 'free play, or interplay, of all the child's powers, thoughts, and physical movements, in embodying in a satisfying form, his own images and interests' (*SS*, p. 118). Free play recalls the doctrine of associationism furthered by earlier educational thinkers in the British empirical tradition such as David Hartley, Francis Hutcheson, John Locke and Lord Kames, and which is given memorable articulation in the works of the Edgeworths, for whom play is central to how practical education arises. Like Maria Edgeworth, Dewey too emphasizes the practical, the hands-on, the free (i.e. that which is chosen, not directed by someone else, not dictated by conscious aims) as well as, crucially, the pleasurable.

Furthermore, Dewey proposes that 'the supreme end of the child is fullness of growth – fullness of realization of his budding powers, a realization which continually carries him on from one plane to another' (*SS*, p. 119). That is to say that the child is motivated not by the end which his activities will achieve, but by the satisfaction entailed in carrying out the activities themselves. This, at one level, is simply another way of saying that the child lives in the present; but it is more than this. It is also a way of saying that the child is liberated from a sense of obligation or duty beyond the task in itself, and consequently can more straightforwardly experience the pleasures of thinking for its own sake. In its most optimal form, this is artistic: 'work which remains permeated with the play attitude is art – in quality if not in conventional designation' (*DE*, p. 214). That is to say that the intermingling of work and play is enriching and fulfiling in both aesthetic and moral terms.

Not only is the child particularly well suited to critical thought, then, but critical thought is particularly well suited to the child, since the child is also peculiarly plastic, capable of 'vibrat[ing] sympathetically with the attitudes and doings of those about them' in ways in which adults, more entrenched in their own habits, are not (*DE*, p. 48). As Robert Coles puts it, in his preface to Gareth B. Matthews's *Dialogues with Children* (1984), 'children, like others called "human beings," summon language in the interests of continuing awareness, in the form of a constant curiosity, an imagination always at work, a full-fledged reflective energy. They join those of us who are older in a desire to edify, to reach others with their messages . . . Children are quite willing, in their pursuit of understanding, to ask sensible, provocative questions. They persist earnestly with those questions until some cognitive and moral hunger is appeased' (p. x). Dewey's account provides us with a means of thinking through in coherent terms not merely *that* but *how* the child might be peculiarly receptive to the ideas which he or she generates through critical thought, rendering critical thought not only more likely, but particularly beneficial during this early phase of life.

Practical criticism

This book highlights the ways in which the nature of the critical activity carried out by literature's children is a *practical* kind of criticism. The term *practical criticism* seeks to bring into a relationship the associations with *criticism* which we find in the work of John Dewey and other advocates of critical thought in education[38] and the associations with *practical* experimentation which we find in the work of Richard Lovell and Maria Edgeworth and other exponents of discovery learning. Coupled together, the words *practical* and *criticism*, of course, also invoke a particular form of decontextualized close reading which was advocated most famously by the Cambridge scholar I. A. Richards in his 1929 work of that name. In each of these three intellectual traditions, the business of asking questions and testing out preliminary suppositions through the analysis of available evidence is proffered as a mode of enquiry which is viewed as liberating, authentic and meaningful. *Literature's Children* explores the possibility that a form of *practical criticism*, albeit one conceived along less rigid lines than those proposed by I. A. Richards, might be a primal, fundamental, original kind of reading activity. It tests a hypothesis that this kind of critical activity might be uniquely commensurate with *childishness* in the sense that decontextualized close reading of the words on the page is precisely what children do. Indeed, when adult readers perform this kind of close reading, there is something anachronistic about it; it involves a contrived attempt to *return* to a set of reading conditions which predates those in which the adult currently exists. That is to say, it involves a contrived, nostalgic, and hence doomed, attempt to replicate circumstances which could only really be possible if the adult were capable of unknowing that which she now, irrevocably, knows.[39]

This book is not a polemic which seeks to advance the cause of practical criticism as a tool for uncovering literary meaning. The particular advantages – and disadvantages – of its methods are already well known. Instead, this book seeks to explore through close reading itself the usefulness of practical criticism for characterizing the nature of the work carried out by the child reader. The exercise is timely, since the practice of close reading has recently come under re-intensified attack. For example, in 2013, Franco Moretti proposed that we need to abandon our attachment to close reading on the basis that it 'will not do' for the study of world literature. The 'trouble with close reading', he asserts, '(in all its incarnations, from the new criticism to deconstruction) is that it necessarily depends on an extremely small canon' (p. 48). If we want to find 'strategies which enable us to read the sheer volume of world literature (not to mention the expansion in the scale of textual material which has been made available to us by new digital technologies', then, he proposes, we need to hone our techniques of 'distant reading – that is to say, focusing 'on units that are much smaller or much larger than the text: devices, themes, tropes – or genres and systems' (Moretti, 2013, pp. 48–9). Moretti's call to arms rests on a belief that we need somehow to move on from – outgrow – close reading; that close reading is passé. 'At bottom,' he asserts, 'it's a theological exercise – very solemn treatment of very few texts taken very seriously' (p. 48). In this, Moretti implicitly aligns close reading with a set of beliefs and practices which are a hangover from a more religious, socially conservative, dutiful era.

Moretti's provocative work has stirred controversy, and his approach has been robustly critiqued from a number of quarters. David A. Brewer has argued that 'flattening the literary field might undo "the monumentalizing that so often accompanies the literary canon", but at the expense of disregarding the varied profiles and presences of literary works in history' (2011–2, p. 162). Jerome McGann forecasts that in the coming decades, as 'the entirety of our inherited archive of cultural works will have to be reedited within a network of digital storage, access, and dissemination', precisely what we will need is 'young people well-trained in the histories of textual transmission and the theory and practice of scholarly method and editing' (2004, p. 410). More recently, Katherine Bode (2017) has expressed concern that in the picture of literary history created by distant reading, the reader falls out of the equation as an active party in the creation of meaning. It is worth noting that Moretti himself has insisted on the importance of integrating traditional methods of reading with new methods made possible by new technologies – his vision is that we take advantage of the different kinds of knowledge made available by both. Be this as it may, his arguments have given those sceptical about the value of close reading a new stick to beat it with.

But in fact, as Eugene Giddens has recently shown, close reading has never played the central role in children's literature studies that Moretti identifies as its traditional role in mainstream literary culture (Giddens, 2017). On the contrary, even prior to the advent of digital technologies, and certainly since, children's literature critics have frequently performed a kind of distant reading: they have been drawn to writing overarching accounts of the histories of particular genres, or eras, or nationalities of children's literature and to draw connections between vast swathes of texts, rather than to present slow, sustained readings of just one excerpt at a time. While there are certain notable exceptions, for example, in the work of the critic Roderick McGillis, which demonstrates the importance of sustained attention to the textual minutiae of literary texts for children, the sheer scope of many studies of children's literature, which take on discussion not of a single text, or a small cluster of texts, but multiple texts at once indicates that the commitment to close reading among specialists in children's literature may in fact never have been as firmly lodged as Moretti's account of our current intellectual climate might lead us to believe.

We can immediately point to a number of likely explanations for why close reading has never played the central role in children's literary criticism that it has played elsewhere. Perhaps it is because, by comparison to many other areas of literary criticism, the study of children's literature is in its relative infancy, and it has been assumed that it is first necessary to map out historical and theoretical trends *before* we can move on to more in-depth analysis of individual texts. Perhaps it is because the study of children's literature has, from the start, been an international project in which scholars reading material written in languages other than their own are not alert to or interested in the localized rhetorical minutiae of particular passages. Perhaps it is because children's literature studies has not grown out of the study of poetry in the way that mainstream literary criticism has done, but has from the start interested itself in myths and stories and the development of narrative. Indeed, comments such as Anna Barbauld's objection to poetry for children – 'But it may well be doubted if poetry *ought* to be lowered to the capacities of children' – have entrenched a firmly established view that the child is capable merely of literal reading, reading for sense, and not analytical reading, which, it has been supposed, is beyond the child's competence (Barbauld, 1781, p. iv). Although in fact much literature which we give to children, whether poetry or prose, is remarkably sophisticated and requires deft analytical interpretation, this theoretical tradition in which we refuse to believe that children are capable of carrying out any kind of reading activity that entails picking up on non-semantic forms of meaning has nonetheless persisted. Perhaps the marginalization of close reading in children's literature criticism reveals a latent belief that the adult critic of children's literature ought to confine him- or herself to tracking what the child reader does, rather than impose something on the text which would (it is assumed) be unavailable to the child. Perhaps, because the earliest practitioners of children's literature studies were often book historians and educationalists, and not literary critics, the field carries the traces of its multidisciplinary origins in its emphasis on thematic content (story; ideology; politics) over rhetorical mode. All of these possibilities have very likely contributed to forming an intellectual landscape in which close reading is not foundational in the ways that it has proved elsewhere in literary studies.

What is certainly not the case, however – though plenty have mistakenly assumed it to be the case – is that children's literature, because it strives to be accessible to children, is transparent. It may be that the textual strategies that children's authors deploy are seemingly simple and rarely call attention to themselves, such that they remain barely visible. But, as Aidan Chambers has observed in his discussion on gaps in 'The Reader in the Book', we ignore what is *not* said at our peril. The assumption that if the textual strategy is practically invisible, then there cannot be a strategy at all, has also given rise to another pernicious myth about children's writing: that, by comparison to writing for adults, it is *easy* to write for a young audience, since writing that is easy to follow must be easy to generate. This is a fantasy which the celebrated children's novelist Ursula Le Guin adroitly punctures: 'Sure it's simple, writing for kids. Just as simple as bringing them up' (Le Guin, 1992, p. 49). It is, of course, a central tenet of literary criticism that literary texts can never be explicitly literal. Indeed, when the textual strategies deployed are more carefully concealed, then it requires all the more effort to uncover them. If anything, then, it is *more difficult* to see the textual techniques at work when the text is *apparently* transparent. But this should not mean, as it seems to have done, that we therefore do not try; it simply means that we need to work harder – or differently – to identify what is going on. As Peter Hunt has written, 'the study of children's texts is technically *more* complex than the study of adult books, partly because the audience is different, and their responses more obviously unknowable, and partly because of the range of texts and the *range* of purposes' (Maybin and Watson, p. 25). And furthermore, if the textual strategies of children's literature are often carefully concealed, or seemingly unremarkable, then the need for the critic to bring them into plain view such that they can be subjected to scrutiny is all the more pressing, if we aspire to be conscious of – and capable of resisting – the ways in which cultural artefacts can weave spells on us.

For all these reasons, to assert that what we might do when we read a literary text is to carry out a form of practical criticism would be a banal commonplace, if asserted in mainstream literary culture; but it turns out to be a curiously unorthodox claim to make in relation to children's literary studies. And yet, as I have suggested, it might transpire that practical critical methods are a peculiarly appropriate means for uncovering meaning in the sphere of children's literature by virtue of the decontextualized ways in which children arrive at literary texts. *Practical criticism is what the child reader does*, since the child, who is likely to lack even basic knowledge about the context of the work at hand, must rely purely on the words on the page as a foundation for the meaning she derives. Like the candidates to whom I. A. Richards gave his unseen extracts, the child reader is unlikely to be equipped with ready biographical information about the author; is unlikely to think to look up, or indeed know what to do with, any information provided about the date of publication; and does not have a vast repertoire of existing literary templates on which to draw in order to make comparisons and contrasts. The child reader thus necessarily relies on their own wits in order to piece together meaning from the clues that they are given, negotiating the gaps both on the page and in their own experience by asking questions and testing out possible answers in an attempt to make sense of what is in front of them. Practical criticism, indeed, is the *only* kind of reading which the child can do. It would therefore seem peculiarly appropriate that the adult critic of children's literature also perform close reading on literary texts for children in an effort fully to appreciate what it is that the child is required to do when he or she judges how to go about responding to the text.

I am not the first to observe that close reading has much to offer to the field of children's literature. David Rudd, for example, characterizes his own recent book, *Reading the Child*, as an attempt to 'maintain the "energetics" of close reading' (2013, p. 9). Indeed, plenty of critics have attended to the localized details of literary texts for children, and the work of John Stephens (1992), Roderick McGillis (1996), and Murray Knowles and Kirsten Malmkjaer (1996) is particularly remarkable for the deftness with which it does this. John Stephens, drawing on discourse analysis, has explored how oral theories of utterances – speech-acts – are particularly fruitful for the analysis of the fabric of children's texts. Knowles and Malmkjaer (1996) bring to bear techniques of linguistic analysis to analyze phenomena such as lexical specificity and the representation of gender (p. 87). While my own case for close reading shares much in common with the work of these scholars, it is distinguished from it in several important ways. All of the above studies, broadly speaking, rest on a shared supposition that the child reader is enslaved to or is controlled by adult ideology, an idea which, at least since Peter Hollindale's taxonomical analysis of the kinds of ideology in operation in children's literature has held sway in children's literature studies (Hollindale, 1988). My own study seeks to shift the emphasis from ideology to ideas, thereby, for reasons outlined above, directing us away from questions of power and instead towards a consideration of the nature of the readerly *activity* at work. In this, the preoccupations that motivate this book are not dissimilar in kind to those that motivate scholars who work in the emerging field of cognitive criticism, notably Maria Nikolajeva (2014) and Roberta Trites (2014), who explore the ways in which narratives for children activate, and in turn are activated by, complex brain operations. But importantly, unlike all of the scholars mentioned above, who tend to place literary works for children in trans-historical contexts, I seek to restore the works under discussion in this book to their historical contexts, in the belief that the linguistic utterances which comprise works of children's literature are necessarily historically determined, as is the readerly activity that they stimulate. Therefore any discussion of how such texts operate must recognize the ways in which the discourses and mental transactions in which such texts participate are, at least in part, a product of their particular place and time. My own close readings, then, seek to acknowledge the historicity and cultural specificity of the textual features manifest in the texts under discussion.

My contention that practical criticism might have more relevance for children's literature than scholars have acknowledged to date might at first sight appear to be motivated by a desire somehow to endow the field of children's literature scholarship with credentials borrowed from the *serious* literary scholarship conducted elsewhere in literary studies. This is an aspiration which has been expressly articulated by critics such as Jerry Griswold, who has asserted that 'when we are able to talk about Children's Literature as literature, we will be able to address others outside our discipline with genuine confidence and authority' (Griswold, 2006). Kimberley Reynolds expresses a similar faith in the power of tried-and-tested literary critical methods to imbue the field with self-evident importance when she writes that 'a great deal of children's literature is *good* literature which can withstand any kind of critical scrutiny'

(1994, p. ix). This concern with the literary quality of children's writing – the consideration of 'how to find the *good* book for the child' – is, Karín Lesnik-Oberstein has claimed (in strikingly Leavisite terms), 'children's literature criticism's purpose, whichever way it is dressed up' (1994, p. 3). But this is not, in fact, my aim. My interest lies not just in identifying what theories about literary criticism might have to offer the study of children's literature, but equally importantly in identifying what the study of children's literature might have to offer theories about literary criticism. The insight that the child might be a kind of critic does not merely impact on how we conceive of the child reader; it impacts on how we conceive of and practise criticism itself.

Literature's children

One of the dangers of introducing a concept as seemingly monolithic as the 'critical child' is that it threatens to push towards simplification and generalization, crudely implying that all child readers behave alike, and what they do can be accounted for via a rigid scheme which has no means of attending to particularity and difference. Jacqueline Rose powerfully made the case in 1984 that it not possible to assume that the conceptual child reader is a 'knowable', unified audience (Rose, 1984, p. 10). While this is undeniably the case – literature's children constitute an audience every bit as plural and heterogeneous as any other audience, indeed, potentially more so, given the fundamental differences in age, competence and maturity which are elided by the all-encompassing term 'child' – at the same time, if we designate a field as *children's literature*, it is convenient, indeed necessary, to have a shorthand with which to refer to the implied reader of such material. It is for this reason that I maintain that it is useful to retain a singular term, a term which, despite its self-evident inadequacy, indeed, perhaps because of it, enables us to formulate pertinent, abstract questions which would otherwise be untenably particularized. It needs to be emphasized, therefore, that my interest in this book focuses on *ideas* about the child reader, seeking to ascertain how we might think about the *concept* of the child reader; in so doing, it does not take into account, indeed, can tell us nothing about, *real* child readers. Any discussion which sought to provide a more satisfactory account of the heterogeneity of child readers would have to proceed empirically and not, as I do here, theoretically. Important work of this kind, which has made great strides in enabling us to see in clearer focus the extent and nature of heterogeneous child audiences has been carried out in a number of different ways. For example, scholars interested in the history of children's literature, including Matthew Grenby (2011), Andrea Immel and Michael Witmore (2006) and Teresa Michals (2014), have shed valuable light on the reception of children's literature, and the different, often unpredictable, uses to which material for children (and material not hitherto associated with children) has been put over the centuries. Teresa Michals's recent study of age in the eighteenth- and nineteenth-century novel has fascinatingly shown that 'when earlier novelists and their readers considered the ideal age of the novel's audience, they tended to claim that the most important member of that audience was "the young person" rather than the adult' (Michals, 2014, p. 2), revealing the extent to which children, both real children and conceptual children, have always been part of the audience of adult literature, just as adults have always been part of the audience of children's literature. Through the collection of empirical data, work by educationalists including Nicholas Tucker (1981) and Morag Styles and Evelyn Arizpe (2003) has enabled us better to understand the variety of, as well as the patterns among, real children's responses to what they read. Such work builds on, even as it challenges, the premise of Arthur Applebee's seminal *The Child's Concept of Story* (1978), in which the reading strategies that children deploy are seen as in correspondence with certain identifiable stages of psychological development (Applebee primarily has in mind those proposed by Jean Piaget (1959). In addition, at least since Brian Appleyard's *Becoming a Reader* (1991), it has become customary to consider the peculiar relevance for children's literature of reader-response theories, in particular those associated with Wolfgang Iser (1974), Louise Rosenblatt (1978) and Norman Holland (1985), on whom Appleyard liberally draws in his effort to sketch out a scheme for the development of the reader based on 'the observable behaviour of readers in the culture we inhabit' (1991, p. 16). Appleyard (1991) charts the child's development through five discernible stages: the *stages of the reader as player, the reader as hero and heroine, the reader as thinker, the reader as interpreter*, and, finally, *the pragmatic reader* (pp. 14–15). In Appleyard's theoretical account of *real* readers, the reader does not begin to judge the material in front of her until adolescence; prior to this stage, the child is deemed 'uncritical' or 'precritical' (p. 2) – she escapes into the material in front of her and is absorbed by it.

My own study, while it is clearly motivated by questions similar in kind to those which motivate the studies discussed above, cannot hope to – indeed, does not seek to – offer an account of the child reader which either corroborates or disproves the findings of scholars who study the *real* reader, since my interest is squarely in the *implied* reader. Here it is helpful to keep in mind the distinction proposed by Wolfgang Iser between the 'real' reader (or as Iser glosses it, the 'real "me" ') and the 'implied reader' ('the alien "me" ' who is ' "occupied" by the thoughts of the author' (Iser, 1974, p. 293). As Iser explains, the 'implied reader . . . incorporates both the prestructuring of the potential meaning by the text, and the reader's actualization of this potential through the reading process' (1974, p. vii); or as Perry Nodelman and Mavis Reimer put it, the 'implied reader' is the 'role a text . . . invites a reader to take on', a role which is circumscribed, even constrained, by the fact that the text implies 'a way of being read' (Nodelman and Reimer, 2003, pp. 17–18). *Literature's Children* thus offers a series of close readings of key children's literary texts in an attempt to ascertain the kinds of practical critical skills which such texts invite the reader to carry out. Inevitably, then, the reader I discuss is always an implied reader and not a real reader; it is a discursive concept of a hypothetical reader, and not a descriptive account of what we know to have really happened to a particular reader. Like Appleyard, then, I too am interested in the activity carried out by the reader – the extent to which such activity might be deemed *critical* – but by shifting the emphasis away from the ways in which children are constructed *by* literary texts towards the ways in which children construct *them*, taking seriously the poststructuralist challenge to the idea that the imposition of the text on the reader is a one-way linear process, my study seeks to open up a space in which it is possible to reconsider, by beginning with a different set of starting points, Appleyard's oft-cited claim that the child reader, by comparison with the adult reader, is *un*critical. By emphasizing the often contradictory ways in which literary texts for children operate on their implied readers, my study insists that the work which the reader carries out simply in order to make sense of the text – albeit even merely to achieve that escape into the text which Appleyard documents – *must* entail a form of critical activity.

In mainstream literary culture, the emphasis long ago shifted away from interest in the author towards interest in the reader. As is well known, the reader is brought squarely into the main frame in theories which we now identify as New Criticism, as well as in those which we tend to characterize as poststructuralist; in theories which we characterize as reader-response theories, the reader takes centre stage. And yet, as I noted above, although in many ways children's literature scholars are especially interested in the reader-question, given that the very field comes into definition by virtue of its reader, children's literature scholars have nonetheless been reluctant to explore the ways in which the reader might play a constitutive role in the meaning-making process, and need not only be envisaged as a stable, passive endpoint. There is a perplexing illogicality to this. The child reader is at once our main interest, and yet we have been cautious about assimilating theories which make the reader pre-eminent, and as a result have held onto the firmly entrenched belief that the child reader will be shaped by the exertion on her of the literary text. Curiously, there is an analogue here in the treatment of the child in the discipline of philosophy. For a long time, it has either explicitly or implicitly been believed, as Avital Ronell puts it, that 'the child constitutes a security risk for the house of philosophy. It crawls in setting off a lot of noise' (Ronell, 2012, p. 156). As Ronell sees it, this view reaches back at least to Aristotle. This has led to what Robert Coles identifies as the 'scepticism of many adults . . . that children are capable of powerfully stated observations, of sustained eloquence, never mind moral reflection and analysis' (Preface to Matthews, 1980, pp. ix–x). While studies such as Anthony Krupp's recent book, *Reason's Children* (2009), have begun to unearth greater interest in the rationality of the child and her capacity to think critically than has previously been acknowledged among mainstream Western philosophers, the challenge to the coherence and linearity of the well-established account that the child has always been perceived to be incapable of reflective thought is in its early stages. The effort to interrogate this received wisdom will no doubt be galvanized by a recent spate of interest, both among scholars of children's literature and among philosophers, in the intersections between children's literature and philosophy. Lisa Sainsbury's 2012 *Ethics in British Children's Literature: Unexamined Life* makes a compelling case for the ways in which literary texts for children stimulate philosophical enquiry. In a different vein, Thomas Wartenberg's *A*

Sneetch Is a Sneetch and Other Philosophical Discoveries (2013) charts some of the philosophical issues which surface in contemporary picture books. Perhaps inevitably, there are frustrations for the literary scholar in reading accounts of children's literature which treat such texts as transparent vehicles for the discussion of metaphysics, apparently oblivious to the fact that literary texts might function in any more complex fashion ('I was actually surprised to discover how difficult it is to accurately characterize the philosophical issue or issues raised by a book' (Wartenberg, p. 5)), or, indeed, that works of children's literature might already have been subject to scrutiny by any scholars outside of the discipline of philosophy. The philosophers who contribute to Peter Costello's *Philosophy in Children's Literature* (2012) are in the main more sensitive to this issue, even though they too mostly proceed as though the ideas inherent in literary texts can be extricated from the forms in which they are articulated. However, the renewed attention paid in such studies to the question of how the child might think – the consideration, even, of the notion that the child might be capable of complex thought – opens up some valuable avenues for enquiry which have the potential to yield useful new insights to ongoing discussions about the work carried out by the child reader, whether that reader be real or implied.

The belief explicitly expressed by Appleyard, also implicit in much children's literature criticism, that the child reader's primary desire is to escape into the text has resulted in particular interest in the notion of the child reader's *pleasure*. Alongside this, the cultural aversion to overt literary didacticism has led commentators of children's literature to prize those texts which most obviously court the child reader's pleasure as quintessential examples of the species. This presumed alliance between pleasure and escapism has prompted comparisons between children's literature and popular literature, that other domain of print culture in which the reader is also often envisaged as a passive victim of the machinations of the text, driven on by unthinking thirst to find out what happens and a sentimental attachment to characters as though they were real people. In relation to both kinds of literature, it is typical to imagine the reader as worked on by the text, rather than as carrying out some kind of work in relation to it, on the basis that active work cannot be compatible with pleasure. The many and various connections between children's literature and popular culture have been explored by critics including David Rudd (2000); Julia Briggs,

Dennis Butts and Matthew Grenby (2008); and Andrew O'Malley (2012). The historical alliance between the two has been celebrated by critics such as Anne Lundin, who has observed the ways in which the professionalization of the study of children's literature in recent decades has entailed an 'evolution of the word "books" to "literature"', which 'reveals the increasing sacralization of discourse on reading for children' (Lundin, 2004, p. 142) – a turn which Lundin laments. However, *Literature's Children* seeks to disentangle discussions of children's literature from those of popular literature on the basis that the comparison is counterproductive to any effort better to understand what children's literature entails (and, I would imagine, vice versa). At the very least, unprejudiced examination of children's literature is compromised by perceived close proximity with a kind of literature which, however unfairly, has a history of association with artistic inferiority. Unappealing though his remarks are, the 'uneasiness' expressed by Henry James in 1899 towards mass-appeal literary texts is alive and well in the literary critical establishment. For James, such works are objectionable on the basis that their popularity reminds us that 'the sort of taste that used to be called "good" has nothing to do with the matter: we are so demonstrably in the presence of millions for whom taste is but an obscure, confused, immediate instinct' (1972, p. 337). But children's literature critics are accustomed to the denigration of their field. What is more serious is that the comparison between children's literature and popular culture promotes a view which (in the wake of theories of the artwork as a manufactured commodity proposed by figures such as Pierre Bourdieu, 1986; Theodor Adorno, 1986; and Walter Benjamin, 2008) has become a powerful means of accounting for the success of works of popular culture: that such texts are necessarily formulaic and manipulative, positioning the reader as a kind of automaton whose torpid quest for gratification blinkers her to the horrors of reality. While this may well be true of some, indeed many, cynically produced works for children, and while some children's literature undeniably functions like, or as, popular literature, and while it may even be true that such works anaesthetize the reader along the lines that Jack Zipes has warned about, it surely cannot be any the more true of *all* children's literature than it is true of *all* adult literature. The assumption that children's literature necessarily functions as popular literature eliminates the possibility that some works of children's literature might operate as works of *art*: that they elicit from us a form of critical enquiry whose pleasure resides in the challenges they pose; in the ways in which they alienate us from ourselves; in the beauty and wonder and doubt they prompt us to feel. Simply because children are novices in the art of reading, it does not follow that they are not capable of engaging with a literary text in this complex and enriching way. Nor does it follow, as Roland Barthes has vividly proposed, that the pursuit of literary pleasure need be – indeed, ever could be – passive. As Barthes has contended, even that which we denominate literary *play* entails a form of readerly work. If we reject the supposition that children's literature is a form of popular culture, then we can move away from the inhibiting assumption that the child reader's pleasure must take the form of a switching off, and not a switching on. In so doing, we can seek to find a vocabulary through which to conceptualize the ways in which the pleasure which the child reader derives through an engagement with a literary text might involve work and not merely play, doubt and not merely affirmation, heightened consciousness about the here and now and not merely escape into alternative worlds, a form of awakening and not a form of shutting down.

This book explores the ways in which the critical reading carried out by the child reader entails an *artful* relationship between work and play. The artfulness of the ways in which the child responds to literature has been obscured, I propose, by the continued dominance in scholarly discussions about children's literature, both explicitly and implicitly, of works which have been taken to adhere to a particular kind of artfulness: one which I here term the art of idealization. Claims that children's literature idealizes take several different forms. First, there are theoretical pronouncements which see *all* kinds of children's literary texts as doing something different from adult texts, and that one of the identifying hallmarks is an idealizing propensity. Second, there has arisen a scholarly convention to refer to a particular era of children's literature as a 'golden age', so called not merely because of the perceived fertility of this era for children's literature, that is to say, the number of memorable works it produced, but furthermore because of the perceived nature of the texts produced during this era, which are seen to present the world in ways which purify, refine, sanitize and comfort. This is the view popularized by Humphrey Carpenter, and it is perceptible in critical work on those same children's literature texts even where critics have found alternative terminology with which to characterize works from this period, for example in Juliet Dusinberre's deployment of the critical label 'modernist' to identify radical experiments in art which 'challenge both the Victorian establishment and its established narratives' (1999, p. 40), or in Kimberley Reynolds's reference to '*fin-de-siècle* nostalgia for childhood' (1994, p. 17). Of course, the two impulses are interrelated: it is precisely because of the tendency to see such texts (e.g. *Peter Pan, The Secret Garden, Alice's Adventures in Wonderland*) as *idealizing* the world that they have been considered *ideal* texts for children, and hence kept in print, giving rise to the idea that a certain era witnessed a flourishing of children's literature, which, by another view, might be thought to have flourished in every decade since at least the 1740s. Thirdly, there is this question of canonicity, and the ways in which there might be thought to be a corpus of ideal children's texts – the best, or the most approved, or the most culturally valuable. Canons are, of course, a feature of all literature, but the notion of canonicity has a particular traction in children's literature because of the ways in which children's literature is tied to school curricula and is overtly (and covertly) used to further educational programmes. Given this, it is perhaps inevitable that the reading list endures as a means of organizing the kind of literature that adults desire to place in the hands of children.

As has been well documented, the ongoing celebration of certain totemic works of children's literature from the so-called 'golden age' entails a kind of collective wistfulness: a preference for the past over the present – even a repudiation of the present. This 'affection' for children's books of the past shows, Shelia A. Egoff has suggested, a '*highly* unusual attachment to the past' which, she contents, '*is no accident*. It derives, rather, from certain more or less constant characteristics of books intended for children' (McGillis, 2003, p. 3). The backwards-looking glance entailed in the gesture which turns to past structures not merely for pleasure but moreover for knowledge tends to be seen as tethered to a politically- and socially-regressive, rather than progressive, agenda. The routine theory invariably put forward is that these works tap into something which we tend to call 'nostalgia': a homesickness for the world as it used to be which comes into play not merely through our alienation from this former world, but moreover through our awareness of our alienation from this former state of existence. There are numerous examples of work carried out in this vein. For example, Elizabeth Thiel, examining the representation of the family in nineteenth-century children's literature, has noted 'our passion for all things "traditionally" Victorian and our nostalgia for a golden age of national pride celebrated by united, supportive families', which, she suggests, 'serves primarily to engender a sense of loss'. Children's literature of this period, she suggests, 'nurtured and perpetuated the myth of the domestic ideal' (Thiel, 2008, pp. 2, 157). But if Thiel is right to identify the importance of nostalgia in our enduring fondness for golden-age literature, then what precisely are we nostalgic *for*? Clearly, at one level we are nostalgic since we may have read these books as children, and therefore we wish to return to these books because they remind us of our own childhoods, and even enable us to gain a foothold on what we take to be a more abstract concept of childhood. But what if in fact we never *did* read these books as children? Many of these books are so seemingly familiar to us that we may assume or believe that we must have read them; but when we come to reread them, we discover that we are in fact reading them for the first time. What we thought was a nostalgic *re*turn to a children's classic turns out simply to be a nostalgic *turn* to a children's classic. If our reading experience is not impelled by nostalgia for our own childhood, then is it impelled by nostalgia for someone else's? As Anne Lundin documents in her fascinating book about the construction of the canon of children's literature, 'Corresponding to aesthetic standards of the adult world, classics are associated with imaginative recreations of humanistic life, an ennobling literature with spiritual resonance' (2004, p. 53). Are we somehow homesick for a home we never had, but wish we *had* had? Does it even make sense to refer to nostalgia as a means of accounting for our yearning towards that which we *never* had?

The term *golden age* has been used by critics such as Humphrey Carpenter to align writing for a child audience to a particular literary mode: the pastoral. This is a mode, as numerous theorists of the pastoral have observed, which seeks to evoke an idealized world even as it simultaneously pulls away from it.[40] It is one which dismantles the idyll it creates even in the process of setting it up. Pastorals, in this sense, are kinds of elegies; they do not straightforwardly idealize – instead, they lament the impossibility of idealization itself. In the field of children's literature, though, all too often the term 'golden age' has been adopted in a way which fails fully to theorize this peculiar hallmark of pastoral. Critics such as Humphrey Carpenter have straightforwardly drawn on the notion of the pastoral in order to bring together works by writers such as J. M. Barrie, E. Nesbit, Kenneth Grahame and A. A. Milne who happened to live within decades of one another, and whose works present us with subject matter that is sufficiently recognizable to remind us of the world we inhabit, but sufficiently distorted to underscore that the world we inhabit is inferior to that represented. Do such works share in common, however, a representational *mode*? Do they dismantle the idylls they create in similar ways to one another – or, indeed, at all?

The ways in which the critical term *golden age* has been used in children's literature scholarship to invoke associations of pastoral without consideration of the ways in which pastoral denotes a literary mode, and not merely a variety of subject matter, cause me to feel uneasy. Of course, at a simple level, any term which seeks to characterize a particular era (when literary history cannot straightforwardly be compartmentalized), or a particular aesthetic (which are always more complicated than any label allows), is doomed to fail. But there is something especially counterproductive about the use of this particular term in the field of children's literary study, since its association with ideas of *ideals* reinforces a misleading impression that children's literature itself is an idealized (sanitized, simplified, purified) literary form. The fact that this is patently not the case in our own age has not prevented scholars from asserting that it still must have been the case in previous eras (and we might note that the use of the critical label has always been applied retrospectively: it was first used by Roger Lancelyn Green to refer to works which were already by then associated with a past age). The notion that children's literature *idealizes* the world is crystallized in titles such as that of Deborah Gorham's 1982 study, *The Victorian Girl and the Feminine Ideal*. But what is the force of the verb *idealizes* in this context? What are the implications of the ahistoricity of the statement? What effect does it have on the critical insights we glean when we insist on seeing our own age as different and anomalous in an otherwise homogeneous tradition which stretches back through time, rather than wondering whether the seeming anomalousness of the present might in fact alert us to the possibility that our sense of the homogeneity of the past might itself be faulty?

The use of such terms causes me uneasiness for another reason. There is something childish about idealism. Idealism is related to children, since children make-believe – they create fantastical alternative worlds for themselves. In addition, adults tell children half-truths – sanitized and rose-tinted versions of the real story – to provide them with comfort or for their ease of comprehension.

But idealism is also childish (in the sense that Hollindale rejects the term)[41] in that it implies an *adult* refusal to be enlightened, to confront truth, to reflect on suffering, to recognize the world as it is – that is to say, it implies a kind of naivety or immaturity, a refusal to concede or to give up hope – a determined confidence even after having confronted reality (optimism).[42] This is the association which Frank Preston Stearns brings out in his 1896 work, *The Real and Ideal in Literature*, in which he advocates literature which idealizes over what he deems to be the then-ubiquitous 'doctrine of realism [which] threatens to crush out everything that is great and elevating in our literature' (p. viii). For Stearns, it is 'the proper business of the artist to represent the real with the ideal shining through it' (p. 16). In so doing, he will enable 'man['s] . . . spiritual nature . . . to again assert itself, and instruct him that the only true rest is to be found in what is invisible and immutable'. In being so instructed, the reader 'will learn once more the lesson of his childhood' (p. viii). It is useful, I propose, to distinguish between these two ideas (the relationship of idealism to children, and its associations with childishness), as its perceived childishness in fact has nothing to do with children, and the use of the idea of childish to ascribe a set of (usually pejorative) connotations to what are in fact markedly adult tendencies serves to contaminate that which actually relates to children, who are not flawed versions of adults, but simply people at an earlier stage on the journey. The same is true, I would contend of their literary culture, which does not present flawed (either naïve or optimistic) versions of adult knowledge, but presents knowledge as it is experienced at an earlier stage of life. To insist that such versions of knowledge are *ideal* seeks to impose adult culture as a kind of normalizing standard against which children's culture is abnormal, or as Maria Nikolajeva (2009) has suggested, *aetonormative*. To think our way out of this repeated tendency to plot children's literature as *not* adult literature, we need to find vocabulary which enables us to see children's culture as serving its *own* ends, and not ends which are formed outside of it, and which reach beyond it. This book attempts to do precisely this.

Literature's Children, then, offers a series of readings of a handful of children's literary texts in relation to all of which claims have been made for their idealizing status. Several of the works discussed here might be considered to have been written during – or under the influence of – what Roger Lancelyn Green termed the golden age, although for the reasons outlined above, this is a category about whose usefulness I remain sceptical. By consequence, where I use the term 'golden age', I do so to acknowledge the ways in which this term has acquired a currency in children's literature scholarship, but not to perpetuate a notion that it is intellectually meaningful to group together only superficially alike works under this banner. The chapters in Part 2 analyze the ways in which idealizing tendencies might be seen to be at work in certain literary texts, making a case for the ways in which the idealizing tendencies they ostensibly present are complicated by the activity entailed in critically reading the text. That is to say that such idealizing tendencies collapse under the critical scrutiny of the child reader. These works, then, are of interest – are *artistic* – precisely on account of this tension. I ought to emphasize that I do not take the literary works discussed in this book as emblematic of patterns beyond themselves. They are all, however, works which share in common the fact that claims have been made about each of them that they *idealize* – and it is these claims, and by extension, the abstract theoretical supposition which underpins such claims – *that children's literature idealizes* – which the close readings offered here together seek to complicate. The chapters in Part 2 seek to demonstrate that the notion that children's literary works, even those which have been famed for so doing, idealize the world is not borne out by an analysis of the kind of critical reading which these texts invite, indeed require, the child reader to carry out. Marah Gubar has recently debunked the idea that the so-called golden age of children's literature gave rise to a host of literary works which 'failed to conceive of children as complex, acculturated human beings in their own right by regarding them either as lost selves or alien Others' (2009, p. vii). Gubar's title, like my own, picks up on the artfulness of children, discussing the ways in which the child is represented as a 'collaborator' in works of the so-called golden age, and is 'not inevitably victimized as a result of this contact with adults and their world' (p. vii). Gubar's account of the representations of child characters in works from this period allows for a greater degree of ingenuity and cunning than is usually acknowledged by scholars who emphasize such child characters' apparent innocence – a word which, as has already been observed, appears with regularity in children's literature scholarship and yet is still in dire need of more systematic theorization.[43] My own book proposes that just as children in literary texts of this era are represented as more in charge of their own destiny than has been generally acknowledged, so too the implied child readers of such texts are more independent than scholarly discourse tends to credit them as being. Merely because a text may appear to *offer* a set of ideals, it does not follow that a reader will *inherit* such ideals. Indeed, to assume that the child reader could do any such thing is a logical impossibility, since ideals are, by their nature, fixed. If we are to concede that reading is an activity which comprises of a set of verbs, and occurs over time, then the reader, whether adult or child, or 'children of a larger growth' (Dryden, 1975, IV.i), *must* translate an ideal (that which is fixed, and hence frozen in time) into an idea (that which is unfixed and hence mobile through time) in order simply to make sense of it – to arrive at a critical judgement. Judgement, as John Dewey's work is particularly helpful in enabling us to see, is the result of a particular kind of thinking in which we test out – play with – different ideas in an attempt to resolve the unresolved. The consideration of ideas presented by a literary text thus entails the reader in a form of critical work which is cunning, wily, clever, active – or to adopt Dewey's terms, *playful* in a specifically *artful* way.

The account of reading offered in *Literature's Children* thus offers a new way of thinking about how literary texts aimed at child audiences might operate both didactically and aesthetically, by viewing critical reading as a united kind of work and play. It offers a way of reconciling didacticism with aestheticism, or rather, seeing didacticism as in itself aesthetic, just as the appreciation of an aesthetic object is in itself an educative experience. In this, it challenges the narrative posed by critics such as J. S. Bratton, who has argued that over the course of the nineteenth century, 'the formulae of didactic fiction, the allegories, romances, historical tales and stories of adventure, became items in the equipment of the professional entertainer; and naturally becoming worn and threadbare with use, they were gradually rendered transparent, until their emptiness was the most obvious thing about them' (1981, p. 208). On the contrary, didacticism continues to be a vital mode for children's literature – and to observe that this is the case need not entail a denigration of the artfulness of the work in question. The works I discuss here are all, I propose, didactic, in the sense that they educate: they encourage the child to think critically, to become a *judge*, not a receptacle of ideology; but crucially they are also all fundamentally aesthetic: they pattern the worlds they present such that the child must delight in the sophistication and open-endedness of his or her own response.

The chapters in Part 1 focus on material from the eighteenth century that is habitually dismissed as didactic, and seek to find new ways of attending to the aesthetic interest such material poses for the child reader. Chapter 1 teases out the complex ways in which the child is invited to engage with poetry in the eighteenth century, identifying the nature of the critical work that children's poetry by Isaac Watts and John Newbery expects child readers to be able to carry out. By identifying the ways in which the child reader is invited to read critically, against the grain, Chapter 2 interrogates the assumption that comic literature for children is delightful and permissive in ways that solemn literature, particularly that produced prior to the mid-nineteenth century, is not.

Part 2 offers close readings of a range of seminal works of children's literature, each of which manifests a different kind of idealizing work which has been seen to be carried out by children's literature since the late nineteenth century. Chapter 3 discusses Kate Greenaway's *Under the Window*, a landmark picturebook volume of poetry, wherein the fusion of images and words forges a new order of aesthetic delight for young people, and opens up lines of sight which trouble Victorian ideals of order. Chapter 4 discusses E. Nesbit's sentimental novel, *The Railway Children*, a novel which seeks to make the child cry even as it acknowledges the incompatibility of tears with happiness. Chapter 5 considers the ways in which Kenneth Grahame's *The Wind in the Willows* functions as a philosophical meditation on the problem of boredom, undecidedly drawing out the simultaneous appeal of two contradictory states: restlessness and inertia. Chapter 6 analyzes the ways in which J. R. R. Tolkien's *The Hobbit* negotiates the child reader's frustrations with language in a form necessarily comprised of the stuff itself. The final chapter, Chapter 7, considers, through the case of Malcolm Saville's *Lone Pine* series, how even apparently literal aesthetics invite, indeed demand, critical participation on the part of a child reader – and how children's works lose their audience when they cease to satisfy the critical child's desires.

Together, the close readings presented in this book aim to contribute to a sharper understanding of the nature of the idealization that takes place in literary texts produced for children, such that we can see in plainer view the critical work that literature's children undertake as they translate adult ideals into childish ideas in their ongoing efforts not to be prevented from thinking.

Part One

The critical child

1

Eighteenth-century children's poetry and the complexity of the child's mind

Isaac Watts's *Divine Songs, Attempted in Easy Language for the Use of Children* (1715) was not the first volume of poems written expressly for children, but it was the first successful one to make the case that something peculiar might be achieved by addressing children through poetic form, and that in order to effectively meet the needs and capacities of a young audience, poetry needed to be shaped with those needs and capacities in mind. By the end of the eighteenth century, Watts's volume had gone through at least fourteen editions, and, as Harvey Darton points out, by the end of the nineteenth century, several of the poems within it had suffered the 'misfortune' of 'being recited by children in public, year in, year out, to the mortification of the reciters and the weariness of the audience' (1982, p. 109). Over the course of the eighteenth century, then, poetry that was specially written or adapted for young people came to occupy a central place in the child's life of the mind. By 1745, the notion that children ought to be conversant with the principles of poetry had become such an established one that John Newbery dedicated an entire volume of his series, *Circle of the Sciences* (1745–6), to the business of introducing young readers to excerpts of poetry and equipping them with strategies for understanding them. The pre-eminent place that adults aspired for poetry to have in children's culture can be construed from the fact that there are no equivalent volumes in the *Circle of the Sciences* series devoted to other species of literature, reflecting the engrained view of poetry's aesthetic and moral superiority to prose or drama. As John Dennis wrote in *The Advancement and Reformation of Modern Poetry* (1701), 'Poetry . . . is more passionate and sensual than prose,' a belief which endured throughout the period, despite concerted attempts to establish the aesthetic and moral credentials of the novel (p. 24). But

Newbery's tacit prioritization of poetry over prose also indicates a widespread supposition that the child reader is capable of carrying out, indeed, desires to carry out, sophisticated critical activity. For it was also widely believed in the eighteenth century that whereas prose is self-explanatory, poetry does not readily yield itself to the reader, and it can only be understood, or at least only understood correctly, after initiation. This is apparent in the use of 'Easy' in the titles both of Newbery's volume, *Poetry Made Familiar and Easy*, and Watts's *Divine Songs, Attempted in Easy Language for the Use of Children*, wherein the emphasis placed on accessibility alerts us to the perceived difficulty of this art form for its intended audience. Careful examination of how these two seminal figures in the evolution of children's literature, Isaac Watts and John Newbery, manipulated subject matter and form in order to render poetry simultaneously accessible to and stimulating for the child reader provides us with a means of viewing some of the period's most prominent ideas about children's literary critical capacities, and reflecting on the centrality and nature of the role established during the period for the critical child.

In the Preface to *Divine Songs*, Watts proclaims, 'I have endeavoured to sink the language to the level of a child's understanding, and yet to keep it (if possible) above contempt' (1716, p. 6). This visual metaphor of height and depth implies a scale in which, as the word 'contempt' drives home, simplicity is aligned with intellectual poverty on the one hand and complexity aligned with intellectual prowess on the other. In this respect, Watts perpetuates a customary belief in the child's ignorance as a gap that must be filled. The influence of John Locke's *Some Thoughts Concerning Education* (1693) in the early decades of the eighteenth century had weakened the dominance of the Puritan view of the child's ignorance as a sign of immorality and ungodliness, seen in the catechism, *Milk for Babes* (1646) by the New England reformer, John Cotton: 'Qu. How doth the Ministery of the Law bring you towards Christ? A. By bringing me to know my sinne, and the wrath of God against me for it' (p. 7). Nonetheless, even in Locke's more liberal account of knowledge, ignorance carries with it the weight of shame, albeit in the secularized political sense that it signifies social redundancy rather than moral perdition. In *Some Thoughts Concerning Education*, Locke argues that '[c]uriosity in children . . . is but an appetite after knowledge, and therefore ought to be encouraged in them, not only as a good sign, but as the great instrument nature has provided to remove that ignorance they were born with, and which, without this busy inquisitiveness, will make them dull and useless creatures' (2007, p. 93). To prevent such psychological and social waste, and to foster instead a 'sound mind in a sound body' (p. 25), is the primary stated aim of Locke's educational treatise. Watts's deployment of 'easy language' thus seeks to tread a delicate path between acknowledging the Lockean belief in children's native desire for intellectual stimulation and the consequent need for literary material to challenge children into readiness to negotiate complexity, while at the same time accepting that the cognitive needs of the preliterate or newly literate are such that they require material devoid of unnecessary complication.

Watts reconciles, at least in part, the possible tension between these competing demands through his recognition that 'language' cannot be reduced to mere diction. He appreciates that since a child's vocabulary is less extensive than an adult's, poetry for children needs to favour terminology already familiar to the child. That this practice has in the centuries since become a customary feature of writing for children should not obscure its innovativeness in 1715. Watts was not responsible for inaugurating it. John Bunyan, for example, whose *A Book for Boys and Girls, or Country Rhymes for Children* (1686) went through nine editions by 1724, had made some attempts to temper his mode of address to his young readership through the incorporation of lines which refer in simple terms to instantly recognizable natural phenomena: 'This pretty Bird, oh! how she flies and sings!' (p. 11). But lines such as these are interspersed with lines elsewhere whose comprehension requires a secure grasp of subtle theological nomenclature: 'The fallen Candles to us intimate,/The bulk of God's Elect in their lapst state' (p. 51). Likewise, James Janeway's prose *A Token for Children* (1676) intermittently ventriloquizes distinctively childish voices, but the polysyllabic circumlocutions he attributes to his juvenile characters belie the adult machinations behind the scenes: 'O Mother . . . it is not any particular Sin of Omission or Commission, that sticks so close to my Conscience, as the Sin of my nature' (p. 6). By comparison, the vocabulary that Watts selects for his child audience is more consistently and calculatedly pared down, so much so that in the decades following the publication of *Divine Songs*, Watts came to emblematize this practice. John Wesley, in his Preface to the 1790 edition of his brother, Charles's, *Hymns for Children* (1763), in which he attempts to defend Charles's sophisticated phraseology, therefore refers back to Watts to set up a counterpoint. Watts, he complains, neglected to teach his readers because he adjusted language to the demands of children rather than requiring children to meet the demands of language: 'There are two ways of writing or speaking to children,' John Wesley writes; 'the one is, to let ourselves down to them; the other, to lift them up to us. Dr. Watts has wrote [sic] in the former way . . . leaving [children] as he found them' (qtd. in Clapp-Itnyre, 2016, p. 61). Similarly, Watts is the implicit target when Anna Laetitia Barbauld in her Preface to *Hymns in Prose* (1781) claims that it is an assault on poetry to adapt it to the child's ear, insisting that prose is a more suitable form for young readers until their cognitive skills are sufficiently developed to enable appreciation of ambiguity. What all of these accounts share in common is a belief that children find it simpler to deal in vocabulary that is already within their purview. At stake is a difference of opinion concerning the pedagogical (and, implicitly, the aesthetical and moral) advantages of catering to, versus resisting, the child's ease. More directly to return to the terms set up in the Introduction, the extent to which the reader should be given the freedom independently to arrive at their interpretation of the text – should be given the opportunity to be a critical child – is the pressing problem which preoccupies poets for children.

It is clear, though, both from Watts's Preface to *Divine Songs* and from the poems themselves that what Watts has in mind by 'language' is not merely which words are used but also how these words are used: that is to say, not just diction or the systems within which words function (what Ferdinand de Saussure would later term 'langue') but also the forms in, or methods by which, words are uttered ('parole') – or to recall John Dewey's terminology, the ways in which the words function as *signs*. Watts gauged that poetic form could be customized to render it a sign-system peculiarly apposite for child readers. Believing that the key pedagogical advantage of verse over prose was its memorability – 'What is learnt in verse is longer retained in memory, and sooner recollected. The like sounds and the like number of syllables exceedingly assist the remembrance' (Watts, 1716, p. 5) – Watts made a powerful argument for the importance of repetition. Patterning the form such that a feature reappears again and again is, he suggests, a means of embedding a thought into the mind, since together, recursive patterns form a memorable tune (a feature that is foregrounded by his decision to identify these poems for children as songs). Accordingly, the metrical lines used in *Divine Songs* are strikingly unvaried and hence easy for the child to anticipate. The majority of the stanzas used are quatrains made up of alternating rhyme; most are lines of tetrameter, sometimes alternated with lines of trimeter to comprise common metre, the traditional metre of hymns. This template was taken up as the usual poetic form of choice by Watts's successors, for example by the anonymous author of *Little Master's Miscellany* (1767), by Christopher Smart in *Hymns for the Amusement of Children* (1771), and even by William Blake in *Songs of Innocence* (1789). Its close correspondence with ballad metre, the metre of so many popular songs and verses disseminated orally during the period, meant that children would likely already be accustomed to the conventions of the form.[1] Watts hopes that encountering subject matter in a form that can be replayed again and again in the inner ear enables his reader, seemingly inadvertently, to catch hold of the ideas carried by the semantic connotations of the words: 'it may often happen, that the end of a song running in the mind may be an effectual means to keep off some temptation, or to incline to some duty, when a word of scripture is not upon the thoughts' (p. 5). Watts's theory of children's poetry thus deals in a kind of proto-unconscious, nearly a century before Samuel Taylor Coleridge imported the vocabulary of the unconscious into the English language, musing in his *Notebook*, 'there is a self, or consciousness of the day, and an opposing self of the night' (1957–73, p. 4409). Watts envisages that the trick of the educationalist must be to instil habits of mind without the reader even appearing to notice. Indeed, for the sleight of hand to be successful, the educator must appear to be doing the opposite, performing what today we might call reverse psychology, or what in his 1784 work, *Studies in Nature*, Jacques-Henri Bernardin de Saint-Pierre, the disciple of Jean-Jacques Rousseau, termed 'contrary effects': 'if the nurse wants her child to laugh, she shrowds her head in her apron; upon this the infant becomes serious' (1796, p. 158). Watts aspires for his language to be 'easy', then, in the sense that its ingestion requires a lack of effort – or at least, a lack of conscious effort – on the part of its reader. It is the critical child's *unconscious* mind that will be at play.

Watts was not the first to perceive the possibilities inherent in manipulating poetic form to enable the child audience to conceive of the work involved in reading as a form of play. For example, the anonymous author of *A Guide for the Child and Youth* (1709), identified simply as 'A Teacher of a Private School', recognizes that 'Prayers, Graces, and Instructions' must be 'fitted to the Capacity of Children' if they are to be accessible to their designated audience, and lights upon poetic form as a fertile mode for communication. However, the writing in *A Guide for the Child and Youth* wears its laboriousness in plain view, resulting in verse that is awkward to read and instantly forgettable. In one poem, the author sets up an anapaestic metre, forcing the word 'Petition' into three distinctly separate syllables in a way that causes the word to be articulated unnaturally, with the emphasis on the first syllable:

First in the Morning
When thou dost awake,
To God for his Grace
Thy Petition make. (1–4)

While in so doing, the author maintains metrical consistency, we are compelled to treat the word not as a carrier of semantic meaning but as a series of pulses in order to complete the line. As Alexander Pope mockingly observed in *Essay on Criticism*, 'But most by numbers judge a poet's song; / And smooth or rough, with them is right or wrong'. The flexibility of the author of *A Guide for the Child and Youth* in relation to the rules of scansion leaves his poetry susceptible to outright rejection. For Watts, though, it was crucial that sound and sense were embroiled in one another in order to enable children to replay the poem to themselves on demand: 'This will be a constant furniture for the minds of children, that they may have something to think upon when alone, and sing over to themselves' (1716, p. 5). The elision here between thought and song reveals the ways in which Watts aspires for the one to yield to the other: the sound will bring to mind the thought, just as the thought will bring to mind the sound. Ann Wierda Rowland has recently demonstrated the ubiquitousness in the eighteenth century of the idea that primitive speech, and by extension the speech of infancy, was proximate to music (2012, p. 88). Johann Gottfried von Herder's *Treatise on the Origin of Language*, for instance, refers to the 'wild, unarticulated noises' of children as a 'language of sensation' (Herder, 2002, p. 66). Crucially, for Watts, the connection between thought and sound at play in poetry is one that not merely expresses but moreover produces the primal sensation of pleasure. For all that Joyce Irene Whalley (1974) has argued that 'to "like" or "enjoy" reading is a comparatively recent concept' (p. 10), Watts anticipates the Deweyan emphasis on child-led education by understanding the necessity that the child be motivated to read by the thrill of the process itself. In Watts's account, though, such pleasure is envisaged as unwitting; indeed, it is generated precisely by the inadvertency of the child's ingestion of the text. The fact that the child does not need to try, the fact that the text burrows its way into the child's ear without the child having to make an effort to learn it, is precisely the point. This marks a clear departure from established Early Modern learning methods such as catechism, which was a key means in the period of ensuring that ideas were imprinted on the child's mind. The ease of Watts's language, then, is not merely a token nod to the child's comparatively narrow vocabulary; it is moreover a means to ensure both the message's safe passage and the child's satisfaction from, perhaps even enjoyment of, the journey itself. It enables the child to carry out a variety of readerly activity which, like Dewey's notion of critical thinking, is purposeful and pleasurable at once, the pleasure ensuing from the fact that the purpose is inherent in the experience of activity itself.

There are certain key insights about the emergent category of the critical child that we can extrapolate from Watts's championing of easy language as the language most fit for the child reader. One is the obvious point which was largely accepted without question in the period: that the child's cognitive capacities were limited to functions that were basic. Hence, Locke (2007) had claimed, 'Children's minds are narrow and weak, and usually susceptible but of one thought at once. Whatever is in a child's head, fills it for the time, especially if set on with any passion. It should therefore be the skill and art of the teacher, to clear their heads of all other thoughts, whilst they are learning of any thing, the better to make room for what he would instil into them, that it may be received with attention and application, without which it leaves no impression. The natural temper of children disposes their minds to wander' (p. 130). One of Locke's many radical interventions into educational thought had been to encourage a view of the child's inability to concentrate for long periods of time as an inevitable feature of childhood cognition rather than as something to be railed against: 'Inadvertency, forgetfulness, unsteadiness, and wandering of thought,' he writes, 'are the natural faults of childhood' (p. 132). While he still labels these characteristics as 'faults', keeping in play an association between inattention and wilful immorality, Locke's promotion of tolerance towards the child's short attention span enabled writers who, like Watts, were interested in addressing children to think with renewed focus about the kinds of poetic techniques that would best suit this cognitive feature. Watts's deployment of 'easy language' also enables us to view in clear sight another belief that predominated in the period: the belief that the child might be inherently lazy or disinclined towards intellectual effort. By the beginning of the eighteenth century, this view of children had become such an established belief that it was often used as a stock motif, with numerous images of the child, both visual and verbal, emphasizing a state of indolence. Advice manuals, such as the anonymously authored *Advice to a Son, Directing Him How to Demean Himself in the Most Important Passages of Life*, popular in the decade when Watts published *Divine Songs*, urged the child against idleness: 'Avoid Sloth, if thou would'st avoid Scorn; Shame is the reward of a Sluggard: Idleness will bring thee to want and beggary' (1716, p. 89). The most well known of the poems in Watts's *Divine Songs*, 'Against Idleness and Mischief', is dedicated precisely to this theme, its very susceptibility to parody, most notably by Lewis Carroll, itself an indicator of its totemic familiarity.

But a radical insight underpins Watts's championing of easy language. Watts's dedication to the child's pleasure reflects a belief, or at least a hope, that intellectual effort is more effective if it is allied to reward. This belief went against the mainstream current: physical punishment was still widespread in schools, despite the fact that Locke had argued its counter-productiveness, and the belief that education was a necessary chore underpinned much thinking on pedagogy and curriculum. Centuries' worth of moral and theological thought had reinforced the attitude, enshrined in scripture, that 'He that spareth the rod, hateth his son; but he that loveth him, chasteneth him betimes' (Proverbs, XIII, 24), and both educational theory and practice largely reified it. Watts does not present his modification of this position as a rejection of such moral or theological thought. Nor is it expressly an endorsement of the aesthetic valorization of instruction through delight that Horace had immortalized in *Ars Poetica* (19 BC) and which was to prove a central guiding principle for much mid-century children's literature by John Newbery and his followers. Watts's implicit argument operates instead at a logical level: the child should enjoy the play of ideas not because it is the duty of the adult to make the child happy (an idea not really articulated with any influence or forcefulness until well into the nineteenth century), but, as John Dewey was later so convincingly to argue, because this is a more reliable way of ensuring that the child learns at all. As Matthew Grenby has put it, the 'entertainment on offer in respectable children's books was generally understood . . . as a catalyst of education, but not, at least until the nineteenth century, as an end in itself' (2011, p. 262). Even in the late eighteenth century, children's writers still felt the need to justify the pleasurable elements of their children's books, by way of such arguments as Mary Ann Kilner's in her Preface to *The Adventures of a Pincushion* (1790): 'the avidity with which children peruse books of entertainment, is a proof how much publications proper for their attention are required' (p. iv). Watts, then, rejects compulsion, and although he does not go as far as embracing the voluntarism of the kind that the Edgeworths would later champion in *Practical Education* (1798), what Watts envisages is a kind of involuntarism, a kind of alchemy that will inevitably occur once the child is exposed to verse. Where Locke had repudiated physical compulsion on the basis that it reinforces concern with bodily pleasure and pain, we might see here in Watts's proto-psychology an unspoken acknowledgement of the importance of bodily appetite – that element which Dewey was later to place centre-stage when he proposed that the child learns through physically *doing*. Here Watts builds on Locke's belief that physical drives are intuitive and that education involves learning how to harness our passions so that we become accustomed not always to pursing sensory pleasure. Watts's *Divine Songs*, then, presents the child with an opportunity to give in to the pursuit of *jouissance* (the thrill of acoustic play) as a means to the end of education. In so doing, Watts's children's poems provide an early example of what Ellenor Fenn in her Preface to *Rational Sports* would later more explicitly refer to as the possibility for literature to 'tincture the mind' by inculcating a 'taste for rational amusement' (p. xiii)[2], and what this book suggests can usefully be viewed as a species of critical activity.

It is one thing to get a rhyme or rhythm into the child's head; it is something else altogether to know that the child has acknowledged the semantic content of those lines and that anything material has been learned. We see in Watts's optimism a faith in children's impressionability, their susceptibility to sensation and affect, which is a belief that recurs throughout the period, articulated by David Hartley in his 1749 *Observations*, when he remarks that children are 'more exquisitely sensible and irritable than adults' (p. 437). He elaborates, 'Children, and young Persons, are diverted by every little jingle, pun, contrast, or coincidence, which is level to their Capacities, even though the Harshness and Inconsistency, with which it first strikes the Fancy, be so minute as scarce to be perceived' (p. 439). Such impressionability carried with it heavy consequences for the educationalist, since it was widely believed that the 'impression of those ideas, which are first engraven on young minds, will influence their characters ever afterwards' (Rosenberg-Orsini, 1785, p. 180). In particular, it was thought that children were unusually affected by passion, and that early education takes place primarily through emotional exchange. Henry Home, Lord Kames, anticipating the connection that William Wordsworth would later draw between the ingestion of love and the ingestion of milk in his famous depiction of the primal scene in *The Prelude* (1798), wrote that an 'infant on the breast discerns good or bad humour in its nurse, from their external signs on her countenance, and from the different tones of her voice' (p. 3). He envisages the child as peculiarly perceptive of the 'internal passions' that are encoded in their 'external signs' (p. 2). Children, then, were perceived to be conspicuously susceptible to external influence. This belief carried into literary theory in the form of an anxiety about, alongside a concomitant optimism in relation to, the child's vulnerability to its reading matter. At the end of the eighteenth century, Ellenor Fenn lamented in her Preface to *School Occurences*: 'Those who are conversant with children, know, that they are more influenced by maxims which they chance to meet with in books, than by those that are inculcated by their parents. It ought not to be so. – But so it is' (p. vi).

It is one thing to observe what kind of readerly activity such 'chance' encounters *seek* to precipitate in their child readers; but close reading of Watts's *Divine Songs* enables us to reflect on the critical activity that these poems *in practice* require. Take, for example, 'Song 1: A General Song of Praise to God', quoted here in full:

How glorious is our Heavenly King,
Who reigns above the sky!
How shall a child presume to sing
His dreadful majesty?

How great his power is none can tell,
Nor think how large his grace;
Not men below, nor saints that dwell
On high before his face.

Not angels that stand round the Lord
Can search his secret will;
But they perform his heavenly word,
And sing his praises still.

Then let me join this holy train,
And my first offerings bring;
Th'eternal God will not disdain
To hear an infant sing.

My heart resolves, my tongue obeys,
And angels shall rejoice
To hear their mighty Maker's praise
Sound from a feeble voice. (pp. 1–2)

The poem rehearses for children a sequence of worshipping manoeuvres. Ostensibly, it appears to open with a series of questions, but grammatically the opening sentence is in fact a statement, one which is aurally indistinguishable from a question, a confusion which is exacerbated by the fact that the subsequent sentence is indeed grammatically a question. The proximity of the two kinds of sentence to one another requires the child reader not merely passively to recognize but moreover actively to experience that observation and interrogation might be bound up in one another, particularly when it comes to the contemplation of the divine. The potentially limitless consequences of this expansive thought, however, are kept in check by the contained nature of the common metre, which provides what feels like a question-and-answer format, wherein the reader is invited to treat the shorter lines of trimeter as solutions of kinds to the sonic problems posed by the longer lines of tetrameter. The poem thus provides its child readers with a means of broaching large abstract questions in a form that promises reassurance and finitude. Locke had written, 'Much less are children capable of reasonings from remote principles. They cannot conceive the force of long deductions: the reasons that move them must be obvious, and level to their thoughts, and such as may (if I may so say) be felt and touched' (2007, p. 65). This poem recognizes the cognitive barriers that might render it hard for children to think in the abstract by carefully managing the transitions between the particular and the general.

The delayed entry of the first-person singular in stanza four, until which point the child is subsumed within a plural first-person voice, 'we', provides the reader with a means of identifying as a plurality, not merely of children, but of people, by virtue of an apparently shared reading experience. The invitation to feel the pulse is proffered as a means of coming together with others – of being initiated into the rites of a culture. As John Dewey was to observe two centuries later, 'Society exists through a process of transmission quite as much as biological life. This transmission occurs by means of communication of habits of doing, thinking, and feeling from the older to the younger. Without this communication of ideals, hopes, expectations, standards, opinions, from those members of society who are passing out of the group life to those who are coming into it, social life could not survive' (*DE*, p. 6). Watts's invitation to join in the song functions not merely in the immediate sense of asking the child to take up the same notes as the people nearby, occupying common time and place with them, but moreover in Dewey's sense as a kind of cultural transmission. It reminds us that for children, especially when literacy is not yet secure, reading is often an aural, communal experience – we read to children and they read to us. The poem emphasizes this aural quality of sound in its references to 'song' and 'voice'. It offers the possibility that simply to sound a note is affirmatory, is delightful – but not in a trivial way: the sound of voice is a powerful, affecting reminder of one another's presence (the parent reading, perhaps?) And yet the poem is not just sound; it is perhaps not even sound, since poems do not have to be read aloud. Indeed, we might pause to wonder where the song of the title takes place. Is the poem the song? Is the child's response to the poem the song? As the abundant use of indicative verbs in this poem suggests, Watts's poem operates in a strange middle space between present tense and abstract idea of the present, or between present tense and future. The coming together of presentness and futurity in the poem ('Then let me') fosters a sense of belonging to a human race – human as distinct from the other creatures in this poem: saints, angels, divine – and calls upon the child actively and voluntarily to subscribe to the values of this race.

For all Watts's emphasis on simplicity in the Preface to *Divine Songs*, there is nonetheless a distinctive complexity at work here. It is a complexity, however, that is shaped by the critical child's inevitable awareness that the words on this page are not his or her own, or at least, not his or hers alone. There is an indeterminacy in the source of the words and the source of the sounds. The poem provides a chorus in which adult voices and child voices are imagined to mingle across time. The complexity at work is thus one of vocal and temporal instability: one which comes into being precisely by virtue of the status of this work as a song for children. For the critical child is required to be out of time – conscious of its alterity to the ideas discussed, the words used, the script which it has not yet learnt – all of which predate the coming of the child reader to them. There is, then, a futurity embedded in the poem not merely by virtue of its address projected onto the child ('Let me') but by virtue of its didactic premise. But in order to activate what the poem offers *in potentia*, the critical child does not straightforwardly (indeed, surely cannot) take up the message to 'sing'; the child must first feel the common rhythms, anticipate the rhymes, compute the question-and-answer format of the stanza pattern before he or she can know how to sound her voice. There is thus an irony at work here. This is a poem which commands the child to sing, but the critical child must infer not just from the premise of the poem but also from the intricacy of its form that their task is not really to sing but in fact merely to listen: to listen now, in the present, and to sing later, in the future. That is to say that the child must perform a sophisticated mental operation; they must compute that the present tense here really signifies the future, the abstract, the general, and not the particularized now.

We can gain a sense of just how sophisticated the mental operations of young critics of children's poetry were deemed, or hoped, to be from the volume on poetry published by John Newbery as part of his series, *Circle of the Sciences* (1745–6). Newbery's aim in this multivolume non-fictional work for young people was to 'diffuse a Light over their Understanding, assist their Reasoning Powers, and lead them on to such Improvements in Knowledge as are to be expected from Years of Maturity' (I.v). It contains volumes on grammar, arithmetic, rhetoric, poetry, logic, geography and chronology and ends with a dictionary. The significance of poetry for Newbery can be estimated from the fact that over the course of his career, Newbery published at least seven books of poetry for children. Close attention to *Poetry Made Familiar and Easy* provides us with insight not merely into what knowledge and skills Newbery considered it to be important for children to develop in relation to poetry, but furthermore into how he anticipated that they would acquire these skills. The volume's narrator asserts that his 'task' is 'to give the Reader some Idea of every Species of Poetry that is worth his Notice' (1776, p. 224). In part, then, the book aims to provide the child with exposure to poetry, the clear implication being that by gaining familiarity with the customs associated with this art, children will gain access to the culture with which these customs are associated. Throughout, the collective pronoun 'our' is used, building a sense of shared traditions, traditions whose custodian the child will one day be. But the work functions as more than merely an anthology of excerpts of poetry; or to put it another way, it does not merely educate in a traditional manner. It seeks also to endow children with ways of asking and answering questions about poetry such that they are left with certain knowledge about it, and such that the child is able to perform certain intellectual manoeuvers in relation to it; that is to say, it places the onus of learning firmly on the student, requiring the pupil to learn through experimentation. There are several pertinent insights that we can extrapolate from close scrutiny of Newbery's book. First, its aims tell us something about why a growing number of authors were beginning to believe that children needed poetry. More specifically, it indicates exactly what intellectual benefits poetry might bring. Second, its priorities provide us with a means of identifying not just *that* but *how* it was deemed important that children did something *to* poetry, and did not merely passively receive it. Third, its own engagement with its implied child reader equips us with a means of viewing in process how eighteenth-century authors such as Newbery envisaged that children might think in the abstract about poetry: that is to say, how they might operate as literary theorists.

The Preface to *Poetry Made Familiar and Easy* suggests that the aim of the book is to enable children to 'soon entertain an adequate idea of [poetry's] real beauties' (n. pag.) – to inform children's taste, and to pass on socially mandated ways of appreciating the complexities of poetry. It is worth noting, if only because it has become so habitual to notice the preoccupation in eighteenth-century children's literature with the child's morality, that the book presents the education of children's moral faculties as an incidental benefit rather than a primary concern: 'should any of our readers be but one virtue the better for these our honest endeavours, we shall not think our labour ill bestowed' (n. pag.). And yet, while the book is impelled by a clear desire to educate, and is founded on a belief that exposure to poetic monuments plays a vital role in shaping the critical faculties of the child, its reverence towards poetry threatens at times to position poetry as a phenomenon of such cultural prestige that children could not hope to gain access to its mysteries. When Newbery insists that 'we must, in a word, be born poets; for this divine art is not to be attain'd by the most unwearied industry and application' (n. pag.), the reader might be forgiven for wondering what is to be gained from the industry and application involved in reading the very book in hand. Such wondering is further fuelled by distinctly anti-Deweyan suggestions throughout that readers are born, not made: 'a person who has a tolerable ear for poetry, will have little occasion for rules concerning the pause and the accents, but will naturally so dispose his words as to create a certain harmony, without labour to the tongue, or violence to the sense' (Newbery, 1776, p. 15). The book therefore puts the child reader in a paradoxical position: children are required to want to labour to acquire the knowledge that the book promises, but simultaneously, they are encouraged to bow to the belief that if knowledge has to be attained through strenuous effort, then the pupil's critical credentials are doubtful. As Andrew O'Malley has shown, if 'the ideal figure of the age was the productive, moral, self-disciplined, healthy, male adult governed by the faculty of reason, the child came to be viewed in many regards as its opposite: the subject interpolated through absence and difference' (2003, pp. 11–12). Newbery's reader, implicitly characterized by way of difference to the adult speaker, seems on first glance destined to be uncritical.

The vexed position in which Newbery places his child reader is reflected in a related uncertainty that suffuses *Poetry Made Familiar and Easy*: indecision about whether the child reader is to be addressed as a future consumer or a future maker of poetry. The stated aims in the Preface make clear that appreciation of poetry is the central goal. Yet, many of the remarks throughout the book ostensibly court the poet apprentice. Questions are posed such as 'On what syllables must the accent fall in this kind of verse?' (p. 11), and rules are supplied in answer, rules which are often more pertinent for learning how to write poetry rather than read it. For example, 'tho' the Alexandrine verse, when rightly employ'd, has an agreeable effect in our poetry, it must be used sparingly and with judgment' (p. 19). The steer here is towards how best to apply this knowledge in the crafting of poetry, encouraging the child to take responsibility for the safe-keeping of poetry's prosperity by writing it in accordance with cultural expectations of taste. There is thus a clear implication that in order to appreciate the genius of those who do not need to learn or practise – in order to become a critic – the child must learn and practise such that he or she is better able to feel awe at the mastery demonstrated by those with innate skill. Reading and writing are implicitly bound together, viewed as embroiled skills; imitation of the masters, it is implied, though never explicitly stated, will itself enhance understanding of them. The deference to authority that underpins this pedagogical principle is also apparent in the frequent quotation of existing commentators on the subject, such as the French historian and educationalist, Charles Rollin, invoked throughout respectfully as 'Monsieur Rollin'. The words of such figures are quoted at length and treated as gospel. On the face of it, this does not constitute much of an invitation for critical resistance.

But one of the striking features of the volume is its invitation to think in expansive terms. Newbery introduces a sweeping historical scope, ranging between summaries of Greek and Roman thought and more recent examples. He therefore supposes that the child is capable of taking a long historical view and perceiving the place that our own age has in a wider temporal context, while also recognizing the inherent challenges in this task for the child, and accordingly simplifying by flattening out historical difference to make it possible for the child to view examples from radically different eras alongside one another and grasp similarity rather than be bamboozled by difference. Expertise in the specifics of history or an ancient language is not necessary; all is brought within the jurisdiction of a novice. More strikingly still, Newbery presupposes that children are capable of and interested in dealing in large, opaque philosophical ideas, including some of the most obdurate literary critical conundra. For example, he begins by asking 'What is poetry?' supplying a gratifyingly succinct answer: 'It is the art of composing poems, or pieces in verse' (Newbery, 1776, p. 1). What is potentially a question of daunting proportions, one which might require prolixity to capture the nuances inherent in even an unsatisfactory answer, is reduced to its most literal and indisputable elements by Newbery's emphasis on the fact of authorship. This tendency to foreground the material and the technical – an attitude signalled by the series title, *Circle of the Sciences* – enables the child critic to be hands-on: to get down to the practical business of noting features relating to scansion or genre. Similarly, chapters are organized around tangible matters such as 'Of the Structure of English Verse; and of Rhyme' and 'Of Satire', and in its attempts to communicate information about these issues, the volume does not hold back from using technical vocabulary, providing full names of rhetorical features and succinct accounts of what they comprise. While the language in which it explains such terms might resemble that which Watts had in mind by 'easy', Newbery deems the child critic capable of learning and understanding the meaning of complex terminology, and furthermore assumes it to be important, indeed essential, that the child be familiar with such terms.

Newbery may make little concession to his child audience in terms of diction, but the modes of address deployed by the narrator of *Poetry Made Familiar and Easy* directly and consistently recognize the child's idiosyncratic needs. Throughout, the narrator makes use of a question-and-answer format, posing rhetorical questions such as 'how seldom do we find so many great and valuable qualifications meet in one person?' (n. pag.), involving his readers in the process of abstract thought and expecting them to generate hypothetical propositions in response. The book therefore solicits its readers actively to participate in the quest for understanding, at times lapsing into the first-person voice and exemplifying the questions that the child might ask: 'Have you any other instructions to give me concerning rhyme?' (p. 9). In this way, it gives the critical child, or 'Pupil', as it frequently calls the reader, an opportunity to learn through child-led experimentation, figuring the child as currently ignorant but keen to change this plight through the deliberate seeking out of answers. Indeed, the imagined curiosity of the child sometimes takes on an urgency: 'Can't you give me some examples of this?' (p. 13). Far from casting the child's ignorance as a sin, the sympathetic alignment between the narrator and the implied reader indicates a view of ignorance as an inevitable affliction which children must bear, one which adults must compassionately seek to alleviate. Newbery's approach shows the influence of Locke's advice that children 'should always be heard, and fairly and kindly answered, when they ask after anything they could know, and desire to be informed about. Curiosity should be as carefully cherished in children, as other appetites suppressed' (p. 85). Just as Locke counsels, Newbery's speaker does not speak down to the child but instead seeks to adapt himself to the child's cognitive and emotional needs. He recognizes, therefore, that the child will become bored by explanations that are too lengthy or which veer from the main point, legitimizing the child's right to experience wandering attention: 'besides, that I fear the Reader will think I have already detained him too long upon this Subject' (pp. 133–4). The speaker recognizes too that the child's understanding of poetry may be impeded by a lack of contextual awareness and discreetly supplies information as needed (e.g. explaining the story of Prometheus) to help the reader fill in any gaps. In so doing, the speaker offers reassurance, implying that the critical child is not to feel ashamed of what he or she does not yet know.

Indeed, far from implying that the ultimate goal is to arrive at a position of omniscience, the speaker reveals his own fallibility, for example by admitting, in relation to an epigram by Alexander Pope, 'For my part, I am at a loss to determine whether it does more honour to the poet who wrote it, or to the nobleman for whom the compliment is designed' (p. 38). In so doing, he leaves the child to determine what to make of the lines. Catherine Macaulay in *Letters on Education* (1790) was later to insist on the importance of the educator matching practice with theory – of parents and teachers leading by example – since, as she puts it, in youth, 'the powers of the understanding are not sufficiently strong to combat the difficulties which in this early season of life it has to encounter. Hence reason loses its energy and becomes no more than the echo of the public voice' (p. 152). Newbery's speaker anticipates this demand for good practice to be modelled, extending his faith in children's capacities to assert their own voices rather than merely echo precedent by encouraging them to practise making their own judgements. He does so not in the spirit that we might associate with late twentieth-century reader-response theory, wherein readers are licensed to constitute the text howsoever they wish, but by nudging his readers to take the cue from the accumulation of judgements – often in the form of assertions offered up as objective truths: epigrams are a 'low species of poetry', for instance (Newbery, 1776, p. 49) – which have sought to shape their taste over the course of the book. Through the process of reading this book, it is envisaged that the critical child will have been made sufficiently familiar with the standards and premises of taste that their own instincts will by now have kicked in, functioning like a sensory organ, invisibly and seemingly without effort enabling the reader to make poetic discriminations.

Newbery's own poetry for children has often been dismissed as didactic, the implication being that it functions straightforwardly to direct the child's morals, situating the reader as a passive and docile recipient of textual transmission. But close consideration of how his verse invites its readers to make use of the powers of discrimination which his non-fiction work seeks to impart reveals that the ease with which the child reader receives instruction through the poetic text might be rather more illusory than such critical verdicts imagine. Take, for example, the poem 'Shuttle-Cock' from *A Little Pretty Pocket-Book* (1744), quoted here in full:

The Shuttle-Cock struck
Does backward rebound;
But, if it be miss'd,
It falls to the Ground.

Moral.
Thus chequer'd in Life,
As Fortune does flow;
Her Smiles lift us high,
Her Frowns sink us low.

As in Watts's 'A General Song of Praise to God', Newbery here sets up a present moment; the poem's epigrammatic style relays an active scene, and the speedy tick-tock of the diameter alerts us to the continuousness of the action which is apparently taking place right before us. The brevity of the poem gives a sense of a small treat; we are being offered a light slice of something fun – a vignette which offers a brief glimpse of amusement. Also like the Watts poem, it sets up a question-and-answer format, a format made explicit by the prominence of the moral, which announces itself in the second stanza. But the relationship between the two stanzas bears closer inspection. For all that it feels like a question posed, it is not altogether clear what problem the first stanza has laid bare; and for all that the second stanza feels like a reply to the first, it in fact exists in a weirdly asymmetrical relationship with it. Formally, there is a satisfying balance in length between the two evenly matched quatrains. But what is signified by the break between them? Is the one scenario an analogue for the other? If so, precisely what attributes are alike? In this analogy, who is the chequered party? The shuttle cock? Fortune? Us? The poem's indeterminacy is generated as much by imprecision (Newbery's formula fails as a sentence, since none of the hermeneutic options it opens up are grammatically coherent) as by multiplicity. But perhaps this does not matter, for we get the general point: life, like a game of shuttlecock, has its ups and downs; it is unpredictable; it can end in contempt, not in elation. The critical child may not know what this poem is advising them to do or how they might alter their behaviour in response, but they have been prompted, through the comparison, to perceive a similitude – to gain a handle on an abstract idea. The two stanzas operate coterminously, and invite the reader to hold them both in their line of sight at once, but not because the first forces the second stanza to perform the function of explaining the first, whatever the term 'moral' might imply.

By leaving the reader without a singular subject position to take up, Newbery's poem, by default, prevails on us to occupy a plural, communal, and potentially general subject position. The critical child is being brought into a fold, membership of which is conducive to pleasure, provided that the rules have been learned. For games are fun; rhythmic language is diverting. For all that the poem presents what we might see as a simplified – an easy – view of life – one underpinned by strictures, methods and truths, it does not coerce us into taking on these values for ourselves. Its mode, rather, is descriptive: it offers up a slice of everyday experience and a glimpse of a routine idea. It re-introduces child readers to the familiar (a shuttlecock) and in so doing, introduces them to the unfamiliar (the unpredictable vicissitudes of life).

Nearly 200 years before John Dewey was to popularize a belief in the critical faculties of the child and the educational benefits – psychologically, socially and politically, as well as intellectually – inherent in cultivating them, Isaac Watts and John Newbery had appreciated that poetic language and poetic form might be contrived to operate on child readers in ways that foster, indeed, insist on, the child's proactive, hands-on readiness to infer and deduce, to analyze and to synthesize, to work at playing. Certainly as early as 1715 it had been accepted by certain notable poets for children that by questioning and probing, testing and discriminating, the critical child can attempt to arrive at judgements of her own that enable her not merely to access but moreover to shape the cultural conversation which literature invites her to join.

2

Laughter and the permission to critique

I wonder, Mrs Morris –
I don't want to be rude –
but I'm just settling the children down,
perhaps you could see a way to leaving now,
mmm? . . .
Wayne that is very rude.
We've talked about kissing before.
If Mrs Morris wants to kiss David goodbye
that's OK and you've no right to
laugh at –
thank you again Mrs Morris, yes
biscuit-making too
That'll be lovely, thank you so much,
goodbye, Mrs Morris. (from Michael Rosen, 'The Register,' n. pag.)

Michael Rosen's bravura dramatic monologue, 'The Register,' from his 2002 collection, *No Breathing in Class*, hilariously depicts the unravelling of a teacher's control over her class during morning registration. The scene exclusively comprises the speech of the teacher, who, harassed as much by the other adults around her (an overbearing parent who will not leave the classroom) as by the ebullient children, is thwarted in her attempts to execute this routine ritual. By requiring us to read the scene through the matrix of the teacher's spoken words without giving us access to her unspoken thoughts, Rosen positions the teacher as the object, and not the subject, of our attention. What fellow feeling we might muster for her doomed campaign to cling on to some semblance of order thus emerges as a form of sympathy rather than empathy, if, following Nancy Eisenberg (2000), we take sympathy to be 'an affective response that consists of feeling sorrow or concern for the distressed or needy other (rather than feeling the same emotion as the other person)' (p. 678). But for all that he invites us to pity the teacher's plight, indeed, even as he does so, Rosen does not spare this supposed figure of authority from the full force of our laughter. Her inability to emerge intact from this trial by child renders her ridiculous, and Rosen's poem licenses us – indeed, positively encourages us – to laugh as her command of the situation disintegrates before our very eyes.

To be permitted to ridicule a teacher is, of course, delicious in its flagrant naughtiness. As the teacher herself points out, it is 'very rude' to laugh at someone, particularly at an adult; and furthermore, 'you've no right to'. In the British culture which Rosen's poem recalls (other poems in the collection lead us to envisage a setting of several decades earlier, the 1950s of Rosen's own childhood), the concept of children's rights was embryonic, with the Declaration of the Rights of the Child not adopted in full by the United Nations until 1959. Why, then, cognisant of the social codes which circumscribe such laughter, is the reader nonetheless drawn to indulge it? In part, we laugh because the poem's anarchic form cajoles us into so doing: the darting, foreshortened changes of direction fling us this way and that in a discombobulating hurly-burly of incomplete experiences. Linearity and purposefulness are frustrated by perpetual interruption, represented visually on the page by the repeated use of the dash. The poem's formal riotousness resembles laughter itself, which wells up inside us unbidden, and pursues its own insouciant path, overwhelming the body until it is spent, or until the laughing subject capitulates to all-out hysteria. Manfred Pfister, in his *A History of English Laughter* (2002), observes that 'the liminal states of laughing and crying function as gateways into and out of insanity' (p. 89). By the poem's end, Rosen's teacher teeters precisely on the brink of threatened insanity, as she histrionically repeats: 'Can anyone see the register? / Can anyone see the register?' Our laughter extends into the silence beyond the final line, filling the gap which her reason has vacated.

But we do not merely laugh because the formal properties of the poem bid us to give voice to the demonic cackle within. The poem's premise lays bare the risibility of our everyday struggles to conceal our private vulnerabilities and present ourselves as intact. The public maternal 'kiss' that poor David endures must be mocked as it represents that once-treasured but still remembered solace, a dependency from which his classmates have by now already weaned themselves – and there is nothing quite so contemptible as a habit which only yesterday we broke ourselves, or, indeed, one which we secretly maintain behind closed doors. We laugh too at the mother's inability to see that which the other children, and the child reader, can all too clearly perceive: that her eagerness to protect her child has precisely the opposite effect to that intended, handing his peers the stick with which to beat him. The thrill of smug prescience that this insight generates in the reader erupts in a self-satisfied smirk at the follies of those less psychologically astute than ourselves – or, as Thomas Hobbes famously put it in his *Treatise on Human Nature* (1650), an eruption of 'sudden glory arising from some sudden conception of some eminency in ourselves, by comparison with the infirmity of others, or with our own formerly' (p. 45). According to Hobbes's logic, our laughter is an expression of momentary delight generated by a comparison which enables us to view ourselves as superior. Rosen's poem harnesses a version of Hobbesian superiority, allying it, for good measure, to the exhilaration of breaking rules. Too late, the teacher reminds us that we are not *entitled* to laugh; that she is the adult, and the children (and by extension the reader) must wait to be allowed. This is a deeply rooted notion; 'no human being is entitled to laugh at the imperfections of others,' wrote the Scottish Enlightenment philosopher Henry Home, Lord Kames in 1781 (p. 152). But of course, the poem has already permitted us to do so. It actively compels, rather than merely sanctions, laughter. It pre-emptively dares us to turn our backs on centuries of moral opinion and to defy the teacher's authority. We laugh since we know that we *should* view the teacher as above reproach, and yet we can but pity her all-too-human inability to demonstrate in practice the power which in principle her position accords her. Our laugh is a chortle of triumph that the supposed exemplar is not after all any the less fallible than ourselves; it is the frisson of sudden realization that if we choose to defy authority – if we simply refuse to grant it – then we can make it disappear. The reader's laughter at the dissipation of the teacher's power destabilizes the very idea of authority, exposing it as a chimera. It is precisely this destabilization of authority that John Dewey worked to effect by seeking to foster in the child the capacity for critical thought. To equip the child with the means to think for themselves – the means to question and to reject received wisdom – is to secure the child's freedom. Laughter, then, is not merely a pleasing by-product of the experience of reading Rosen's poem. The reader's laugh is an intrinsic part of the very fabric of the text; its presence indicates that the poem's anarchic politics, or in Deweyan terms, its commitment to the democratic potential of critical thinking, have taken root inside the child reader where they defiantly lie beyond the reach of adult control.

In British children's poetry today, this potent, transgressive act of making the child laugh is not merely permitted, it has become conventional. Comic children's poetry is ubiquitous. Poets such as Michael Rosen, Wendy Cope, Allan Ahlberg, Roger McGough, and Benjamin Zephaniah, who primarily specialize in comic writing, dominate the children's poetry market, both through single-author volumes and through their high visibility in anthologies. As Morag Styles observed in 2001, it is hard to 'think of *any* poets writing for children who are not amusing at least some of the time' (p. 140). On the one hand, the popularity of comic verse for children indicates that there is an entrenched belief (or optimism, perhaps) that the association of poetry with laughter secures an attendant association between poetry and pleasure. But children's poetry has been associated with pleasure for much longer than it has been associated with laughter, and so the omnipresence of children's comic verse cannot merely be read as a shift in our pedagogical approach – our own age's means of executing the Horatian creed that poetry must entail delight in order to secure instruction. To provoke laughter, as Manfred Pfister (2002) observes, is to set up a 'triangular relationship between (1) the "laughter-maker", i.e. the one who incites laughter by making a joke or drawing attention to some absurdity, (2) the "butt of laughter" as its target or victim, and (3) the "laugher(s)", i.e. the laughing audience'. This is 'always also a social triangle, constructed along parameters of gender, class, race, age or other crucial differences operative in the respective culture' (p. vi). If we accept that laughter is necessarily social, entailing, as Pfister identifies, the interaction of 'different' parties, then to provoke it is also always necessarily a political act, since the social differences that are 'operative' (gender, class, race, age) bring with them imbalances of insight, experience, and knowledge. Our weddedness to comic poetry for children, then, indicates a deep-rooted *political* commitment to the project of democracy. This democratic project of making the child laugh through the medium of poetry is all the more noteworthy when we bear in mind that in our own age we have a decidedly ambivalent attitude towards the project of making the adult laugh through the medium of poetry. Indeed, the trajectories of children's poetry over recent decades have followed a markedly different route to those of adult poetry, wherein the comic has largely been relegated to the realm of popular culture and we tend to esteem as signs of literary significance qualities such as complexity, density and weightiness. Percy Bysshe Shelley's supremely earnest vision of poets as 'the unacknowledged legislators of the world' (p. 535) has cast a long-reaching shadow over the enterprise of writing poetry, one which has pushed to the margins of respectable literary culture poetry that does not take this responsibility seriously. The vogue for using poetry to make the reader laugh, then, and our anxiety about failing to keep up with this vogue, is these days largely concentrated in the idea of the child. This vogue, and the anxiety it induces, coincide with, indeed, are no doubt largely fuelled by, a wider cultural worry about whether laughter is a fittingly adult response to the serious business of high art. Not only does the popularity of comic verse for children highlight the urgency of our desire to ensure that the child's existence is carefree (the child *must* laugh) but by the same token, it indicates our fear or suspicion that laughter is incommensurate with maturity; the adult – the critical adult, at least – cannot afford to laugh.

These poetic alliances between childishness and laughter on the one hand and maturity and seriousness on the other are not, however, inevitable. In fact, they mark a striking inversion of the customs that shaped literary taste during an earlier era of British literary history, the first decades of the eighteenth century. If we were to seek to identify a moment in literary history when humour was prized as a vital component of *adult* poetry, uppermost in our minds would surely be the early decades of the eighteenth century, which bore witness to what has been termed the great age of British satire, an age whose providence, as Martin Battestin has put it, was wit.[1] Among poetic luminaries of this age, most famously the members of the Scriblerus Club, including Jonathan Swift, Alexander Pope and John Gay, and their acerbic detractor, Lady Mary Wortley Montagu, the capacity to manipulate humour with precision and finesse such that the ensuing laughter unearthed supposed hidden truths was prized as a hallmark that distinguished poets from mere hacks. It is against this very same backdrop that some of the earliest influential volumes of poetry for children were produced: Isaac Watts's *Divine Songs* (1715); Thomas Boreman and Mary Cooper's *Tommy Thumb's Pretty Song Book* was published in 1744. Remarkably, given that this age has come to be identified by literary historians precisely by way of its conspicuous celebration of literary humour, the comic mode is almost entirely absent from poetry written for children during the same decades. Eighteenth-century children's poets, in fact, go to great lengths to *avoid* making the child laugh; it is striking how feebly the child reader is ostensibly invited, or permitted, to snigger in their work. As Andrea Immel has noted of John Newbery's works for children, 'Cultivating wit, politeness, and amiability in children was demonstrably more important to Newbery than getting belly laughs' (2009, p. 149). The same is true of Newbery's imitators. Indeed, to check the child's laughter was sometimes even an express aim of eighteenth-century poetry written for children, a solicitous gesture apparently made with the child's well-being in mind. That is not to say that such authors did not put a premium on the child's pleasure. On the contrary, Isaac Watts in his landmark collection, *Divine Songs* (1715), cites as first among the four advantages of writing in verse 'a greater Delight in the learning of Truths and Duties this way', adding that there is something 'so amusing and entertaining in Rhymes and Metre, that will incline Children to make this part of their Business a Diversion' (n. pag.). The child's amusement, though, does not include, indeed, at times expressly excludes, the experience of laughter. Laughter in Watts's collection is equated with 'raillery' and 'jeering', and as such is envisaged as a form of cruelty, unjustifiable in Christian and moral terms. Moreover, to laugh at another involves assuming a kind of power over them and as such was seen to entail arrogance. Entitling a child, necessarily ignorant and inexperienced, to wield such a dangerous weapon could, it was feared, have harmful effects on the individuals concerned, and worse, on society at large.

By the time that Watts came to publish *Divine Songs*, Anthony Ashley Cooper, the third Earl of Shaftesbury, had already published *Sensus Communis: An Essay on the Freedom of Wit and Humour* (1709), his liberal defence of raillery. Shaftesbury overturns Hobbes's argument against laughter by advocating it as a tool for political cohesiveness. Anticipating Dewey's advocacy of the social and political importance of critical thinking 200 years later, he insists that laughter is a socially constructive response to an argument with which one disagrees on the grounds that if the argument survives the attack, then it cannot be without merit, and if it does not, then its erroneousness will have been more benignly and effectively exposed than through destruction by any other means. Arguments such as this armed literary artists with a compelling set of moral and political justifications for writing in the comic mode, and the wealth of comic literature written during the early eighteenth century indicates the extent to which literary artists were prepared to reject Hobbes's account. However, Isaac Watts, writing just three years after the publication of *Sensus Communis*, expressly warns children against the very thing that Shaftesbury's influential treatise had sought to promote:

'Against Scoffing and calling Names'
Our Tongues were made to bless the Lord.
And not speak ill of Men:
When others give a railing Word,
We must not rail again.

Cross Words and angry Names require
To be chastiz'd at School;
And he's in danger of Hell-fire,
That calls his Brother, Fool.

But Lips that dare be so prophane,
To meek and jeer and scoff
At holy Things, or holy Men,
The Lord shall cut them off.

When Children in their wanton Play
Serv'd old *Elisha* so,
And bid the Prophet go his Way,
Go up thou bald head, go;

God quickly stopt their wicked Breath,
And sent two raging Bears,
That tore them Limb from Limb to Death
With Blood and Groans and Tears.

Great God, how terrible art thou,
To Sinners e'er so young!
Grant me thy Grace, and teach me how
To tame and rule my Tongue. (*Divine Songs*, pp. 25–6).

It would be banal to observe that Watts's poem 'Against Scoffing and calling Names' is not a comic poem, for this would miss something vital about the relationship that such a poem has with the premise of comic writing. To be sure, this poem does not seek to make the child laugh. But it would be more accurate to observe that the poem seeks *not* to make the child laugh. The child addressee in the poem, and by extension the child reader of the poem, are, through the very process of reading the poem, being taught how not to laugh. The exactitude of the poem's ballad meter, maintained with precision throughout, requires words to be placed just so. This obtrusive example of verbal poise models the control that the child is encouraged to exert over his or her tongue, and specifically the control that the child is encouraged to exert over his or her desire to use words to provoke the laughter of others. But there would be no need for Watts to make the point if the lesson which his poem attempts to deliver was one which the critical child had already learned. By its very existence, the poem testifies to a perceived need for the child to be reminded of this instruction; that is to say, the poem presupposes that the child, prior to reading the poem, is inclined towards laughter, and needs, through the poem, to be shown how to stop. In this way, the poem represents a kind of anti-comic verse. While the premise of Michael Rosen's 2002 poem is that the child may not laugh unless the poem intervenes to provoke that response, the premise of Watts's 'Against Scoffing and Calling Names' is the exact reverse: the child may not *stop* laughing unless the poem intervenes to prevent it. Both poems reflect a belief that the critical child's laughter can be managed, indeed that it might be in need of such management, by poetry.

What is at stake here, just as in Rosen's poem written nearly 300 years later, is authority ('tame and rule'). Yet whereas Rosen's poem is concerned with the fragile authority of the adult over the child, Watts, like John Dewey, is concerned with the authority of the child over him- or herself. Alexander Pope might well claim of his own 1717 poem, *The Rape of the Lock*, that it sought, in relation to his warring protagonists, 'to make a jest of it, and laugh them together again' (n. pag); but Watts fears that scoffing and calling names has the opposite effect, resulting in rifts and division rather than cohesion. While Pope, then, tasks poetry with the job of bringing people together by making them laugh, Watts accorded to poetry the responsibility for preventing people from falling out by helping them to stop laughing. As Watts sees it, showing the child how to control his desire to jest is a means of helping him to reach upwards towards the divine, as opposed to revelling in the profane. For, as Watts's word 'tame' insinuates, there is something seemingly visceral and untaught about the impulse to laugh. As Anca Parvulescu observes in *Laughter: Notes on a Passion* (2010), laughter 'is one of the extra-reasonable, animal-like activities of the mouth, alongside eating, breathing, spitting, or kissing' (p. 9). It is a giving over of control to something non-human, and certainly, in Watts's scheme, all-too-worldly. The incommensurability of laughter with human rationality is a theme that preoccupied numerous commentators on laughter during this period. In his essay, 'Laughter', published in *The Spectator* in 1711, Joseph Addison writes, 'Laughter, while it lasts, slackens and unbraces the Mind, weakens the Faculties, and causes a kind of Remissness and Dissolution in all the Powers of the Soul. And thus far it may be looked upon as a Weakness in the Composition of Human Nature' (n. pag.). For Addison, this human quirk is at once a 'weakness' and a solace, rendering 'Man . . . the merriest Species of the Creation' when 'all above and below him are Serious' (n. pag.). He proposed that we should tolerate our proclivity to laugh, even indulge it, mindful of its therapeutic benefits. But those, like Watts, who looked to the Bible for a doctrinal steer on the question of how to manage this particular human frailty found much to unsettle them about the apparent incompatibility of laughter with moral virtue and Christian worship. As has been frequently noted over the centuries, 'We read that Jesus wept; we do not read that he laughed' (Montagu, 1830, p. 17).[2] Furthermore, we read that Jesus was laughed *at* on the cross. For those like the Reverend Isaac Watts, eager to counsel children against blasphemy, the curse uttered in Luke's gospel, 'Woe to you who laugh now!' (Luke 6:25) provided a fearful warning. It is small wonder, then, that Watts's poems for children seek to steer his readers away from the perils of laughing.

Watts's insistence that laughter is a form of cruelty indicates the ongoing influence that Hobbes's (albeit secular) account of laughter continued to have over the domain of eighteenth-century children's poetry. Hobbes had identified laughter as one of the many manifestations of our unbounded self-love which must be reined in if the seeds are to be sown for an ordered civil society. Abraham Bosse's well-known frontispiece to Hobbes's *Leviathan* (1651) encapsulates the author's idea of a civil society in which each individual forfeits certain of their self-interests in return for the collective interest of government (see Figure 2.1).

In Hobbes's analysis, each political subject voluntarily enters into this social contract to avoid *summum malum* (violent death), the avoidance of which Hobbes took to be our ultimate driving force. Hobbes's *Leviathan*, written in the inter-regnum following the Civil War, advances the case that monarchy is the least objectionable means of ensuring civil order. Hobbes therefore embodies the idea of the nation state in the figure of the king, a king comprised of his subjects. In Bosse's visual representation of the body politic, the king's subjects all look inwards towards their monarch, their faces shielded from our gaze. In the original manuscript edition, however, Bosse had drawn the figures such that they looked outwards and their faces were visible to the reader. Through this revision, whereby Hobbes deliberately conceals the citizens' faces from our view, the author underscores his point that orderly governance must entail not merely the suppression of passion but moreover the suppression of the *expression* of passion. Since our passions are individual, and hence give rise to self-interests that are in competition with one another, to indulge, even to communicate them freely would precipitate a state of anarchy: a war 'where every man is Enemy to every man' (Hobbes, 1997, p. 70). Hobbes saw laughter as a particularly insidious expression of passion, since, as the longstanding rhetorical history of the metaphor of wit as a weapon reminds us, laughter wounds. Hobbes believed that an eruption of laughter was a sign of aggression – a pre-emption of the war of all against all. Laughter, for Hobbes, therefore vividly reminds us (visibly, acoustically, affectively) that all of our interests are in conflict. It foreshadows, and so brings to mind, that *summum malum*, the violent death, which he saw as our overriding objective to avoid. Sacrificing our inclination to laugh, or, as Hobbes views it, surrendering our inclination to revel in the misfortunes of others, is a price he urges us to pay if we wish to live peacefully and harmoniously among others. For Hobbes, laughter is not merely immoral (though this is implicitly the case), but more to the point, it is politically disruptive.

Why, then, did Hobbes's antipathy to laughter exert such especial influence over poets writing for children, when so many poets writing for adults were prepared to reject his central premise? One explanation might lie in the terms of debate that were used by those who offered some of the most persuasive counterarguments to Hobbesian egoism. For example, the moral philosopher Francis Hutcheson, in his *Reflections upon Laughter* (1750), sought to discredit Hobbes's superiority theory by insisting on the moral and social benefits that laughter produced. In his analysis of the causes of laughter, he shifted the focus away from morality and towards cognitive activity, proposing that we are made to laugh by the disruption of 'associations of ideas made in our infancy' (p. 17). We laugh, Hutcheson claims, when our ideas of 'dignity and meanness' are inverted, belittling that which we customarily regard with respect, and vice versa (p. 21). Hutcheson puts childhood at the heart of his theory of laughter, since it is back to childhood that we refer each time we laugh and find ourselves alienated from the understanding which we laid down then. The logical extension of Hutcheson's theory, however, is that such laughter is an intrinsically adult phenomenon, since it requires childhood to serve as a phase of preparation for pleasures to be reaped later in life and not to act as a period during which those pleasures can be enjoyed in the present. The logical extension of Hutcheson's theory, if carried into the literary realm, is that during early life, children will be in need of literature which establishes conventions. It is only when they grow older that they will be capable of deriving pleasure from literature which disrupts such conventions – that is to say, comic literature.

The kind of thinking that we see at work in eighteenth-century children's poetry is closely in line with the views expressed on the subject by the period's most influential pedagogues and educational theorists. In *Émile* (1762), for example, Jean-Jacques Rousseau envisages a strikingly limited role for laughter in childhood. He conceives of it as a tool that, through carefully managed associations, will teach Emile, like Pavlov's dog, control over his emotions. The lesson Rousseau describes involves a mask, and its aim is to overcome the initial fear induced by the mask. 'I would laugh,' Emile's tutor explains, 'the company should laugh, and the child would laugh with the rest. . . . By artful management, he will thus be brought to laugh' (p. 67). In Rousseau's educational programme, laughter is a means to an end and not an end itself. He takes it to be something which can be, and hence should be, controlled by the adult teacher and not left in the hands of the child. Rousseau is no more in favour of children taking it upon themselves to generate laughter than Locke is more than half a century earlier in *Some Thoughts Concerning Education* (1693). Here, Locke warns that 'because the right management of so nice and ticklish a business, wherein a little slip may spoil all, is not every body's Talent, I think those who would secure themselves from provoking others, especially all young people, should carefully abstain' (Locke, 2007, p. 157). For all that Locke and Rousseau popularized the notion that the child needs freedom to 'play', neither saw laughter as a necessary or desirable dimension of such play. Indeed, it was common to bemoan the perceived indulgence of young people, particularly girls, when they were left free to laugh at will. Mary Wollstonecraft in *Thoughts on the Education of Daughters* (1787) singles out for especial criticism young women 'who are termed good-humored' but who are in fact, to her mind, 'frequently giddy, indolent, and insensible; yet because the society they mix with appear seldom displeased with a person who does not contest, and will laugh off an affront, they imagine themselves pleasing, when they are only not disagreeable' (p. 65). Rather than seeking to extend the right to laugh – or the right to make others laugh – to those currently denied it

Figure 2.1 Detail from frontispiece of Thomas Hobbes's *Leviathan*, by Abraham Bosse (1651).

(women and children), Wollstonecraft seeks even more stringently to impose existing prohibitions.

For educationalists such as Wollstonecraft, it was in part the suddenness with which laughter was believed to take over the body that led to such anxiety about it. This anxiety was tied up with the perennial worry about the mind's lack of control over the body, and in particular, the precariousness of our capacity to control what we attend to. For educationalists who feared that the child's capacity to concentrate was inferior to the adult's, and believed that childhood ought to be the time in which what Locke called good 'habits of thinking' were instilled, this was a particularly pressing concern. In its very abruptness and unpredictability, laughter threatened to undermine education. Further, to laugh is to betray the fact that one is at 'leasure'. As has been well documented, Locke's influential ideas on the importance of play during childhood meant that by the eighteenth century it was much more acceptable than in previous ages for children, especially those of the middle classes, to be at leisure. But Locke's idea was that the child would fill this leisure time with play which reinforced rather than contradicted his lessons. Much as Locke valued liveliness in childhood, he had no desire to encourage children to be frivolous. As Wollstonecraft's association of good humour with giddiness suggests, the two were perceived to be closely embroiled. In addition, children, as Andrew O'Malley has shown, were commonly aligned in the period with criminal classes and the insane, who shared in common a perceived incapacity for judgement (2003, p. 11). As the rather humourless German educationalist, Christian Gotthilf Salzmann, proclaimed in 1782, 'a foolish child laughs at every thing it does not understand; a good one never forgets that it must live many years in the world before it can distinguish right from wrong' (1799, p. 167). Among especially conservative thinkers, children were perceived to be in need of the same harsh treatment as the intellectually or morally bankrupt: to be locked up and kept out of trouble, safely away from the contaminating influence of a joke. Certainly, they were not deemed capable of the complex mental operations and supple command of language and judgement required to execute wit. Children, who comparatively lack literacy or sophisticated command of language, and thus will fail to understand, or worse, misfire jokes, would be safer avoiding them altogether. Eighteenth-century concerns about laughter were not merely centred on the question of the child's well-being; there was also the question of the adult's well-being. Laughter, it was believed, made one unattractive, prompting disgust among others. Its innately physical origins, the contortions of the mouth it entails and the offensive noise it creates, call attention to the body. As the eighteenth-century conduct writer Justine Gräfin Rosenberg-Orsini (1785) makes clear, it was considered polite for women and children to render their bodies as immobile and unobtrusive as possible: 'Frequent laughing . . . dilates the features, furrows the forehead and cheeks; it tarnishes the enamel of the teeth, by exposing them too often to the air, and even causes little wrinkles on the lips, which spoils the freshness of a pretty mouth' (pp. 177–8).

But how are we to reconcile the period's apparent resistance to the idea of comic poetry for children with the observation made by the mid-eighteenth-century philosopher David Hartley (among others) that it is a source of delight to the adult to cause the child to laugh? Even in infancy, Hartley declares, through 'tickling' and 'clapping the hands frequently, reiterating a sudden motion etc' (1749, I: pp. 252, 437), triggering a child's mirth is one of the parent's proudest tricks. Furthermore, eighteenth-century references to childhood reveal that then, as now, there was a widely held belief that laughter is endemic to childhood, so much so that the motif of the laughing child was frequently used as a stock rhetorical device to denote that which is natural. Hence the conduct book writer John Coltman could declare that 'the child that cries is as sure alive, as the child that laughs' (p. 116), and the moral philosopher John Studholme, in a discussion of the bodily expressions of emotions, could draw on the simile that for the face to express pleasure when the body is in pain is 'as unnatural, as if a Child should laugh when in Pain, or be angry and cry when pleased' (p. 48). The 'peculiar attribute' of 'infancy', it was proclaimed, 'seems to be that of laughing' (Anon, 1769, p. 26). Richard Lovell and Maria Edgeworth in their ground-breaking educational treatise, *Practical Education* (1798), could thus insist that the child's 'laugh and cry are such common expressions of delight or anguish, that they can not be mistaken, even by the illiterate' (pp. 620–1). Laughter, one might conclude, was held in the eighteenth century to be a child's native state – symptomatic, even, of childish innocence. Hence, for

Christopher Smart, in the poem 'Mirth', from his 1771 collection *Hymns for the Amusement of Children*, to express merriment through laughter is a form of worship:

'HYMN XXV.
MIRTH'

If you are merry sing away,
And touch the organs sweet;
This is the Lord's triumphant day,
Ye children in the gall'ries gay,
Shout from each goodly seat.
It shall be May to-morrow's morn,
Afield then let us run,
And deck us in the blooming thorn,
Soon as the cock begins to warn,
And long before the sun.
I give the praise to Christ alone,
My pinks already show;
And my streak'd roses fully blown,
The sweetness of the Lord make known,
And to his glory grow.
Ye little prattlers that repair
For cowslips in the mead,
Of those exulting colts beware,
But blythe security is there,
Where skipping lambkins feed.
With white and crimson laughs the sky,
With birds the hedge-rows ring;
To give the praise to God most high,
And all the sulky fiends defy,
Is a most joyful thing.

Here, the inescapability of laughter is underscored by its attribution to the landscape: it is the 'sky' that laughs at the coming of spring. It is worth noting that the laughter Smart depicts is not directed *at* anyone but is instead directed *to* a purpose: 'to give praise to God'. This is a form of laughter not with an object but with an objective. Smart is reconceiving laughter as something anthropological and not necessarily, or merely, social, as Hobbes had envisaged it. In drawing on this image of the sky laughing, Smart invokes a longstanding poetic tradition, indeed, one which we might even identify as something of a cliché, if we accept Joseph Addison's verdict that it is *the* most established and universal metaphor in the toolkit:

> the Metaphor of Laughing, applied to Fields and Meadows when they are in Flower, or to Trees when they are in Blossom, runs through all Languages; which I have not observed of any other Metaphor, excepting that of Fire and Burning when they are applied to Love. This shows that we naturally regard Laughter, as what is in itself amiable and beautiful. (1711, n. pag.)

On the one hand, Smart's use of this routine metaphor serves to create an impression of the familiarity, and hence the customariness, of laughter in childhood. However, we might pause to attend to the poem's grammatical mode. This is not a poem which describes a child's laughter, nor is it one which seeks to trigger it. It is rather a poem which anticipates the imagined pleasure of the child's laughter and invites the critical child to visualize what it might feel – and sound – like to be licensed to laugh unguarded. In fact, the children in the poem are precisely *not* presently able to laugh; they are enclosed in a church, and the noises they make are constrained by the rules which govern church conduct. The imperative, 'It shall be May to-morrow's morn, / Afield then let us run', temporally situates the child's unbounded movement and noise in the future. The laughing child thus remains an ideal available to the critical child only in the realm of fantasy. Smart uses the medium of the children's poem to animate an already well-established association between childhood and laughter to foster pleasure in the idea of the laughing child; but this is a pleasure that will stay firmly in the interiority of the child reader's imagination and not one which will erupt in the reader's bodily expression of the thing in question: mirth.

Therefore, despite the fact that the idea of laughter in childhood held clear appeal for late eighteenth-century poets, and despite the fact that over the course of the century, the laughing child had become entrenched as a poetic symbol to represent naturalness, even divinity, the image of the laughing child remained shot through with those same anxieties that preoccupied Watts several decades earlier. This is true even when laughter takes to the centre of the stage, as it does in William Blake's 'Laughing Song' in *Songs of Innocence* (1789):

'Laughing Song'

When the green woods laugh with the voice of joy
And the dimpling stream runs laughing by,
When the air does laugh with our merry wit,
And the green hill laughs with the noise of it.

When the meadows laugh with lively green
And the grasshopper laughs in the merry scene,
When Mary and Susan and Emily,
With their sweet round mouths sing Ha, Ha, He.

When the painted birds laugh in the shade
Where our table with cherries and nuts is spread
Come live & be merry and join with me,
To sing the sweet chorus of Ha, Ha, He. (pp. 27–8)

Although Blake's positioning of this poem in his *Songs of Innocence* apparently asserts the harmlessness of laughter in childhood, evoking the pleasure it involves for the laughing subject, the characteristically dissonant harmonics sounded by the music of this song trace the period's complicated attitudes towards the idea of the laughing child. By referring to, and acoustically enacting, the children's laughter as a form of music, the poem reminds us that laughter is aural; its medium is the voice, and its instrument the mouth, that orifice which is also responsible for the ingestion of food. Both activities, laughing and eating, which in this poem coincide, call attention to the child's body in its messiest, noisiest, most mobile and intrusive form – a form which eighteenth-century conduct manuals for children sought hard to keep out of public view owing to its capacity to irritate and disgust the polite adult.[3] More unsettling still is the unpredictable, wayward rhythm in which nearly every line in the poem performs a different kind of tetrameter. This unstable rhythm registers the anarchic potential of laughter, which follows no rules, darts capriciously and is in constant flux. The futile attempt to render the sound of laughter in linguistic form, resulting in a line of seeming nonsense ('Ha, Ha, He') highlights its palpable irrationality – its incompatibility with meaningful thought. When the child does speak, it is to issue a command: 'Come live & be merry and join with me'. The laughing subject has assumed power over those around it, in particular power over creatures smaller than it – grasshoppers, birds – precisely those creatures to whom children, at least according to John Locke, routinely display cruelty (2007, p. 132). The poem thus casts the laughing child as omnipotent, or, more specifically, it casts laughing child*ren* as an omnipotent critical mass; for the refrain, sung in unison, reminds us of how infectious laughter is – of how the individual loses autonomy when following the laughing crowd, and mimics the sounds made by others, either voluntarily or involuntarily, either caught up in its own pleasure or dragged in by the need to please others. The cacophonous sounds that the children utter intimate the ludicrousness that lurks beneath the supposedly ordered human world.

As is demonstrated by both Watts's dire warnings of the consequences of incurring divine wrath in *Divine Songs* and Blake's unflinching depictions of the abuses of children in this life in *Songs of Innocence and Experience*, poets writing for children at both ends of the eighteenth century were prepared to be frank with children about the perils and sufferings ahead of them. But it is another step altogether to acknowledge to children that life is a game the purpose of which we have not yet discovered, which we play without knowing the rules, and over which no one has any real control. While eighteenth-century poets for children went to great lengths to shield children from this insight, designating childhood as a space from which readers of poetry could be protected from the perceived perils of laughter, and requiring the critical child reader to work independently and proactively to find it for herself in the disjunctions between subject and form, today's poets for children seek precisely to reveal the ludicrousness that lurks beneath the supposedly ordered human world, turning to laughter as their means of so doing. We have become accustomed to seeing this act of entitling the child to laugh as an act of benevolence which prioritizes the child's delight. In Deweyan terms, we can view it as an act of liberation – a sign of the child's permission to be critical. But how might we take up this invitation for the child to critique without disdaining children's poetry which fails or refuses to let the child laugh – without recoiling with embarrassment from the very precursors of the form in question. In congratulating ourselves in the twenty-first century for giving literature's children permission to laugh, we need to be careful that we do not find ourselves looking back on earlier kinds of children's poetry and indulging that Hobbesian 'sudden glory arising from some sudden conception of some eminency in ourselves, by comparison with the infirmity of others, or with our own formerly'. For it was precisely through encounters with works such as those by Isaac Watts, Christopher Smart and William Blake that the child reader acquired a taste for critical thought, a taste that only in later centuries (owing, among other influences, to the impact of Deweyan educational philosophy on cultural ideas about the importance of the child's freedom to think) could emerge as full-blown laughter; for, as John Dewey frequently reminds us – and as vanguards of liberalism such as Anthony Ashley Cooper had already discovered over two centuries before – to teach a child to think critically is the surest safeguard for democracy – our collective freedom from autocratic authority – that there is. This, literature's children, laughing critics and critical laughers as they are, hardly need to be told.

Part Two

The art of idealization

3

On seeing: Kate Greenaway's *Under the Window*

The work of Kate Greenaway encapsulates the eerie stasis – and the accompanying, discomfiting, erotic allure – of childhood when it is rendered as an idealized phantom. The appeal of Greenaway's girl-ghosts was felt among her early readers in even the most unexpected quarters. 'Her spirit and bright thoughts and smiles will live for all time,' wrote an unlikely admirer, Algernon Charles Swinburne, on learning of her death in 1901 (Swinburne, 1944). Her early biographers, M. H. Spielmann and G. S. Layard, record the widespread association of her work with the saccharine, observing that 'about the name of Kate Greenaway there floats a perfume so sweet and fragrant' (Spielmann and Layard, 1905, p. 1). Indeed, the term 'ideal' and its cognates – idyll, perfection, innocent – are repeatedly evoked in critical attempts to characterize Greenaway's work. Joyce Whalley and Tessa Chester, in their landmark *A History of Children's Book Illustration* (1988), refer to her 'impossibly clean children' who 'live in an idyllically neat and sunny countryside (p. 107). They claim that her 'settings, like her clothes, were idealized: a dream world where it was always sunny, with tea on the lawn, and where children never got dirty' (p. 209). Similarly, Ina Taylor, whose work, *The Art of Kate Greenaway*, is subtitled *A Nostalgic Portrait of Childhood*, homes in on Greenaway's 'romantic' tendencies:

> Kate Greenaway's art conjures up an imaginary world where children dance in flowery meadows and nursery rhyme characters find a life which is forever beautiful and innocent. In the Greenaway world, it is nearly always May and the early summer sun is encouraging the apple and hawthorn to blossom. Children are tempted out of doors to play, wearing their new sprigged muslin frocks and summer bonnets. Older sisters take afternoon tea in

> formal gardens where Nature has been thoroughly tamed. Geraniums and lilies bloom in geometrically shaped beds contained by neat box hedges and gravel paths; the trees are a model of the topiarist's art, and roses fastened to white trellising scent the air. . . . If only life were as innocent or as beautiful as in her nursery books. (p. 8)

For Taylor, it is the presence of summer-blooming flora which roots the Greenaway world in an expressly romantic tradition. But this is no wild Wordsworthian sublime. On the contrary, Greenaway's version of the pastoral is, as Anne Lundin identifies, a 'prettified world' (McGavran, 1999, p. 155). If this aesthetic recollects or redirects a brand of romanticism, then it is a brand of 'feminine romanticism' (p. 159). Greenaway's picture books, Lundin suggests, 'modelled childhood for the late Victorians as a garden idyll, with winsome children frolicking in pasturelands or village greens surrounded by verdant images' (p. 159). Greenaway has substituted the 'mountains, . . . lakes, And sounding cataracts, . . . and mists and winds/That dwell among the hills' (Wordsworth, 1974, ll. 424–6) for the cultivated flowerbed and, crucially, adorned them with the presence of human beings. More specifically, as Lundin notes, the humans that Greenaway repeatedly depicts are youthful and they are female; her drawings present 'an idyllic childhood inhabited by children and young maidens in sophisticated rural simplicity' (p. 160). We are a long way away from the feral *ingénues* who populate Wordsworth's *Lyrical Ballads*. The 'simple child' (l. 1) of Wordsworth's 'We are Seven' – a figure who might stand as an emblem of Wordsworth's romanticization of childhood – is 'a little cottage Girl' (l. 5) who is 'wildly clad' (l. 10) and has a 'woodland air' (l. 9). Greenaway's diminutive females, while also cottage dwellers, are genteel and refined: 'Some wore their hair in pigtail plaits, / And some of them wore curls' ('The Twelve Miss Pelicoes', ll. 15–16). From their bonnets to their dancing shoes, they are decked out in the accoutrements of polite society, albeit anachronistically in the fashions of their grandparents.

And yet Greenaway's earliest enthusiasts – whose powerful advocacy secured her widespread popular appeal – were oddly in denial about this facet of her work. John Ruskin, whose fascination with Greenaway's work has been subject to intense scrutiny,[1] and who enjoyed a lifelong friendship with its author (perhaps a mentorship, perhaps a romantic liaison), identified the appeal of

Greenaway's prelapsarian world in its apparent pre-industrialism: 'There are no railroads in it, to carry the children away,' he wrote in *The Art of England*; 'no tunnel or pit mouths to swallow them up . . . no vestige of science, civilization, economic arrangements, or commercial enterprise' (Ruskin, 1884, p. 152). But while Ruskin's assessment neatly identifies the ways in which Greenaway has excised the scars of manufacture and commodification from her natural landscapes, it ignores the ways in which these scars are etched onto her depictions of children. The repeated assertions that Greenaway's world is idyllic, then, rest on an insistent incorporation of the human subjects into the settings which Greenaway conjures for them, and furthermore, on a view that such settings encode what Ruskin's contemporary, Gleeson White, called 'the legend of the gentlefolk' (1897–8, pp. 39–40), to produce what James Holt McGavran calls 'England's idealized past – its national childhood – but fashioned into an eclectic contemporary style (McGavran, 1999, p. 165), and what Anne Lundin describes as an 'idyllic village back in time, in an England that never was' (Lundin, 1993, p. 51). But what of Greenaway's people? How do her human subjects inhabit the settings she gives them?

Greenaway herself recognized that there were processes of distortion and sanitization operating in her work, although she put this down to the condition of art itself, rather than then the peculiar condition of *her* art: 'I can never define what art really is,' she mused in a letter of 1896. 'It isn't realism, it isn't all imagination, it's a queer giving something to nature that is possible for nature to have, but always has not.' She locates the idealizing tendencies of her work in her treatment of the environment, and not in her treatment of the figures which inhabit these environments. Referring to Edward Burne-Jones's roses, setting up an implicit comparison with her own, she writes, 'They don't often grow like that, but they could' (quoted in Spielmann and Layard, 1905, p. 209). As her use of the conditional highlights, the world Greenaway outlines is not a throwback to the past, much as Ruskin and others have been able to project this nostalgic regression onto it, but an aspiration forwards: the plotting of what John Dewey identifies as a 'model'. Greenaway's worlds, as art critic, William Feaver, reaching for the same word, proposes, also 'model' (1977, p. 17). They reach towards that Kantian notion of the maximum idea imaginable – or, as Martin Hardie, the pioneering early critic of illustration, was to put it, Greenaway's work represents 'the best in the best of all possible worlds' (Hardie, p. 277).

Kimberley Reynolds, among others, has cautioned us to remember what children's works of this era often neglect to make explicit: 'that for most of the population, childhood continued to be an inconvenient, often brutal, phase to be got through as quickly as possible' (1994, p. 17). It may well be the case that Greenaway's world reflects 'an idealised perception of the young embraced by middle-class adults in the closing decades of Victoria's reign', as historians such as Peter Cunningham have suggested (Watson, 2001, p. 305); but if we accept what is presented as a generic, ahistorical prototype of a perfect world, without bringing into plain view the ways in which this prototype encodes a *particular* account of a *particular* world, then we remain blinded to the peculiarity of the view which Greenaway's work invites the reader to take up. Moreover, we evade the question of the ways in which her work, precisely by presenting particular, mobile ideas as fixed, frozen ideals, demands a certain kind of work from her child audience – work which, as this chapter will demonstrate, the critical child reader is as likely to resist as to carry out, since the complex nature of the works themselves pulls the reader in competing directions. Instead of reasserting the by-now familiar position *that* Greenaway's work idealizes, this chapter attempts to understand *what* Greenaway idealizes, and in so doing, to illuminate what is at stake for the critical child in the repeated identification of such ideas as ideal.

To start with, it needs to be observed that a vital thread running through the critical remarks quoted above is a consistently held assumption that Greenaway's works are feasts for our eyes. We gaze on Greenaway's children. If Greenaway's worlds are appealing, then they are so on account of the impressions they make on our faculty of sight. The fact that even in her own age, Greenaway images were lifted from their original contexts and reproduced on household items such as crockery and buttons testifies to the widespread visual allure of her creations. And yet Greenaway's initial success derived from the popularity of her breakthrough work, *Under the Window* (1879), a book of illustrated poems to which she supplied not merely the images but also the verse. It is unsurprising that Greenaway has been remembered primarily as an illustrator, since illustration, both of her own work and, more typically, of other people's, comprised the vast majority of her output. However, the focus on

Greenaway's illustration has resulted in a near total disregard of her verse, and although her position in the history of children's picturebooks has been long-appreciated, her position in the history of children's poetry has been almost entirely overlooked. Moreover, where critics of children's literature have paused to pass comment on *Under the Window*, they have focussed almost exclusively on its images, rarely pausing to consider not merely the ways in which the poems function as poems, but additionally, serve to complicate, and not just to reinforce, what is conveyed by the images.[2] The dearth of critical interest in Kate Greenaway as a poet is not in itself remarkable, given the general lack of scholarly interest in the domain of children's poetry.[3] But it is also worth noting that the scholarly tendency to view rather than to read Greenaway's landmark volume indicates the extent to which Greenaway's works themselves establish the pre-eminence of watching – and indeed, the extent to which reading is set up as a line of sight. This section will consider the ways in which Greenaway germinates apparently perfect conditions for watching and examines what is at stake in offering these up – and indeed, in the critical child's acceptance of them – as conducive to visual pleasure.

The importance of gazing is established by the volume's title, *Under the Window*, the lettering embedded into a frontispiece in which a garland of children circles around the words. The children share in common that all of them either look away or look directly at one another, absorbed in their own activity, seemingly immune to the scenario of being watched – all but one little boy who breaks the fourth wall, staring straight out blankly to meet our eye. Words and image intertwine, then, to immobilize a particular view: under the window. The very phrase itself, of course, situates this view, invoking that which is immediate and everyday, right there beneath our eyes. And yet the word 'under' also hints at what is routinely missed – that which might typically lie beneath notice. The window is thus evoked not as a transparent piece of glass but as a microscope which enlarges the miniature and enables us to see what the naked eye struggles to make sense of. The conceit of the window locates the work squarely within an existing literary tradition of frontispieces dating back at least to John Newbery's *A Little Pretty Pocket-Book* (1744), and recalling that other seminal coupling of verse and image, William Blake's *Songs of Innocence* (1789). Newbery's window lies behind the children, who sit in a comfortable drawing room at the knee of their mother or nurse, reading. The clear implication is that enlightenment (such as that provided by Newbery's work) as yet eludes the child but will be gleaned through reading the work. Blake, by contrast, has his children sat with their nurse outdoors; no window is required, for the children dwell in the light, and have no need for a window to bring it to them. By reintroducing the frame of the window, Greenaway not only recalls the enlightenment tradition which Blake had challenged but also reanimates the Horatian cause (instruction through delight) which Newbery's work champions.

There is a crucial reversal, however, at work in Greenaway's scene. The children in *Under the Window* reside not in an interior illuminated from without. *They* are outside; it is *child critic* who illuminates them as he or she summons them to his or her notice through the frame of the page. Like Blake's innocents, Greenaway's ghost-girls dwell in the elements; but as the title makes clear, the reader does not reside outside too, but is positioned inside looking out. The viewer is thus from the start alienated from the child subjects; the critical child peers *at* them but does not look *with* them. Whereas Blake's children are caught in the act of childhood, Greenaway's children are caught in the act of presenting childhood; carefully arranged into a neat row, they are defined by their awareness of the watching eye. Alike in appearance, and conjoined at the hands, they are a critical mass facing the reader head-on. Unlike Newbery's one-way enlightenment – for, once educated, one has no need for the murky inchoateness of barbarianism – Greenaway's window offers a two-way view: the reader looks out of the window at the children, but they, should they choose, should they dare, can look back at the reader to confront the spectacle of the reader watching them. Unlike Newbery's window, then, Greenaway's is transparent; it is a vehicle for, and not a constitutive agent in, the acquisition of knowledge. The act of looking mimetically reflects rather than produces what is there. The allusiveness of Greenaway's frontispiece thus reverberates both with an enlightenment idea that seeing results in understanding (a form of understanding which, in the Newbery tradition, takes the form of rules and maxims to be learned) and with a romantic idea that the child is an epistemological subject and not merely an object. But Greenaway importantly reconfigures our line of sight and by implication the modes through which the child critic knows. In Blake's *Songs of Innocence*, the child figures have access to ontological knowledge that the reading and viewing subject does not. Greenaway's children know something very particular: they know that their function is to be watched. The child critic knows that they know this, because they are persistently represented as watching the reader watch them.

Much has been made of the erotics of watching in Greenaway's work. Anna Silver, in particular, observing that Greenaway's child subjects tend to be prepubescent females, has emphasized the relevance of Greenaway's relationship with John Ruskin. Ruskin, whose penchant for scantily clad prepubescent girls has been well-documented, was a fervent admirer of Greenaway's work and is known to have written to Greenaway begging her to draw him images of children without clothes. Silver (2000), analyzing what it is about Greenaway's work that so captivated Ruskin's imagination, has proposed that it is her skill in portraying 'girls before they lose their innocent girlish loveliness' (p. 37). According to Silver, for Ruskin, the 'key quality that contributes to a girl's character and shape . . . is her orderliness' (p. 38), and to this end, Ruskin figured 'the girl's body as an object that needs to be disciplined, and growth as something that needs to be controlled' (p. 38). Inferring that it was these qualities that Ruskin found and responded to in Greenaway's work, Silver concludes that 'passionlessness and serenity are the keynotes of her drawings' (p. 42). Silver's observation of the ways in which the Victorian so-called 'cult of the child' fetishes the child as an erotic object is not, of course, new and has been explored in depth by commentators including James Kincaid and Jacqueline Rose, among others.[4] As these scholars have discussed, such an account of childhood foregrounds the delight of the onlooker, and in so doing, it places the child in an impossible bind: the child is moulded to satisfy the erotic desires of the adult and is taught from an early age that this is its role.[5] At the same time, fundamental to the adult's desire is the child's apparent innocence – that is to say, its unconsciousness of this fact (as in Blake's frontispiece). The child must therefore strive to be watchable without revealing awareness of being watched. Of course, the child critic cannot un-know what it knows; but its capacity to act as if not being watched is the source of the onlooker's delight. The critical child, then, understands that he or she must feign unawareness of being watched in order to satisfy the adult delight of watching those who do not know that they are seen.

Rose has famously concluded that, in placing the reader in this predicament, such literature cannot include the child within its audience. Greenaway's work, like J. M. Barrie's *Peter Pan*, the subject of Rose's prolonged discussion, invites the child reader to adopt a point of view which positions children as exotic specimens, attractive in their very foreignness. In so doing, *Under the Window*, like *Peter Pan*, proffers as ideal a mode of viewing in which the reader derives satisfaction from the spectacle of the child's unselfconscious absorption in her own activity. But such reading of Greenaway's work would only be possible if we were to ignore the fact that her work presents a matrix of *reciprocal* watching, one which exposes, and hence challenges from within, the inadequacy of the very critical paradigms which Rose uses to analyze children's literature. By depicting children not merely as objects to be viewed, but as viewing subjects in the act of *flouting* the rule of feigning unawareness of being watched, Greenaway invites the critical child to witness in a state of disintegration those mobile ideas which only *ostensibly* masquerade as ideals. The child critic, then, in order to make sense of Greenaway's poems as poems, and not merely as descriptions of the visual elements of the work, must necessarily question, and not simply accept, those rules which are presented as fixed – and will derive aesthetic pleasure precisely from the gaps between what *might* hypothetically be, and what *is*, in the particular instance of *this* work, the case.[6]

Advice literature which laid out the rules for children and parents in the second half of the nineteenth century places a strong emphasis on the importance of ensuring that a child is fit to be looked at. In particular, this entails looking neat and orderly. As the author of *Path to Pleasure for Good and Dutiful Children* writes, 'If it were not for our mothers, sisters, and female servants, what ragged and miserable objects should we often appear!' (n.d., n. pag.). The Hobbesian premise underpinning this sentiment is one which presumes the natural state of things to be disorderly and decaying. The implication is that cultivating a tidy appearance, even if it may not reflect a tidy mind, might at least help to create one. Note that the responsibility for ensuring such a neat appearance falls squarely in the female domain, and that the period of life in which efforts should be channelled into ensuring such exactitude stretches right back to childhood. Appearance is a feminine concern, both since the appearance of women is of paramount importance to men and since the appearance of men rests on the extent to which female care-givers instil the right values early on.

The emphasis given to a neat physical appearance is in line with a more general emphasis in advice literature of this period on the importance of behaviour which attracts rather than repels others. That is to say, advice literature of this period is preoccupied not by how the child should be but by how the child should be *seen* to be. Precepts governing how the child should behave such that they satisfy requisite standards tend to be characterized as rules for *politeness*, a concept which came into vogue in British discourse of the early eighteenth century and remained a dominant concept in discussions of childhood throughout the nineteenth.[7] As Felix Urban, in *The First Book of Manners: Or, Introduction to Polite Behaviour*, asserts, 'Childhood is, without question, the age at which Good Manners ought to be inculcated and acquired; otherwise, a number of habits are in danger of springing up in children, which may materially affect their course in after life' (1856, pp. iv–v). The mode typically envisaged for the acquisition of such behaviour was the learning of rules. Consequently, there are numerous books from the period which make available in plain form the rules of courtesy which it was deemed important for the child to learn. For such a process to be successful, the child's pliancy was vital, as the prominent Victorian bastion of respectability, the Reverend Lord Sydney Godolphin Osborne, wrote to *The Times* in 1865 to underscore, insisting that the child's obedience was as one of the 'two cardinal virtues of nursery life' (the other being 'love') (1865).

Many works in this genre take a rather rudimentary form which is often comprised simply of lists of rules. But while the shapelessness and directionlessness of such listing can create a seeming haphazardness, authors of such manuals repeatedly insist, as does the pioneering educator and humanist, Frederick Gould, that the 'rules of courtesy are not arbitrary; they spring from our social relations' (1899, p. xi). Indeed, far from being spurious, such rules are seen to be inevitable and unquestionable, as Felix Urban's use of the singular reveals in his declaration that by '"Manners" is meant "the way" of behaving towards others' (1856, p. 11), the singular here admitting of no equivocality in determining what good behaviour might entail. Urban's treatise goes on to explore some of the reasons why manners are important, dwelling on the social shame – the 'embarrassment and mortification – possibly even loss, shame, and suffering' (p. v) – of failing to adhere to social protocol. Further, as additional reasons why politeness must be instilled in young people, he cites the practical dangers of 'being led aside into the ways of the unruly and the vicious' (p. v); the political expediency of 'preventing disunions' and fostering 'civility' (p. 14); the utilitarian motive that, once acquired, manners serve as a 'permanent letter of introduction and recommendation', enabling one to get ahead in the world (p. 14). Other courtesy book authors underscore the moral incentive of doing one's 'duty', which is the reason emphasized by William Denison, formerly Governor of Madras, in his *Advice to Children* (1871, p. 15). For F. J. Gould, even the small matter of the survival of the species hangs in the balance, since good manners 'tend to the preservation of the person and the race' (p. xii).

However, the chief reason which commentators on the subject repeatedly provide for the necessity of cultivating *politesse* is the avoidance of repugnance. What is fundamentally at stake is not another's hurt, or safety – but their irritation, or worse, revulsion. Felix Urban writes, 'If children be accustomed betimes to the practice of polite behaviour, they may be spared from occasioning much discomfort and annoyance to others' (p. v). This is the theme taken up by Dr Adam Blekinsop, whose *A Shilling's-Worth of Advice, on Manners, Behaviour and Dress* seeks to show how 'Gents' may become gentlemen and young ladies more attractive. He concludes his piece with the 'earnest advice' that 'never by word, deed, or look' should a young lady 'give rise to the most trifling feeling of disgust. However trivial each individual act may be, they will be of serious import in the aggregate. Disgust once established, aversion will not be far behind. Bear in mind this little maxim: – "There is no place where real politeness is of more value, than where we mostly think it would be superfluous"' (pp. 29–30). As Blekinsop makes clear, the primary culprits – those most likely to nauseate – are young women. The ways in which women can torture those (males) around them by their failure to take sufficient preventative measures are numerous and severe, as Blekinsop indignantly notes:

> I have heard that there are, even in these days, females who come down with their hair in paper – nay, remain in that state all day. I am incredulous to this; and even entertain strong doubts upon the better authenticated existence

> of morning wrappers. The latter may be endured with internal grumbling, and for the sake of peace and quietness – as we put up with washing days, fried chops, and a clothes-horse by the parlour fire – but no sensible woman will ever inflict them upon the most patient Job. As for curl-papers, they almost justify any man in wishing himself a widower. There is a point at which forbearance ceases to be a virtue; and that point, I apprehend to be somewhat short of curl papers. (p. 29)

Underlying Blekinsop's physical repulsion is a palpable sense of betrayal that a woman who reveals the machinations involved in assembling her coiffed exterior betrays that this exterior is an illusion – one carefully contrived to satisfy demanding husbandly standards. In refusing to render herself fit to be gazed on, she launches an assault on the very nature of a relationship between a man and a woman. Worse, she does so for no apparent reason: 'there is no necessity to disgust your husband . . . ; . . . even if Fate should have made you a drudge, don't show it. Keep up the poetry of life, even if it is upon hashed mutton' (pp. 28–9). Implicit in Blekinsop's account is that any reason which might dictate how a woman manipulates her appearance which does not prioritize the interests of the men around her is invalid. Blekinsop's advice, however, is not directed at the nation's wives but at the nation's young; children, then, especially female children, should from the beginning groom themselves with the gaze of their future husband in mind.

Good manners, then, relate first and foremost to 'the Care and Government of our Person' (Gould, 1899, p. 15). Paramount is 'the government and cleanliness of the person; lest anything should arise therefrom either inconvenient or disagreeable to others' (p. 16). Important, too, is tidy clothing, since 'careless, slovenly habits will render any one unacceptable – nay, sometimes, almost repulsive; while there is a certain general neatness of appearance which conciliates good-will, and renders a person acceptable with even the plainest clothing' (p. 27). But it is not merely how well scrubbed and dressed the body is; what is also important is what one does with it once it has been prepared for public view. For example, one must never 'suffer the ends of the fingers to be introduced into the nostrils. This is a disagreeable, revolting habit, which very little children are apt to fall into, and of which they cannot too quickly be broken by their parents, and all others who may have the charge of them' (Gould,

1899, p. 25). In addition, carrying the body without 'running, or . . . walking with a hasty precipitate step' is desirable. 'Let your pace be moderate and uniform,' recommends Gould, 'unless any urgent occasion should require a quicker step' (p. 54). But crucially, what is really vital is that the young female does not 'display' – 'coquetry, like flattery, is only effective when not discovered' (Blekinsop, p. 25). Herein lies the paradox: the female is made to be looked at, and must strive to look presentable; but it is crucial that she does not reveal her awareness that this is the case. The ultimate in vulgarity is to reveal her awareness that her looks have the potential to meet with approval. The rules of politeness, then, particularly as they pertain to the female child, are formed so as to enable her to attract rather than repel others, particularly adult males. At the same time, they enable her to perfect a façade of ignorance as to the effects of her exertions on others. She must cultivate a heightened alertness to the negative effects that her appearance might have on the men around her, but complete indifference to any positive effects that she might create.

Given the precariousness of the balance which is to be achieved, it is unsurprising that conduct manuals of the period provide rules for the most nuanced details of behaviour. Any aspect which might be noticed by another must be subject to careful organization. Thus, for example, *The Polite Academy* provides the following step-by-step instructions for young women on how to walk gracefully:

1. Hold up your head without any stiffness.
2. Keep your whole person upright.
3. Let your shoulders fall easily.
4. Drop your arms easily and gracefully down to the waist.
5. Then place the hands on one another, with the palms turning upward, and a little inward.
6. Take short steps, and do not lift up your feet too high.
7. Let the foot that was up be brought down slowly, and with an easy motion.
8. In this manner you may easily courtesy to any one passing by.
9. Join the back foot to the fore one, then sink gently, and rise up again gradually: after this, continue walking as before.

10. Never stare as you walk, and always look down when you courtesy. (Anon., n.d., pp. 82–3)

In case the words alone fail satisfactorily to convey an impression of what is required, they are safeguarded throughout with images, 'a set of Genteel Figures of Masters and Misses, in easy proper Attitudes adapted to the Rules' (p. 69). This reinforces the sense that what the child must bear in mind is that she is a creature to be viewed; she must perpetually anticipate how she will be seen from the outside, and not be distracted by what she sees as she looks out. Part of managing her looks involves managing her look*ing*. Manuals such as this therefore give special attention to the question of what the child is to do with her eyes. Indeed, this is one of the first questions that the anonymous author of *The Polite Academy* addresses: 'To accomplish [the rules of decency, modesty, and good manners], I shall first recommend it to my little Readers, whether in company or out, to avoid all particular or affected motions of the head, all wanton or oblique glances of the eyes, all ogling or winking, dimpling of the cheeks, or priming of the lips' (pp. 5–6). The implication here is that the child is to avoid finding any use for her eyes besides those which are strictly necessary in order for her to see where she is going. This reduces watching to a purely functional activity, not one from which the child is expected to gain any aesthetic pleasure. *She* ought to be the source of aesthetic pleasure in any scene in which she finds herself. Hence, conduct manuals such as this are littered with rules governing how, when and where the child should direct her eyes: 'Never stare at any one who is speaking; but listen with a decent behaviour' (p. 56); 'Look into the face of the person you speak to, and the same when he speaks to you; but do this modestly and decently' (p. 59); 'If you see any thing that surprizes you, do not stop to stare at it, but look upon it and pass on' (p. 60). Since it is the child as viewing object and not viewing subject which politeness manuals of the period are keen to cultivate, it follows that the child's eyes are not deemed to be windows into the child's soul – or, at least, the extent to which the child communicates anything of her own soul to the outside world through her eyes is carefully circumscribed, on the basis that it is not her soul which will provide pleasure (or its obverse) to those around her, but her body. There is thus an inherent irony in the injunction that the child should 'let [her] eyes and [her] looks agree with [her] words, and shew [her] respect is real and sincere' (p. 38), since the method via which she achieves this semblance of authenticity is by withholding what her eyes might communicate. Signalling respect for others is thus precisely not 'sincere', since it entails masking and not exposing 'real' thoughts and feelings. It is only sincere in the sense that it reflects what the child sincerely *ought* to be like, not what she actually is like. Intriguingly, the moral duplicity involved in good manners is something with which conduct writers of the period are perfectly reconciled. As the author of *The Polite Academy* asserts, 'Politeness makes us appear outwardly what we should be inwardly' (p. 113). The notion of fabrication is thus inscribed within the very concept of good manners. Indeed, a lack of artfulness is perceived, in conduct literature of the period, to be a positive disadvantage, since it is impossible to get ahead socially without adjusting one's behaviour to secure the desired ends. Hence, in direct repudiation of that central tenet of romanticism, *The Polite Academy* informs us that 'rusticity' is exactly what we should be steering our children away from, as it 'debars [them] of all easy access or familiar intercourse with persons of delicacy' (p. 113). Good manners, then, are a means to an end, and that end is pleasing others – not, however, for altruistic ends, but, on the contrary, so that they might open doors for us and enable us to join the ranks of the comfortable middle classes, which, it is assumed, is the unquestioned ambition of the reader of such a text.

The fulfilment of this ambition is the promised reward for all the hard work required to master the rules of politeness, for, just like John Dewey's hard-won capacity for critical thought, good manners do not come easily, but are fostered by concerted practice and self-control. Gould writes, 'The effect of repetition of movement is observed even in the inorganic world, as in the wearing of a channel by a river, and it is amply displayed in the lives of animals' (1899, p. xii). We have here a curious mixture of working against the grain and working with it: the sheer effort involved in honing the habit of good manners indicates that mastering the rules of politeness is counter-intuitive and a product of hard graft rather than instinct; but by drawing a parallel with the repetitions involved in the natural world, Gould implies that the patterns of behaviour he advocates are themselves organic and inevitable. Implicitly, then, the outcome – a scenario in which, as in Lucy Lyttleton Cameron's 1820 novel, *The Polite Little Children* (which was persistently popular throughout the nineteenth century), where the child protagonists become 'kind, affectionate, and truly Polite' (p. 36) – is also figured as one which is natural and inevitable. The ideal is thus proposed as the norm; it is its failure – impoliteness – which is the perversion. This process whereby the artificial ideal appears to the child as the given occurs through the child's internalization of the rules of etiquette. As Gould explains, 'the best kind of people' go 'the right way because they are bidden to do so' not 'for fear of an EYE watching us' but 'by THEIR OWN CONSCIENCE' (p. 5). The 'eye' here has shifted from the erotic gaze of a passer-by admiring the modest posture of a child walking to a Foucauldian internalization of a Benthamite panopticon, such that what the child sees when she looks out is inseparable from (has become the same as) what the passer-by sees as he looks at her. The ideal mode of viewing, then, which such politeness manuals advocated, is one in which the child appropriates as her own line of sight the line of sight which another would adopt in relation to her. Put simply, she looks at herself, and not at others; as viewing subject, she sees only herself as object. What she will see, if all the rules have been followed, is order, a point which Gould is keen to stress: 'ORDER is the rule of the sun; and ORDER is the rule of the child' (p. 91):

> Order gives us life, health, comfort, safety, intelligence, science, and beauty. You might almost think order was a magic fairy that went about the world, doing all kinds of wonderful deeds, and changing ugly things into handsome. Order lays the table neatly, and makes father, mother, and children smile as they sit down to meals. Order dresses boys and girls and men and women in such a way that it is pleasant to the eyes to behold them. Order keeps the furniture polished, and the windows bright, and the garden cheerful. Order makes the streets of the city clean. Order guides the crowds in the roads so that they do not jostle or annoy. Order brings our letters to the door, runs the train into the station at the right minute, and makes machines work correctly, and master and man live happily together. It is true that the world is not in the order it should be. There is *dis*order where the people are sad, and poor, and ragged, and ready to steal and do many evil deeds. We must all of us help to put the world in order. Yes, you boys must help to bring order into the world. You girls also. (p. 92)

This rousing call to arms might stand as a characterization of the world which Kate Greenaway's work depicts, a world in which, as Anne Silver has observed, 'passionlessness and serenity are the keynotes' (2000, p. 42). But while *Under the Window* is ostensibly preoccupied with order, Greenaway's convoluted lines of sight place the critical child in a fractious position: she must simultaneously uphold and thwart the modes of viewing which such Victorian codes of politeness entail:

> Under the window is my garden,
> Where sweet, sweet flowers grow;
> And in the pear-tree dwells a robin.
> The dearest bird I know.
>
> Tho' I peep out betimes in the morning,
> Still the flowers are up the first;
> Then I try and talk to the robin,
> And perhaps he'd chat – if he durst. (p. 15)

The status of this scene as idyllic is assured not merely through the choice of sentimental diction ('sweet', 'sweet') but moreover through its repetition, which indicates that the only thing that could further improve an already perfected scene is its multiplication. This impression is reinforced by the superlative, 'dearest' – that reaching after the maximum possible. Greenaway sets up here all those clichés of the domesticated pastoral world to which her chocolate-box designer admirers were so drawn: the robin, the garden, the tree. The children all look out at the world below them, and the child reader watches their apparent pleasure in a scene which the possessive pronoun indicates belongs to them, or at least, to one of them. The fact that we have just one voice, in the singular, and yet three children to look at, all uniform with their identikit blonde tousles, neatly frilled with ruffs and podgy arms, implies that the poetic voice speaks on their behalf: it is the voice of a child, any child, *the* child. This invests the voice with a representative quality. It purports to answer that perennial adult wondering, brought to the heart of the discussion several generations earlier by William Wordsworth and contemporaries including Samuel Taylor Coleridge and Charles Lamb: what does the child think? *How* does the child think? Here, as in Wordsworth's *Lyrical Ballads*, we have a singular child speaking for children as a species. What F. G. Gould identified as orderliness is everywhere apparent in the accompanying image: in the meticulous grids in the window panes; in the lines of the square print of the gingham curtains; in the careful arrangement of the children, spaced at regular intervals apart, displayed in descending order of size. While the poem identifies the source of the scene's delight in the reliability of the natural cycle, the inevitability of the annual crop of fruit, the invariable proximity of a robin, the image directs our view not at the garden scene but at the scene of the children looking out at the garden. This, the implication is, is the source of the *reader's* delight. The apparent neatness of the whole is sealed by the tripping nursery rhyme forms in which lines of tetrameter are alternated with lines of trimeter, a form which recalls the form most frequently adopted in the *Mother Goose* rhymes.[8] Greenaway slots her poem squarely into an existing tradition, drawing on the credit of timelessness and simplicity which this association lends.

And yet, even here at this sugared opening juncture to the volume in which the child reader gazes at children gazing at the natural world, the critical child might note that the verb which the speaker uses to describe the act of looking is 'peep'. The voice of the poem, a singular 'I', sits at an odd angle to the illustration, suggesting that the act of an individual child stealing a surreptitious glance occurs outside the moment which the image captures in which several children openly gaze. The poetic child hints at a distrust of the scene at hand, a desire to catch it out; the poem documents her refusal to accept at face value its inevitability – her readiness, even her keenness, to flout the rules. Not satisfied with merely seeking to witness the breakdown of natural rules, the child actively seeks to force this breakdown, attempting to elicit human conversation from the bird, boldly and adamantly reaching after that which the robin 'durst'. The use of this verb here, with its implication of knowing transgression, attributes a desire to resist order onto this symbolic feature of the natural world, the robin. Even the robin, it is implied, is feigning his participation in this scene, a scene which purports to an innocence that is merely a charade. There are complicated layers of knowingness set up here, wherein the adult authorial voice mimics a child who mimics similarity with a robin who mimics incomprehension. The seeming candour and directness of the gaze depicted in the picture is thus subtly, but palpably, at odds with what in the poem is presented as a covert, solitary peek behind the curtains when the window is shut. So what is the child reader, the critical child, to make of this dissonance which is sounded even in the very poem which gives the collection its title?

Confronted with the competing perspectives which the combination of word and image provides, the critical child must decide for herself which (whose) point of view to adopt. Therefore, when certain poems, such as 'Five Little Sisters Walking in a Row' present the scene via a voice which is decidedly adult in inflection, it is not a given that the critical child will accept as such what this voice passes off as wisdom:

> Five little sisters walking in a row;
> Now, isn't that the best way for little girls to go?
> Each had a round hat, each had a muff,
> And each had a new pelisse of soft green stuff.
>
> Five little marigolds standing in a row;
> Now, isn't that the best way for marigolds to grow?
> Each with a green stalk, and all the five had got
> A bright yellow flower, and a new red pot. (p. 28)

The girls in this scene appear to be enacting to a tee the guidelines prescribed for walking gracefully offered by the author of *The Polite Academy*. It is presumably in their diligent fulfilment of such standards of good manners that the way in which the girls go can be deemed 'best'. As with the prescriptions given in *The Polite Academy*, the poem's exclusive concern is the outward appearance of the figures: their uniformity, their neatness, the luxurious fashionableness (albeit in an outdated form) of their clothes. The comparison to flowers eschews that longstanding poetic convention which Gertrude Stein was later to deride ('Rose is a rose is a rose', 1968, p. 187) wherein women are equated with the heady, mysterious passion that their perceived beauty engenders in men; instead, Greenaway's girls are likened to potted plants – flowers whose appeal resides in their contained movement and growth. Their appeal resides in the fact that their prettiness is precisely knowable. Like the monochrome faces of marigolds, the girls' faces are impassive; dutifully, they keep their eyes on the path ahead and are not distracted by the passing view. Eerily, though, since the image presents the girls head-on, it creates the impression that they are walking directly towards us – indeed, into us; their walking is figured as an onwards, inexorable march; one which will continue, come what may; one which, finding us in its path, will require us to jump out of the way. Static though this picture is with the child in the middle, the biggest child, leading the way, foot forward, it is on the brink of lapsing into movement. The girls, contained as they are, like the marigolds, by the feminine apparel which marks the contours of their childish forms, will, as they move towards us, growing ever bigger, move out of the centre of the frame and out of our line of sight. Furthermore, confronting us head-on, these girls can see the child reader; they can see what lies behind the child reader – that which the reader cannot see because they have their backs turned to it. So what is it that is 'best' about all this walking neatly in a row – is it the sight of it, or might it in fact be the view with which it provides the critical child? The tugging of the poem and the image in different directions requires the child reader to consider this unanswered question and decide for herself.

Elsewhere in the collection, Greenaway elaborates further on what it is that the children might see when they look out rather than merely be looked at. The pair of poems – 'Margery Brown, on the Top of the Hill', from close the beginning of the collection, and 'Heigh Ho! – Time Creeps but Slow', the penultimate poem of the volume – expressly addresses this matter of what the child sees through those eyes whose excessive use conduct writers were so keen to curtail:

'Margery Brown, on the top of the hill,
Why are you standing, idle still?'
'Oh, I'm looking over to London town;
Shall I see the horsemen if I go down?'

'Margery Brown, on the top of the hill,
Why are you standing, listening still?'
'Oh, I hear the bells of London ring,
And I hear the men and the maidens sing.'

'Margery Brown, on the top of the hill,
Why are you standing, waiting still?'
'Oh, a knight is there, but I can't go down,
For the bells ring strangely in London town.' (p. 22)

The poem captures the child in a state of restless curiosity, one akin to that experienced by the child of *Under the Window*; neither child is satisfied by the accounts that she has been given – the rules whose validity they have been required to accept on trust – and both are determined to learn for themselves the answers to the questions which preoccupy them. As the author of *The Polite Academy* warns, 'Curiosity' is lethal; it is the 'main temptation which is likely to off-balance young women in this endeavour' to acquire good manners; it 'is a dangerous enemy, that lurks within their own breasts, to assault them on the weakest side when most unguarded, and in private; nay, when reflecting on their own innocency, they think they cannot easily be tempted' (p. 11). In spite of her curiosity, Margery Brown outwardly conforms to the rules which dictate how she should behave. The image conveys a child standing elegantly and with composure, apparently static, not imposing herself on the scene. Such an image could serve as a plate designed to illustrate exemplary deportment in a manual such as *The Polite Academy*. And yet the child stands with her back to the reader; it is a silent protest, one in which her comportment is apparently faultless save for the fact that her entire body, modestly packaged as it is, is facing the wrong way: she is violating that central principle that she is required to keep her eyes fixed on the matter at hand and not flagrantly gaze out into the unknown. Furthermore, it is not clear how the reader is to reconcile the inertia depicted in the image with the undissipated energy motivating the poem's questioning voice. To whom does this voice belong? Is it the voice of another child, bewildered by Margery Brown's unabashed refusal to adhere to social protocol? Is it the voice of a gently chastizing adult, functioning catechistically to prompt Margery Brown to see the error of her 'idle' ways? But if it seeks to do so, it does so unsuccessfully, for although the poem reveals a gap in Margery Brown's logic – it is ultimately *not* clear why she is standing gawping at the city below her – by drawing the reader's attention to the oddness of the rule which seeks to curtail her from so doing, it causes the critical child to question the validity of such a rule. It exposes the reality of the social protocols inflicted on girls: they result in static, frozen, wistful images. They turn inactivity into a virtue. To this end, it is interesting to note that the verb 'wait' is used with abundance in this collection, and indeed, it comprises the central activity of this poem. But if standing still is the height of politeness, how is this compatible with the injunction everywhere apparent in children's literature in the Protestant tradition to be useful, to work hard, to help others? We need only think of *The History of Goody Two-Shoes*, or Maria Edgeworth's *The Purple Jar*, or Sarah Trimmer's *Fabulous Histories* – just some of the many works which children of the second half of the nineteenth century were encouraged to read and imitate – to note how prominently such an idea loomed in children's culture of the period. Is standing elegantly, then, a form of waiting akin to that immortalized in Milton's 'Sonnet XVI' ('They also serve who only stand and waite'), where patient endurance is itself a form of worship? Or, to recode a similar idea in the more secular vocabulary of Victorian children's culture, is waiting itself morally good? Although these arguments might be brought into play in response to the child's questions, the poem nonetheless strains against them, hinting that there is something void – intellectually redundant, socially inert, morally vacuous – about simply making oneself a pretty object, but not *doing* anything with it.

At one level, then, what the reader sees, or seeks to see, is the city of London, sprawled out below her. At another level, though, what the critical child sees is the ethical dubiousness of the stories spun to her by adults. She perceives that 'the bells ring strangely in London town' and she 'can't go down'. The city, indeed, *that* city (which is a byword for adult experiences of which the child is supposed to have no knowledge) grips her with a yearning; she longs to visit, despite her apprehensions that she would not, after all, discover there the 'knight' of whom she has been told. The poem thus raises ethical questions about the predicament not merely of watching – as commentators such as Silver have pointed out – but furthermore, of being watched. Not only is it potentially immoral, but it is also illogical. The questioning voice insists that Margery Brown provide a reason for simply standing, but the reason which the poem offers makes no intellectual sense. The child alludes to the stories and legends and half-truths which she has been led to associate with London, her 'For' proposing them as some kind of explanation for her behaviour. And yet the explanation is no such thing. This logical grammar which encases an illogical thought sequence beautifully mimics the authoritarian behaviour of the caregiving adult, who routinely prohibits that which the child desires (a trip to London) for undisclosed (no apparently valid) reasons, and provides in their place inadequate *non sequitors* which the child must simply learn and repeat, for she does not have a hope of comprehending them.

In the later poem, 'Heigh Ho! – Time Creeps but Slow', the child's suspiciousness of the adult gaze, which consigns the child to a state of protracted time-killing, has evolved into outright accusation. The illustration sets up a scene of a perfectly rotund child, bonnet perkily pointed upwards in seeming optimism, looking out over the garden gate and away from us into the distance. Engrossed in the country scene ahead of her, the child is a stock pastoral figure inhabiting a quintessentially picturesque Greenaway landscape. But in dialogue with the accompanying poem, which provides commentary on the child's activity from her point of view, and not merely from the vantage of catching her at it, the child's absorption takes on a much less enchanting significance:

> Heigh Ho! – time creeps but slow;
>   I've looked up the hill so long;
> None come this way, the sun sinks low,
>   And my shadow's very long.
>
> They said I should sail in a little boat,
>   Up the stream, by the great white mill;
> But I've waited all day, and none come my way;
>   I've waited – I'm waiting still.
>
> They said I should see a fairy town
>   With houses all of gold,
> And silver people and a gold church steeple; –
>   But it wasn't the truth they told. (p. 60)

The poem vibrates with the child's betrayal at the hands of the adults around her. The rules which 'they' have laid down for her – the stories and promises she has been told – have not been kept by those who have prescribed them. *This* is what the child sees as she gazes over the fence: that 'it wasn't the truth they told'. The child's voice identifies – and berates – the hypocrisy of the adult who lies to the child, insisting on the delightfulness of imaginary creatures, feeding her with aspirational narratives about the life that lies ahead of her as an incentive for being good. While Wordsworth's child figures have 'intimations' of mortality, Greenaway's child intimates, indeed confronts head-on, the decay and corruption of the world around and ahead of her. This, it transpires, is what engrosses her as she resolutely fails to meet the eye of the watching presence behind her. Like 'Margery Brown, on the Top of the Hill', this poem too is uttered in the first-person voice, creating the impression that this description of what lies in the child's line of sight (or, more accurately, what does not) has been rendered in her own words. But what do we make of the fact that, by virtue of the form in which they are contrived, these words come out in rhythm and rhyme? Assimilating her impressions into a contented jaunt ('But I've waited all day, and none come my way'), the child seemingly absorbs the impact of the body blow, pressing the mess she finds into a soothingly ordered form. The result is almost self-deprecating in the hollow notes it sounds; we hear the child's forced laughter at her own folly in having expected more. It is as if she sentimentalizes her own naivety in having believed what 'they told' in the first place. Certainly, the rerouting of existential disillusionment into quotidian frustration ('Heigh ho!') aestheticizes it and, in prettifying it, tames it.

What is the critical child to make of this aestheticization of childhood disenchantment? Is she to infer that it is an exemplary way of dealing with such emotion: to narrate it; to sing it; to empty it of pain by channelling the feelings it engenders into formulaic rhythms and rhymes, and in so doing, make it generic and depersonalized? The image strains against this reading; it pulls against the enclosure that the alternating rhyme scheme of the poem performs. The child stands squarely facing away from us in a pose of watching – waiting for something out of sight (the background is blankly white) to come into view. There is a comic deliberateness in the exactness with which the child has turned her back on the onlooker, as if in petulance she has striven to find the precise angle at which she will be furthest from the scrutiny of the adult eye. And yet there is a poignancy to this too. The child cannot meet the eye of the onlooker; she refuses to be witnessed in this state of emotion. It is as if she is embarrassed at being afflicted by her thwarted hopes – annoyed not with the perpetrator of the lie but with herself for having fallen for the trick. The image thus captures a snapshot of a child who hides her face in shame. While the static image cannot indicate when this moment takes place – its duration;

its chronology; its sequentiality – the poem, through the use of grammatical tense ('I've waited – I'm waiting still') confirms that this is not a watching which once took place but a watching which continues to take place – a watching which stretches into the present. The child, the poem implies, is *still* waiting. The repetition of the ambiguous 'still', a repetition which occurs in both poems, requires the critical child to determine – in Dewey's terms, to hypothesize, to test, to weigh up the evidence, and ultimately to 'judge' – whether the term functions to describe the static posture of the child or the static fate of the child. In navigating a path between them, and perceiving their interchangeability, the critical child is invited to reflect on their reducibility. The child's shame is ongoing as is the child's outward bodily conformity to the protocols of politeness.

The child thus conforms to that which she has inherited and reinvests it with her own meaning. Appreciating that the truth is simply that which we say it is, she appropriates this logic, offering up her own inadequate certainty in the place of the inadequate certainty supplied by her parent. This comprises the central premise of 'Indeed It Is True, It Is Perfectly True':

> Indeed it is true, it is perfectly true;
>   Believe me, indeed, I am playing no tricks;
> An old man and his dog bide up there in the moon,
>   And he's cross as a bundle of sticks. (p. 24)

The child, who has been raised to view 'obedience' as the cardinal virtue, copies the adult example. In so doing, she imitates adult illogic – our capacity for self-deception and incoherence, but in spite of it all, our rigid insistence on the validity and necessity of the rules which have caused us to arrive at this faulty end point. *Under the Window* represents children mimicking adult behaviour not merely in the improbable clothing Greenaway dresses them in, and in their manners, but, as a consequence, in their mental practices too:

> My house is red – a little house,
>   A happy child am I,
> I laugh and play the livelong day
>   I hardly ever cry.

I have a tree, a green, green tree,
    To shade me from the sun;
And under it I often sit,
    When all my work is done.

My little basket I will take,
    And trip into the town;
When next I'm there I'll buy some cake,
    And spend my bright half-crown. (p. 61)

Greenaway's illustration portrays a rust-coloured scene in which the child, clad from head to toe in colours the same rust shade as the roof of her home, is harmonized with her surroundings. The implication is that her presence is key to the idyll: the idea of the domestic scene, with the house nestling in gentle rolling hills, garden trim and adorned with a bed of blooming flowers, is perfected by the figure of the girl, frozen in the foreground. Her presence to the right of the picture counterbalances the tree to the left; both stretch vertically, growing upwards, perpendicular, like chimneys, the neatly painted blue fence, and the flowers in the immaculately weeded bed. By the same token, the implication works in reverse, as the poem makes clear: the child's enviable psychic state ('A happy child am I') seemingly ensues from her ownership of the house (not, it might be pointed out, on the modest scale that the word 'little' might indicate; this is no pokey cottage, but a sizeable family property.) And yet the grammatical sequencing here is strange: 'My house is red – a little house,/A happy child am I'. What sense is the child reader who questions, probes, seeks answers, to make of the apparent relationship between the ownership of the house and the contentment of the child? Is the relationship one of chronology? Analogy? Is the one symbolic of the other? The association of the two recapitulates a familiar capitalist narrative, one which, as Jack Zipes has argued, underpins the history of children's literature, wherein the child who is virtuous is rewarded by material gain, which bestows happiness (2001). But the artificiality of this contrived narrative is betrayed by Greenaway's awkward word order, her inverted syntax ('am I'), which sets up the rhyme with 'cry', thereby making it a dominant word in the stanza, even as the child is denying its prominence in her life. The child's understanding of happiness is shaped by her evident knowledge of the reverse: tears, exposure to the glare of the sun, work. The poem provides the reader not merely with a glimpse into her present state of mind but moreover a glimpse of her aspirations for the future. What the child plans to do as soon as she is safely out of the sight of adult surveillance is to run off into town ('trip' – no sedate walking for her), to treat herself to cake. The reader might suspect that the rules of eating so painstakingly laid out in the many conduct manuals of the day will not be closely adhered to as the child consumes this snack – no doubt in public. The poem reveals the child's desperate urge to break the claustrophobic rules laid out for her even as she adorns what is presented as an idyllic picturesque. Further, it provides a rationale for so doing. Having endured the ordeal of perpetually measuring her movements, laughing demurely, playing prettily, refraining from crying, generally rendering herself watchable, she is entitled to a reward, the reward being temporary release from the rules which she has supposedly internalized such that she no longer sees them as imposed from without. By presenting the child's escape from the scene as consistent with its logic, and not as a departure from it, Greenaway implies that this is a scene which is on the brink of disintegration. The child is about, any minute, to walk out of the picture and abandon the rules which result in the vision we find appealing. The dramatic excitement of the scene is thus located in the future – in what happens when the poem has finished, when the static image has been made mobile again. The 'brightness' of the scene derives from the coin, that glistening symbol of future, and not past, happiness – a symbol, in fact, of past hardship.

And yet any hopefulness in the future is ultimately shrouded in *Under the Window*. Take, for example, the poem 'In Go-Cart So Tiny':

> In go-cart so tiny
> My sister I drew;
> And I've promised to draw her
> The wide world through.
>
> We have not yet started –
> I own it with sorrow –
> Because our trip's always
> Put off till to-morrow. (p. 29)

This poem, like 'My House Is Red – a Little House', hardly expresses unfettered delight in the possibility of a world in which children can eventually overthrow the shackles of constant adult scrutiny. In fact, it suggests that children simply import into the realm of childhood (the relationships they have with one another) the broken promises which so characterize the adult world. The speaker of the poem beautifully encapsulates the meaninglessness of performative language, mocking her own inability to conceive of any alternative to the derelict vow by articulating it in the passive voice ('our trip's always/Put off till to-morrow'). The child's shrug in the face of her sister's suffering suggests her cynicism: she has already recognized that deliberate betrayal is a condition of the world. The accompanying image provides its audience with a full view of the face of the older child, implying her knowingness; by contrast, the face of the younger child, sat in the go-cart, is shrouded by a huge bonnet which figuratively connotes her inability to see what her sibling has already apprehended. The child in front – one of the collection's few boys – exaggeratedly marches onwards anyway, leading the way, despite the futility of the expedition; the older sister, holding the handle of the go-cart, inclines her face away from him, as if embarrassed by his unabashed optimism, seemingly straining away from the direction in which he leads them, looking half back at the direction from which they have come, and half outwards, towards us. She is trapped in a 'sorrow' in which she knows that she cannot fulfil that which she will go on promising, trapped partly as the author of her own misfortune, and partly as the object of the reader's pity. This is a child who knows that she has made herself an object of pity, and yet makes her sister an object of pity even as she reveals this knowledge. Greenaway's *Under the Window* thus registers the child's searing capacity to scrutinize and to criticize, indeed, to turn that scrutiny, the critical gaze, on herself. The critical child does not merely see what the adult does not tell her, and what the adult does not want her to know; she sees, moreover, what she does not herself want to know.

In the final plate, the children dance obligingly out of the collection, the static tableau confirming our delight not in their moving forms but in the stillness of forms which are frozen on the brink of their exit from view. Dutifully adhering to the rules of politeness prescribed to them, the girls' eyes are cast down, their steps are gracefully small. This is demure, modest, mannered movement, disclosing none of the boisterous exuberance which the accompanying poem encapsulates:

> Ring the bells – ting!
> Hip, hurrah for the King!
> The dunce fell into the pool, oh!
> The dunce was going to school, oh!
> The groom and the cook
> Fished him out with a hook,
> And he piped his eye like a fool, oh! (p. 64)

The poem functions as an injunction to be noisy. Its redundant end-sounds ('oh!', 'oh!'), which the scansion of the poem requires the reader to read with rude emphasis, revel in the fun of vocal sound for its own sake. Likewise, the nonsensical sentiments of the poem, in which disconnected ideas ('hurrah for the King!'; 'The dunce fell into the pool, oh!') are forced together for the sheer pleasure of having some words to chant in rhythmic form. The sound of the poem – visceral, urgent, joyful – pulls against the restrained unsmiling dance depicted in the image. It offers a counter-ideal to the ideal of being watchable – an ideal in which children are *heard*. The poem's noisy children make no sense (just like the noise of the adult world), but they insist on sounding their noises anyway (just as adult noises are given a place to be sounded). It is entirely apposite that the final line of the volume would document what the child speaker identifies as a contemptuous use of the eye ('piped his eye like a fool, oh!', the word 'pipe' an archaic verb meaning to watch, notice or look at). The implication here is that the inability to use the eye to watch closely is a sign of intellectual dysfunction. The packaging of this idea in a jaunty nursery rhyme gives it seeming universal status – every child knows it to be the case. The poem thus celebrates the unabashed noisy disorder which the children's outward conformity to the rules of politeness conceals. And yet even the image pulls against the ideal it ostensibly presents: the children, conjoined hand-to-skirt, are a critical mass. We sense their cooperation with one another, the strength and solidity of their silent mutiny. But there in the centre of the image is a child who gazes straight back at the reader even as the reader watches her, undoing the intactness of a scene in which literature's children, both characters and readers, are supposedly engrossed in their own apparent merriment, passive recipients of the rules designed to dictate their behaviour. In so doing, she betrays that both parties – the self-conscious character and the critical child reader – are nothing of the sort. Both know full well how to refuse the lines of sight plotted out for them, and both defiantly look their onlooker in the eye, daring them to summon the futile courage to tell them where to look next.

4

On crying: E. Nesbit's *The Railway Children*

> *Why we expect children to be more tranquil than a parliamentary body or a ministers' meeting I do not know and cannot imagine. (Abbot, 1908, p. 93)*

The child is born crying. Indeed, during its early encounters with the world it appears to do little else, creating a mystifying disharmonious music whose apparent futility has perennially baffled us: 'Soft infancy, that nothing canst but cry' (*Troilus and Cressida*, II.ii.105). Since the baby speaks in tears, so tears are seen to be infantile, and the vernacular has us 'crying *like* a baby', a conceit memorably entrenched in the literary imagination by the desolate Alfred Tennyson, who cast himself in *In Memoriam A. H. H.* as 'An infant crying in the night:/ An infant crying for the light:/ And with no language but a cry' (LIV). The seeming inevitability of the child's tears means that one of the primal duties – perhaps even one of the fundamental rights – of the parent is to stem them. As Tom Lutz has written, 'tears help create and sustain the attachment that is the salient fact of the parent-child relationship' (Lutz, 1999, p. 159). But the parent's desire to stop her child's tears is not merely founded on an aspiration for intimacy with the newborn child; the vocabulary with which we routinely describe the process ('soothe', 'calm', 'placate') indicates a deep-seated belief that to arrest the child's tears brings it comfort. The quiet child (synonymous with the good child) must be a happy child. Despite the fact that in our post-romantic age we have ostensibly debunked the notion of original sin, such language presupposes that the child comes into the world with an innate knowledge of suffering; that its tears are the expression of this suffering – and not, for example, the child's 'song' (Lutz, 1999, p. 158) – and moreover, that the adult, and more specifically the parent, can, and therefore should, ease the child's suffering by ending its cries.

Whereas by the end of the eighteenth century the influence of, among others, Jean-Jacques Rousseau and William Wordsworth had popularized a belief that childhood is a period as yet uncontaminated by pain and ambiguity, by the end of the nineteenth century, this had transmogrified into a widespread belief that children *must* be protected from pain and ambiguity – that childhood *ought* to be a period of happiness. For all its reputed sentimentalism, the Victorian fascination with childhood as the domain of pleasure and play is motivated by a palpable scepticism which highlights a significant departure from its eighteenth-century antecedents (marking a difference which is missed by commentators such as James Holt McGavran who see the Victorian 'cult of the child' as a late-flowering manifestation of Wordsworthian romanticism. While Wordsworth had perceived the child to be incapable of suffering, the assiduousness with which parents of the late nineteenth and early twentieth century were advised to fabricate the happiness of their children betrays an underlying suspicion that without adult intervention, the child's inherent capacity for suffering will resurface, shattering the ideal. 'A happy childhood means everything,' writes the author of *The Way They Should Go: Hints to Young Parents* (1896, p. 62). 'An unhappy childhood may so fill the life's fountains with bitterness as to sadden all the after years,' warns the Reverend J. R. Miller (1888, p. 46). 'Let a child's *home* be the happiest *house* to him in the world,' counsels another. 'It is sad enough to see dismal, doleful men and women, but it is a truly lamentable and unnatural sight to see a doleful child!' (Chavasse, 1886, p. 125).

Such incendiary doom-mongering places a heavy responsibility on the parent, in whose gift the child's idyllic state – her happiness – lies. Small wonder that parents at the end of the nineteenth century and the beginning of the twentieth turned in their droves to the burgeoning genre of the parenting manual, a form of publication which sought to give practical tips on how to manufacture model happy childhoods. The sheer amount of space dedicated in these manuals to the problem of the crying child testifies to the stress – and indeed the tears – caused to parents by the challenge of providing the comfort which is supposedly their *raison-d'être*. The 1874 parenting manual, *How to Rear and Train Them*, says, 'Be wise, for even an infant soon discovers its power, and will prove itself the veriest tyrant if it finds you relent at the sight of a few tears' (E. C., 1874, p. 68). Similarly, in 1908 Ernest Abbott, who, like many writers in this genre, taxonomizes the various cries (the plain cry, the colicky cry, the tired cry), having painstakingly identified their differences, nonetheless lumps them altogether when he writes, 'Not to run to a child every time he cries is the beginning of learning not to yield to a child every time he wants something. In many cases authority is thus exercised by doing nothing' (Abbot, 1908, pp. 15–16). This echoes a point made emphatically three decades earlier in *The Mothers' Home-Book* (1880):

> If children are suffered to cry unheeded, their tempers become soured, and their dispositions gloomy and peevish. If they are accustomed to have their own way, and indulged in whatever they cry for, it makes them domineering and violent, unable to bear the contradictions and disappointments which they are sure to meet with in their career through life. (p. 229)

What is at stake for this writer, as for so many who enter into discussions about the proper relations between adults and children, is authority, here a form of parental control that should on no account be surrendered by the adult to the child, not, ostensibly, so that the parent might get some sleep, but because the child, unlike the adult, is deemed incapable of knowing (or at least enacting) what is in its best interests.

The case that the accession of the child's will to the adult's might result in the child's comfort can be made by figuring crying as a malady which the parent (particularly if she follows the advice laid out in these guides) is able to cure. Thus the team of specialists behind the big-selling *The Book of the Home: A Practical Guide to Household Management* (1901) write of crying in children that 'treatment to be successful must vary with differently-constituted individuals' (Davidson, VII: p. 41), diagnosing tears as a kind of syndrome necessitating systematic therapy. The link between crying and ill health is further consolidated by the prevalent anxiety that tears might trigger disease, a danger underscored by the medical authority, Pye Henry Chavasse, whose *Advice to a Mother on the Management of her Children* sold in the thousands in the last decades of the nineteenth century: 'A mother . . . should always bear in mind, that a rupture of the navel is often caused *by* much crying' (Chavasse, 1886, p. 13). Some of the more liberal parenting manuals attempt to innovate less draconian methods for coaxing the child to dry her eyes. Bernard Myers, for example, writes, 'Simply to scold, as so many nurses have the unfortunate habit of doing, will only add to the child's tears and the nurse's discomfort, whereas by quickly and pleasantly hanging the conversation to something to be seen in the distance, or to a game they are going to play on their arrival home, the effect is often instantaneous' (Myers, 1909, p. 115). And the Swedish radical, Ellen Key, famed for her child-centred philosophy of parenting, proposed that 'the crying child [should be] immediately isolated'; it should be 'explained to him at the same time that whoever annoys others must not be with them' (Key, 1909, pp. 125–6). That the child must be muzzled in the first place is taken as read, since crying, which shatters the peace of those within earshot, is selfish; it must be ceased because it oppresses those who must bear witness to it.

So why is crying so heinous? The answer provided by late-nineteenth- and early-twentieth-century parenting manuals, among whose authors clerics and Christian do-gooders rank highly, is that crying is blasphemous. Since earthly suffering is merely a temporary condition, and all will be recompensed in the next life where 'there is no crying at all' (Ryle, 1859, pp. 5–6), to bemoan one's lot shows a want of faith. Open crying challenges the beneficence of God. But even while they forbid tears, advice manuals in this tradition acknowledge their inevitability: 'Yes, rich and poor, young and old, have wept! The whole world is watered with tears', writes the Reverend George Everard (Everard, 1886, p. 5). There is 'no way to heaven but by the weeping cross', goes the proverb. Hence the child, who is born crying, must learn not to cry so as to have a happy childhood – or, since suffering is inevitable, as it will discover, it must learn to cry in private, so as at least to enhance the happiness of those around it. 'The first lesson to be taught by example as well as precept,' writes J. E. Panton, 'is to suffer in silence, to control one's self, and to be master or mistress undoubtedly of one's own miseries' (Panton, 1896, p. 148).

The gift of an idealized childhood thus involves a rather more fraught exchange than might initially meet the eye. Adults, according to these parenting manuals, must work strenuously to give happy childhoods to their offspring; and in accepting these gifts, children undertake not to suffer, or at the very least, to conceal any suffering that won't go away. Marcel Mauss famously characterized the 'gift generously offered' as one whose 'accompanying behaviour is formal pretence and social deception', the exchange of which is based on 'obligation and . . . self-interest' (Mauss, 1954, p. 1). In the giving of a happy childhood, as in any gift exchange, the giving costs the giver, as these parenting manuals vividly show; strenuous effort is required both at a practical level – in contriving the correct size of the nursery, colour of its walls, distance of cot from fire – and at an emotional level – since the parent must downplay her own suffering (something of an inconvenience, given its inescapability). What is less obvious, and is a dimension of the gift exchange on which parenting manuals of this period are almost entirely mute, is that receipt of the gift is not straightforwardly gratifying to the child either. The child, obliged to repay the debt incurred by its parents' sacrifice, must strive to make the giving of the gift worthwhile.

While parenting manuals of the late Victorian and Edwardian period almost universally refrain from enquiry into the implications of this gift exchange for the child (that is to say, the child during its childhood, and not merely the future adult whom the child will one day become), there *is* a form of writing in the period which does consider the question from the child's point of view: the children's novel. As has been well documented, landmark novels by authors including Louisa Molesworth, Lewis Carroll and George MacDonald acknowledged the complicated affective life of the child; but it was Edith Nesbit, prolific novelist and poet, who most boldly experimented with the novel form to attempt to broker a means of speaking for, and not merely speaking of or to, the child. Julia Briggs alludes to the 'little revolution in children's writing' effected by Nesbit's *Bastable* trilogy (1899–1904), which was followed by the *Psammead* series (1902–6) and, in 1906, the enduringly popular *The Railway Children* (Briggs, in Avery and Briggs, 1989, p. 244). Nesbit's idiosyncratic style has often been noted, but she is nonetheless frequently grouped with authors writing in the same decade – especially Kenneth Grahame – who are seen to evoke a literary analogue for the happy, separate, time-limited sphere of childhood advocated by medical, social and theological commentators of the day.[1] Clumsy use of the 'golden age' banner to force together works which are only superficially alike has served to obscure the ways in which Nesbit's novels mount a strident critique of the idea of happy childhood so prized by her age. Certainly, Nesbit did not seek to collapse the distinction between childhood and adulthood; her writing persistently testifies to what she called 'a freemasonry between children, a spontaneous confidence and give-and-take which is and must be for ever impossible between children and grown-ups, no matter how sympathetic the grown-up, how confiding the child' (*Wings and the Child*, p. 4). But, when she found that her novels (somewhat to her surprise and discomfort) chiefly appealed to a child and not an adult audience, she felt keenly that she owed it to her child readers to document not merely the pleasures but also the pains of childhood. 'When I was a little child,' she wrote in her memoir, 'I used to pray fervently, tearfully, that when I should be grown-up I might never forget what I thought and felt and suffered then' (*Long Ago*, p. 27). She saw it as her duty to reinsert the tears that had fallen out of so many contemporary accounts of childhood, both non-fictional, as in the parenting manuals of the age, and fictional, epitomized by works such as Kenneth Grahame's celebrated *The Golden Age* (1895) and *Dream Days* (1898).

To write *of* or *to* the child is, as Jacqueline Rose has argued, an impossibility, since 'the adult comes first (author, maker, giver) and the child comes after (reader, product, received), but . . . neither of them enter the space in between' (pp. 1–2). This may be so, but Nesbit fashioned an extraordinary narrative voice which strove, as Marah Gubar has observed, to dissolve 'any strict division between author and audience' (Gubar, 2001, p. 412). Certain divisions are of course insurmountable; but by inscribing the child's point of view in the very fabric of the narrative even as the narrator appears to be addressing us in an adult voice, and by using this perspective to expose the outer limits of the adult's field of vision, Nesbit goes some way towards speaking *for* the child. She invites her reader to enter into a conspiracy with the child protagonists even as we place ourselves in the hands of the narrator, creating a kinship between the two founded on a capacity for insight which they share, and which the adult characters lack. Inasmuch as the narrator brandishes authority, the authority she brandishes is not discernibly 'adult'; it is not the authority of the 'giver' of childhood but somehow the authority of its recipient. By analyzing how Edith Nesbit's *The Railway Children* casts the child as an active agent in this process of exchange, one who is not merely conscious of it but furthermore in control of it, this discussion aims to expose what the parenting manuals of this period conceal – but what the critical child, restlessly sceptical and intent on discovery, will nonetheless uncover – the costs involved when the child gives up her right to cry.

Early on in *The Railway Children*, before the conflict proper has begun, we witness a routine domestic incident: Peter's toy train suddenly goes 'off with a bang' (p. 10):

> All the Noah's Ark people who were in the tender were broken to bits, but nothing else was hurt except the poor little engine and the feelings of Peter. The others said he cried over it – but of course boys of ten do not cry, however terrible the tragedies may be which darken their lot. He said that his eyes were red because he had a cold. (pp. 10–11)

On one view, this is a trivial episode which, since it concerns merely the breaking of a toy, will soon be forgotten. This view – the view which the child knows *ought* to be his – is registered by the narrator's use of hyperbole which, in likening the incident to a 'terrible' 'traged[y]', indicates Peter's awareness of what this is not. The abstraction, 'boys of ten do not cry', gives us access to the method Peter uses to arrive at this rational conclusion – a method whereby he distances himself from the scene to enable him to measure his reaction according to the social codes to which he is expected to conform, and not according to the emotions with which he contends. Peter encounters the scene not as its subject but as an analytical observer of other unnamed hypothetical child subjects. This enables him to enter into, or at least to deflect, the inevitable laughter that ensues from the transparency of his efforts to conceal his tears. But in fact, this trivial incident is not so quickly forgotten; indeed, it haunts Peter's imagination far more actively than does the later unexplained disappearance of his father. While Peter mimics adult slang, 'broken to bits', in a valiant effort to pass off as comic that which he experiences as tragic (on the basis that the opposite of a tear must be a laugh), his metaphorical designation of the Noah's Ark animals as 'people' reminds us that for a child, toys are not mere inanimate objects, and are not even merely *like* animate objects: they *are* animate objects, their deaths mourned as such. And yet this is not a passage of first-person narrative. The speaker is the same intrusive narrator whose interchangeably omniscient and selective view guides us through the whole novel. By sliding almost imperceptibly into free-indirect-discourse at this point, Nesbit erodes any significant difference between her narrator and her child character. Consequently, much as the narrative tempts us affectionately to ruffle Peter's hair along with the amused adult, who can congratulate herself on what a happy childhood she must have bestowed on her son if *this* is his gravest worldly concern, the critical child will recognize all too acutely the emotional cost to Peter of rendering himself an object of comedy rather than an object of pity. While Nesbit's narrative, as is typical of what Barbara Wall calls 'dual address' (Wall, 1991, p. 36), gives the reader access to knowledge that eludes the child (knowledge of his failure to pull off the fraud), it also – more subversively – gives her access to knowledge that eludes the grown-ups. Specifically, it gives her access to (or reminds her of) the sacrifice involved in keeping your tears to yourself so as not to disturb the equilibrium of those around you.

The feasibility of this awkward pact wherein the child undertakes only to cry in private in order to ensure his parents' peace of mind is threatened by the child's troubling realization that adults themselves cry. So effectively do the adults in *The Railway Children* conspire to deny this fact from the younger generation that the eventual realization comes as a traumatic surprise: 'I never saw a man cry before,' says Bobbie to the doctor, reporting the distress of the Russian refugee. 'You don't know what it's like' (p. 91), she adds, with poignant irony. The attempt to protect Roberta from pain has merely compounded it; her blind faith in adult truthfulness has made her discovery isolating in its seeming rarity. In *The Book of the Child* (1907), Frederick How remarks on how 'sometimes a perception of a great sorrow will force its way to the mind of a child, and nothing more pathetic can be witnessed than the dumb perplexity with which a child faces such trouble' (How, 1907, p. 148). How's sentimental concern with the ways in which this 'pathetic' scenario might distress the adult onlooker ('it reminds one of the wistful expression in the face of a favourite dog' (Carpenter, 1985, pp. 148–9)) casts the child at the mercy of the knowing adult. Nesbit, however, refuses to make the child an object of pathos. When Roberta, the eldest child, senses her mother's grief at the loss of her father (who has been wrongly imprisoned for fraud), the scene is focalized through Roberta such that the child protagonist becomes the subject and not the object of emotion: 'Oh, Mother,' she whispered to herself as she got into bed, 'how brave you are! How I love you! Fancy being brave enough to laugh when you're feeling like *that*!' (p. 21). In a striking reversal of fortune, Nesbit depicts the ignorant character in this scene not as Bobbie but as the mother; the mother unsuccessfully conceals her grief from Bobbie, while for her part Bobbie successfully conceals from her mother the fact that she has seen through her mother's deception. This narrative format cushions the character from the indignity of the reader's pity, inviting the reader instead to empathize with the ethically compromised position in which Roberta has been placed. Faced with her mother's (albeit well-meaning) duplicity, Roberta has no choice but to misrepresent her own feelings too. 'If Mother doesn't want us to know she's been crying,' she said to herself as she heard through the dark the catching of her mother's breath, 'we *won't* know it. That's all.' (p. 15) In order to satisfy her mother's need for her child to remain untouched by (innocent of) the tragedy, Roberta enters into a deliberate lie. The mother's determination to uphold her own virtue by securing for her daughter the blanketed childhood advocated by parenting experts results in the child's determined corruption. Bobbie, of course, like her mother, is merely doing what is required of her by clerics such as Reverend Miller, who informs the nation's young that if they were to 'remember always that their parents have cares, anxieties and sorrows of which they know not, it would make them gentle at all times towards them. Here is an opportunity,' he prompts, 'for most helpful ministry' (Miller, 1888, p. 52). But Nesbit exposes the moral, and indeed religious, ambiguity which Miller's account of this 'ministry' does not pause to consider: that its execution implicates the child in wilful dishonesty, in flagrant contravention of that fundamental Christian tenet, 'thou shalt not bear false witness' (*Deuteronomy*, 5: 20). Humphrey Carpenter misses the point when he asserts that Nesbit essentially 'accepted the attitude, prevalent in the 1870s and 1880s, that children are delightfully naïve' (Carpenter, 1985, p. 135). On the contrary, Nesbit presents childish innocence as a sleight of hand – a gift given to the parent by the child that costs the child her integrity.

There is an acute irony here: in seeking so sedulously to preserve the parent-child relationship as one founded on the parent's capacity to stem the child's tears, Bobbie's mother anaesthetizes herself from her daughter's suffering. Perversely, in their mutual determination not to burden one another with their sorrow, both deny themselves the possibility of giving – or receiving – the solace they otherwise might:

> Bobbie understood a little bit the thoughts that were making Mother so quiet – the thoughts of the time when Mother was a little girl and was all the

> world to *her* mother. It seems so easy and natural to run to Mother when one is in trouble. Bobbie understood a little how people do not leave off running to their mothers when they are in trouble even when they are grown up, and she thought she knew a little what it must be to be sad, and have no mother to run to any more. (p. 55)

In one sense, Bobbie and her mother are in parallel; both cry in private, where they yearn for the comfort once promised by a parent, a comfort which both now recognize to be illusory. But there is a crucial difference. While Roberta can perceive the similarity between their positions, this similarity is lost on the mother. Nesbit entirely reconfigures the traditional patterning of children's literature in which a figure of adult authority presides over childish ignorance; here, it is the child who is in possession of superior knowledge – knowledge which the adult does not even know she lacks. Nesbit's transference of knowledge from the adult to the child prevents the children in her novel from merely being passive recipients of their mother's gift; while Bobbie cannot refuse the gift, she can seize control of the terms of its exchange, carving out a role for herself as a giver too:

> 'Poor old Mammy, you *are* tired,' said Peter. Bobbie said, 'Come on Phil; I'll race you to the gate.' And she started the race, though she hated doing it. *You* know why Bobbie did that. Mother only thought that Bobbie was tired of walking slowly. Even Mothers, who love you better than anyone else ever will, don't always understand. (p. 131)

In a strange reversal of the primal gift given by the parent to the child, the stopping of tears, the gift which Bobbie offers her mother is space in which to cry. But unlike the parent's gift to the child, which projects onto rather than elicits from the child what its chief needs are, Bobbie's gift to her mother is founded on an astute and well-judged reading of her mother's evident desires. So effective is her ability to anticipate what her mother needs that her mother remains unconscious that a gift has even been given. Bobbie's gift is therefore doubly generous; not only does she give her mother licence to cry, but she furthermore allows her to continue believing that her own sorrow has not contaminated her daughter's innocence. Nesbit thus documents the strains that the parent's need for her children to be happy places on those children; but she also depicts the active strategies that children deploy to shape the meaning of, and not merely react to, adult behaviour. Moreover, the child's insight is not simply portrayed as different to the adult's; it is clearly identified as more accurate than the adult's. The second-person address, '*You* know why Bobbie did that,' flatters the reader with possession of knowledge that Roberta's mother fails to grasp, knowledge which the narrator brands as 'understanding'. The American writer of *Parent and Child* (1910) proposes what at the time is a relatively unorthodox idea: that a 'thing that is due to children is that they should be told as far as possible the exact truth' (Lodge, p. 23). Nesbit's 1906 novel, *The Railway Children*, had already made a powerful case for the advantages of so doing – if for no better reason than that the critical child will root out the truth regardless.

And yet, when Bobbie finally discovers the truth of her father's wrongful imprisonment, she instinctively withholds the 'terrible secret' (p. 177) from her younger siblings. 'Why didn't you tell me, Mammy?' she demands,

> 'Are you going to tell the others?' Mother asked.
>
> 'No.'
>
> 'Why?'
>
> 'Because –'
>
> 'Exactly', said Mother; 'so you understand why I didn't tell you. We two must help each other to be brave.' (p. 178)

All the evidence that Nesbit has accrued over the course of the novel would point towards the benefits of passing on knowledge of suffering. Quite apart from the Christian precept of honesty ostensibly prized by the novel, Nesbit has repeatedly testified to the emotional ordeal – both for the parent and for the child – of falsely insisting on the child's innocence; and then there is the fact that the child will anyway find out, since the child possesses acute powers of perception. And yet, not merely does Roberta's mother, repeatedly held up by the narrator as well as the other characters as a moral example, persevere in her dogged refusal to expose her children to tears of suffering, now Bobbie too takes up the mantle. So why does Bobbie deny her siblings knowledge which she had herself so craved? The narrator never reveals her reason. But over the course of the novel, Bobbie has learned two important lessons about tears. The first is that everyone sheds them, even the grown-ups; the received wisdom that we grow out of them, that we are capable of stopping them, is a confidence trick. And the second is that tears are contagious:

> Mother was extremely angry. . . . But it was much worse when she suddenly began to cry. Crying is catching, I believe, like measles and whooping-cough. At any rate, everyone at once found itself taking part in a crying-party. (p. 63)

Perhaps the second can be accounted for by the first: faced with the realization that even one's mother cries, and that one's mother's capacity to stop one's own tears is based on a sham, then there is not much for it but to cry. But if everyone was to cry all the time, then life would quickly descend into a farce – a 'crying-party' (as it does in the scene when Roberta, Peter and Phyllis lay on a surprise birthday party for Perks, a scene which pastiches the worst excesses of Victorian sentimentalism, as, overcome by the kindnesses of the child protagonists, one character after another succumbs to tears). While in the sentimental tradition, harking back to eighteenth-century novels of sensibility by writers such as Laurence Sterne and Henry Mackenzie, the shedding of tears is itself a gift, something with which the character, and by extension, the critical reader, can offset the embarrassing debt owed to those who suffer, in Nesbit's novel, tears are ultimately impotent. Like the parent who seeks to shelter her child from suffering but is unable to do so, crying cannot, in and of itself, compensate pain.

It is perhaps our consciousness of this impotence which accounts for the tears that so many readers have shed, as Susan Anderson has documented, at the pivotal climax of *The Railway Children*, the moment which reunites Roberta with her father on the station platform:

> 'Oh! my Daddy, my Daddy!' That scream went like a knife into the heart of everyone in the train, and people put their heads out of the windows to see a tall pale man with lips set in a thin close line, and a little girl clinging to him with arms and legs, while his arms went tightly round her. (Anderson, 2007, p. 239)

Bobbie has learned, as has the reader, that her father is no more capable of protecting his daughter from suffering than anyone else, and yet her incantatory 'Daddy', 'Daddy', reminiscent of the child's first words, reduces him to his role as parent, coercively, pleadingly, investing him with the means to comfort her.

The words assume a kind of performative function, making him that which she says he is. However much we come to recognize the limitations of our parents' power to protect us, we nonetheless continue to subscribe to the myth. 'Think if it was your Daddy' (p. 180). Roberta had earlier written to the old gentleman, his whiskery age apparently no bar to his still being a child to *his* father. The emotive injunction has the desired effect; before long, the old gentleman has overturned the miscarriage of justice and returned Bobbie's father to his children.

Everything turns out all right in the end. But *en route* Nesbit has required her critical children to confront global atrocities: Russian labour camps, the fallibility of the English legal system, surgery without anaesthetic. Edith Nesbit's Fabianism has been well documented, and the novel clearly reflects a political agenda of sorts.[2] But *The Railway Children* is not infused with the spirit of optimism which often characterizes Fabianism. Nesbit refuses to infantilize her child audience by conciliating them with the superficial consolation of falsehoods. Instead, *The Railway Children* makes clear not merely that everyone, the child quite as much as the adult, suffers but also that no one party is ever really able to comfort the other – to allay their tears – because all are so busy struggling to conceal their own. While in the Christian tradition, there is at least some solace in the promise of an afterlife, Nesbit does not have recourse to a future of this sort. Indeed, her novel ends in a discomforting retreat into the present tense, leaving us in a curious state of suspension, knowing that the future is as yet undecided: 'He goes in and the door is shut. I think we will not open the door to follow him. I think that just now we are not wanted there. I think it will be best for us to go quickly and quietly away' (p. 240).

Perhaps, though, the critical child might derive some comfort from the knowledge – the truth – that everyone secretly cries. Nesbit's real legacy for children's literature, a legacy that lasts into this day, is the forging of the children's novel as a therapeutic space made possible not through pretence that suffering does not occur but precisely by enabling the child critic to work out that it does. While Edwardian parenting manuals busied themselves with trying to stem the child's tears, Nesbit gives the child dispensation to shed these tears under cover of the critical imagination.[3]

5

On being (bored): Kenneth Grahame's *The Wind in the Willows*

He who seeks rest finds boredom. He who seeks work finds rest. (Dylan Thomas)

Critics have repeatedly characterized Kenneth Grahame's *The Wind in the Willows* (1908) as 'utopian' (McGillis, 1984–5) – a celebration of 'the ideals of English style' (Lerer, 2009, p. 61). It has variously been described as 'an image of happiness perfectly combined with innocence' (Fred Inglis, 1981, p. 120); a 'pastoral celebration of animal life' (Kathryn Graham, 1998, p. 181); 'Arcadian' (Peter Hunt, 1994b); and a 'pastoral idyll' (Sarah Gilead, 1988, p. 148). Geraldine Poss delights in its 'innocent pastoral milieu' (1975, p. 84), and Roger Sales rejoices that it enables us imaginatively to live 'in a timeless snugness' (1983, p. 168). Grahame's biographer, Peter Green, reads the novel as escapist – as a psychological retreat from a job that Grahame hated and a miserable marriage (Green, 1959). Humphrey Carpenter goes further still, asserting that 'of all the Victorians and Edwardians who tried to create Arcadia in print, only Grahame really managed it' (1985, p. 155). In identifying the novel as a pastoral, such critics tend to emphasize the ways in which the novel presents a particular version of *place*: the river bank, a hangover from a premodern world in which human existence, like that of animals, derived its rhythms from the ebb and flow of natural currents. Carpenter emphasizes another, related feature of this place: that it marginalizes female figures; it is a '*bachelor* Arcadia, unencumbered by women' (1985, p. 156). The emphasis accorded to place has led critics to debate the extent to which the novel, in its close listening to the discreet patterns of the natural world, mourns the passing of pre-modernity or embraces the vibrancy of urban clatter. Such a debate is made possible by the novel's indeterminacy. As is typical of the pastoral mode, despite the notes of scepticism that the novel sounds about social progress, at the same time it provides ways of critiquing the bucolic scenarios which it ostensibly celebrates. It thus both amplifies and mutes the quiet ways of being it overhears, equipping the critical child with the means of questioning the idyllic status which the pastoralism inherent in Grahame's form invests in them. As Gilead has suggested, the 'narrative strand with which Grahame will close rejects the fantasy of a childhood kingdom where pleasure principle and reality principle do not clash' (1988, p. 150). Indeed, in its sounding of a note of failure and mourning, the end of the novel exposes as unattainable the lifestyle that the rest of the novel has fetishized.

But while, in this way, the conflict which the novel plays out can certainly be read as a political one – progressivism versus conservatism; capitalism versus socialism – at the same time its central preoccupation is decidedly apolitical. That is to say, *The Wind in the Willows* animates a species of philosophical contemplation that rests on indifference to the political. More specifically, reinvigorating a tradition that stretches back beyond Plato, taking in thinkers as diverse as Michel de Montaigne and Samuel Johnson *en route*, Grahame's novel positions itself in a transhistorical conversation about the perennial problem, the inescapability, the perverse pleasure, of boredom. Thematically and formally, conceptually and linguistically, the novel vacillates undecidedly between activity and inactivity, absorption and *ennui*. Betwixt and between, it ostensibly idealizes a middle way – motion as distinct from *commotion* on the one hand and *inertia* on the other. The kind of activity that the novel celebrates, however, is a quintessentially Deweyan one: one that is motivated by pleasure in motion as and for itself and not contaminated by a need to escape the tedium of one's own existence. The word 'restless' recurs totemically, threateningly, throughout the book, egregiously emblematized in the character of Toad such that Toad's character is identified by way of it: '"Once, it was nothing but sailing," said the Rat. "Then he tired of that and took to punting. Nothing would please him but to punt all day and every day, and a nice mess he made of it. Last year it was house-boating, and we all had to go and stay with him in his house-boat, and pretend we liked it. He was going to spend the rest of his life in a house-boat. It's all the same, whatever he takes up; he get tired of it, and starts on something fresh" ' (Grahame, 1961, p. 19). Movement is central to Toad's way of life; he seeks out vehicles that speed things up; he is constantly on the go; even his prose runs more quickly than other characters'. But Toad's movements are frenetic and volatile; he moves suddenly and urgently. The wayfarer, by way of contrast, is also constantly on the move, but his movement marks an opposite extreme: his movements are constant and aimless; he walks slowly and dispassionately. Toad moves anxiously between different homes (Toad Hall; the caravan; prison), while the wayfarer abjures any permanent place of rest. The movement of both is motivated by *boredom*, boredom which results in restless curiosity on the one hand and restless incuriousness on the other. In its own restless fascination with oppositions, *The Wind in the Willows* requires the critical reader to play out a philosophical conversation about that most fundamental of human questions: what is it to *be* without being *bored*? How can the ideal (stasis) and the idea (motion) coexist?

But what, though, is boredom? The early twentieth-century psychologist, Otto Fenichel, one of the first psychologists to observe the importance of boredom and to attempt to theorize it, proposed that boredom is 'an unpleasurable experience of a lack of impulse' – a 'damming up of libido' (1854, p. 302) which is 'characterized by the coexistence of a need for activity and an inhibition of activity' alongside 'a craving for stimulus and dissatisfaction with the proffered stimuli' (Fenichel, 1854, p. 292). This is why boredom 'makes some children cry' (p. 296) – the object which the child has been led to expect or desire is not forthcoming. Similarly, the cultural historian, Peter Toohey, suggests that boredom 'is an emotion which produces feelings of being constrained or confined by some unavoidable and distastefully predictable circumstance and, as a result, a feeling of being distanced from one's surroundings and the normal flow of time' (Toohey, 2011, p. 45). Being bored is no small matter, though; indeed, Erich Fromm insisted that boredom is 'one of the greatest tortures. If I were to imagine Hell,' he wrote in *The Dogma of Christ*, 'it would be the place where you were continually bored' (Fromm, 1963, p. 150).

It is interesting to observe that it is something of a rhetorical pattern for commentators on boredom to turn to examples about children in order to substantiate their case about the fundamentality of boredom – its importance, or its originariness – an argument which rests on the observation that, as

Anton Zijderveld puts it, 'children experience it quite often' (Zijderveld, 1979, p. 76). Peter Toohey, for example, begins his book *Boredom: A Lively History* (2011) with the opening questions: 'Who cares about boredom? It's trivial, and it's something that children suffer, isn't it?' (p. 1). He then proceeds to discuss what he calls boredom's 'stigma of childishness', implying that it is its association with children that accounts for the fact that it is often dismissed as a trivial concept, unworthy of sustained scholarly enquiry (p. 4). Additionally, the citing of evidence about increased reports of boredom in children is repeatedly used to substantiate a case that boredom is a 'growing metaphysical void at the center of Western civilization', as Sean Desmond Healy (1984, p. 87) puts it in *Boredom, Self and Culture*. This point is corroborated by Zijderveld, who sees boredom as a 'typically modern characteristic' (1979, p. 77) and by Lars Svendsen who claims that it is 'a typical phenomenon of modernity' (2005, p. 11). Patricia Meyer Spacks cites evidence that 'high-school teachers report that students' complaints of boredom constitute a growing pedagogical problem; mothers moan that their young children constantly demand relief from boredom' to demonstrate the same phenomenon (1995, p. 4).

But let us suppose that such evidence about a propensity for boredom among modern young people tells us something not about the universality of boredom, or about a cultural increase in the incidence of boredom, but instead something about the *child* – something which strikes us as new either because it *is* new, or because it is something which we have somehow failed to notice before now, perhaps because we have lacked the vocabulary with which to articulate it. Suppose the child has a peculiar relationship with boredom? If, as Spacks has suggested, 'boredom [is] a response to the immediate' (1995, p. 12), then it is conceivable that its prevalence among children is something that is especially difficult for adults to perceive, because now that we, as adults, are no longer subject to the immediate factors which might once have inspired boredom, we forget that we ever were. Consequently, our amnesia about our own childhood boredom might blind us to the ways in which the very same factors might trigger boredom in our own children. Cultural amnesia – or even denial – might explain the continual surprise encoded in scholarly observations about the reportedly high incidence of boredom in childhood. It would also explain the tendency in scholarly literature on boredom to draw historical narratives wherein the boredom of children is seen to be something new – something on the increase – rather than something with which children have always contended.

As the speculative nature of such propositions suggests, the status of boredom in childhood has been dramatically under studied. Despite the frequency with which writers on boredom, for rhetorical effect, propose some kind of deep-rooted connection between boredom and childhood, very few experts on boredom have given sustained attention to the nature of these connections. One of the few scholars to have done so is the psychoanalyst, Adam Phillips, who, in his seminal work, *On Kissing, Tickling and Being Bored: Psychoanalytic Essays on the Unexamined Life* (1993), has claimed that children are peculiarly susceptible to boredom.

> Children . . . ask with persistent regularity the great existential question "What shall we do now?" Every adult remembers, among many other things, the great ennui of childhood, and every child's life is punctuated by spells of boredom: that state of suspended anticipation in which things are started and nothing begins, the mood of diffuse restlessness which contains that most absurd and paradoxical wish, the wish for a desire. (Phillips, 1993, p. 71)

What is striking about Phillips's account of boredom in childhood is what he perceives to be its normativity. He refers to 'the child's ordinary experience of being bored' (p. 71), characterizing boredom as a 'banal crisis' (p. 72), a 'precarious process in which the child is, as it were, both waiting for something and looking for something, in which hope is being secretly negotiated; and in this sense boredom is akin to free-floating attention' (p. 72). It would appear from Phillips's account that when the child is bored, what is lacking is movement or activity, specifically, *ongoing* movement; no *processes* of activity are set in motion. Phillips's use of the passive voice ('things are started and nothing begins') brings into play an implication that boredom is an affliction for which one is not oneself responsible; it locates the origin of activity as outside the child, proposing that the child is bored because nothing external to it has caused it to be interested. Indeed, Fenichel suggests that even a 'small child recognizes that there emanate from the outside world stimuli which can be used for instinctual gratification' and hence will be bored when 'adequate objects' to fulfil 'instinctual aims' are not available (1854, p. 293). Boredom is thus a rational recognition that one's own expectations have not been met. In this way, it is bound up with socialization – with the fate of one's own needs in a context which involves other people. For Phillips, this cuts to the heart of the matter, and indeed, since boredom plays a role in the acclimatization of the child to the fact that they function in a social world, to have one's expectations unmet is not necessarily detrimental: the 'child's boredom starts as a regular crisis in the child's developing capacity to be alone in the presence of the mother. In other words, the capacity to be bored can be a developmental achievement for the child' (1993, p. 72). If, as Fenichel suggests, the child perceives that he or she has a 'right' not to be bored – a right to '*expect* "aid to discharge" from the external world' – then the child needs to learn that this right is unwarranted; such assistance will not automatically be provided (1854, p. 301). Assuming that people *do* learn such lessons over time, then it would follow that children would indeed be more inclined to experience that which the adult has learned better to manage. The adult, then, might be less susceptible to what Fenichel distinguishes as 'manifest restlessness or fidgetiness' (p. 296) – even if she is unable entirely to banish 'the manifest quiet of boredom' (p. 294). In the child, though, at least for Fenichel, these conditions are 'hardly distinguishable'. Or, perhaps, alternatively, as Peter Toohey suggests, it is simply that children 'have no shame when it comes to complaining of being bored. Adults, though never immune, are quick to deny they suffer from boredom – they're too grown up' (2011, p. 11). Either way, the child, who has been less thoroughly schooled in the strategies she will in due course acquire to manage her own psychological conditions, comparatively lacks the resources to deal with her own boredom. As a result, as Phillips puts it, 'the bored child quickly becomes preoccupied by his lack of preoccupation. Not exactly waiting for someone else, he is, as it were, waiting for himself. Neither hopeless nor expectant, neither intent nor resigned, the child is in a dull helplessness of possibility and dismay' (1993, p. 72). That is to say that, perceiving the problem to derive from outside, and lacking the inner resources to turn the situation around, the child might not merely be peculiarly susceptible to boredom, but moreover, peculiarly unable to overcome it when it occurs.

But is it a given that boredom is necessarily experienced as an affliction? In fact, Adam Phillips is not alone in viewing boredom as an 'opportunity' for self-discovery (1993, p. 73). Indeed, the adult's perennial desire to keep the child occupied and to save her from her own inclination towards inertia is, Phillips proposes, counterproductive. 'It is one of the most oppressive demands of adults,' he writes, 'that the child should be interested, rather than take time to find what interests him. Boredom is integral to the process of taking one's time' (p. 73). For Phillips, then, the non-activity entailed in being bored is not a form of unproductivity; on the contrary, it allows a period of time in which deliberation can take place, ensuring that the child's subsequent choices are fully thought through. The process Phillips outlines is reminiscent of the process John Dewey outlines in his account of the importance of time for critical thinking; *not* leaping hastily to the next stage enables that stage to be reached in a more calculated and chosen manner, minimizing the likelihood of making erroneous decisions. If pausing – taking one's time – is important in critical thinking, then it follows, as has already been discussed, that it is also a vital component in critical *reading*. Boredom, then – the freedom to take time before electing what to be interested in – plays a plays a key role in the process of the child's critical reading.

Since the child is peculiarly susceptible to boredom, the child reader too is likely to be particularly prone to it. If Phillips is correct in his assertion that the child *expects* not to be bored – feels that it is her right not to be bored; even feels anger if her expectations are not met – then this has significant implications for children's literature. The threat (or the possibility) of the child reader's boredom places unique pressures on the writer of literature for a young audience. Indeed, perhaps we could even go so far as to suggest that the adult's awareness of the child's susceptibility to boredom, and the concomitant desire to retain the child's interest – is a major factor in determining what children's literature is: that is to say, our understanding of the subtle ways in which literature for children might be different in kind to literature for other audiences needs to take into account the role played by boredom. Patricia Meyer Spacks, writing about adult literature, has suggested that there is anyway a peculiar relationship between boredom and literature: 'as action and as product, writing resists boredom, constituting itself by that resistance. In this sense all writing – at least since 1800 or so – is "about" boredom, as all physical construction is "about" entropy. The act of writing implicitly claims interest (boredom's antithesis) for the assertions or questions or exclamations it generates' (1995, p. 1).[1] Literary writing, and literary reading, thus take place in the context of boredom, either of 'boredom impending or boredom repudiated'. Literature can be understood 'as impelled by the effort to withstand boredom's threat' (p. 2). Spacks's observation that boredom is integral to the processes of writing and reading leads her to notice that boredom also 'recurs insistently as literary subject' (p. 3), especially in literature since 1800. However, compelling as Spacks's account is, when we turn to literature written for children, it is hard to plot a similar narrative. Whereas, as Spacks demonstrates, many novels for adults written contemporaneously to *The Wind in the Willows* expressly invite us to reflect on the condition of boredom – think of the works of Oscar Wilde, or Joris-Karl Huysmans, or Virginia Woolf, which precisely claim our interest through their preoccupation with boredom as a literary subject – a quick survey of notable children's books written in the same era would suggest that children's writers, whether consciously or not, judged that the prolonged analysis or depiction of boredom has no place in the children's novel. It is hard to think of a children's counterpart to *Mrs Dalloway* – that is to say, a novel in which the character's lack of interest is the source of the reader's interest. Even if one takes a more expansive comprehension of boredom to include not merely the mundanely tedious but the excessively melancholic – what some commentators on boredom have called *ennui* – it is hard to think of a children's text from this era which expressly addresses the theme. Certainly, there are novels such as Frances Hodgson Burnett's *The Secret Garden* (1910) which acknowledge the existence of depressed mental states, but they do so through demonstrating the appeal – and the inevitable return to – the obverse. In fact, such is the absence of boredom as a dominant literary subject in children's literature from this era that we might be tempted to suggest that its very marginalization, particularly at a moment of literary history – crudely put, the modernist era – in which boredom became a major site of interest in mainstream culture, tells us something important about where the lines demarcating children's literature from this mainstream literary culture lie. This evidence would suggest that there was a tacit understanding during this period that a children's book which dwells in protracted, incurable, inactive mental states does so at its peril. Put another way, children's literature of this period presents idealized versions of the world in which the mental states which people experience are primarily active, rather than inactive, ones. But what are the imagined perils of the express representation of boredom, we might ask? Is it boring to the reader to read about being bored? Or, since the history of adult literature suggests otherwise, is it peculiarly boring to the *child* reader to read about being bored? If we look more carefully at works of children's literature in this purportedly idealizing tradition, however, we might reflect on the fact that a lack of *express* representation of boredom does not constitute a lack of interest in boredom per se. Indeed, we have already noted the possibility that the children's text might have a peculiarly intimate relationship with boredom, since the child has a peculiar capacity to succumb to it. If children's novels of this era do not directly or exhaustively analyze boredom, then how *do* they register their acute awareness of the relevance of this mental state for the child?

Adam Phillips suggests that in boredom, 'in the process of waiting for the mother the child discovers a capacity for representation as a means of deferral. Representation – fantasy – is the medium in which he desires and waits' (1993, p. 79). Chapter 3 explores the ways in which Kate Greenaway depicts waiting as a vexed, even pained, condition. Phillips, though, suggests that the child invents coping strategies which alleviate the anguish of the absence of external stimuli. Specifically, he proposes that the child uses his imagination, acting out interactive activities in the absence of having real ones to distract him. Representation is, of course, the very medium of literature. In particular, fantasy is one of the most dominant modes of children's literature, especially children's literature of the era in question. Following this logic, we can propose that rather than representing the child's boredom, the children's novel might instead seek to act out – *represent* – the activities in which the child otherwise lacks the means to interest himself. This gives the children's literary text a very specific function: to alleviate or defer boredom by providing motion where there is otherwise none. As Toohey suggests, children 'don't give very much thought to [the] status [of boredom]. Nor do they begin to try to name it. At the very most all they think about is escape' (2011, p. 34). While adult novels of the same period seek to alleviate boredom by staring it in the face – seeking to name it – children's novels of the turn of the twentieth century seek to alleviate the same condition by modelling a means of overcoming it. If Phillips is correct in his suggestion that through being bored, the child eventually learns how to manage his own independence, then children's novels have a vital educative function, not by telling the child what to do but by mimicking how fantasy (making up activity which is unavailable to you) is a resource, indeed, the *ideal* resource – available to the child as a means of occupying himself when bored.

The child's demand not to be bored, whether this sense of entitlement is reasonable or not, whether it is derived internally or projected onto it from the world beyond, is a central condition of children's literature of this *fin-de-siècle* moment. By the same token, such children's literature demands that the reader *work* at acquiring the capacity for fantasy which the text models. As Friedrich Nietzsche observed, 'to escape boredom', man invents work that is 'play, that is, work that is designed to quiet no need other than that for working in general' (Nietzsche, 1995, p. 288). This in a sense is what the critical child does when she turns to a literary text in the hope – expectation – that it will mitigate boredom. She actively participates in this quest to be mobile, to keep things moving, to use her imagination – or she slides back into boredom. Thus a pastoral fantasy such as *The Wind in the Willows* – a text which, in its iconic status, is one of the handful of novels which have come to *stand* for golden-age children's literature – presents the reader with alternative modes of how to manage boredom. The various possibilities are offered up to the critical child: Mole's holidaying; Rat's dreaming; Toad's retail therapy; the wayfarer's wandering. The critical child must navigate a path between them and determine for herself what kind of movement is most conducive to the alleviation of boredom. In charting the characters' peculiar attempts to escape from boredom, the critical child undergoes a trajectory from boredom to stimulation and back again, not merely – indeed, not even – because this is the trajectory plotted for the characters (since it is not, at least not unequivocally so), but because the critical attention involved in distinguishing between the trajectories of the characters entails a form of work which will distract the reader from her own inertia. Like the characters in the novel, the reader is enabled to forget about being bored, is dragged away from boredom by the animating energy of the fantasy it presents. It is this, quite as much as its pastoral setting, which provides the impression of an idyll which critics have so persistently observed: the particular ways in which the novel evades that ubiquitous and disabling mental condition. In fact, interestingly, Toohey has observed a kinship between nostalgia and boredom; both are based, he claims, 'on a feeling of mild disgust with the present' (2011, p. 162). Just as we can read *Wind in the Willows* as a pastoral impelled by nostalgia, we can also read it as a fantasy impelled by boredom. The rest of this chapter will explore the ways in which the novel performs an idealizing function by enacting a retreat from boredom, considering the work that the child critic undertakes in making sense of the idealized status of this fantasy.

The Wind in the Willows represents its characters vacillating between 'want and boredom,' which, at least for Arthur Schopenhauer, can be seen as 'the twin poles of human life' (1976, p. 45). Toad and the wayfarer pursue seemingly oppositional kinds of activity, but they are linked by the fact that they are both motivated by the same basic need: the need to avoid boredom. In between, we have Rat and Mole, who delight in bustle as and for itself, a form of being which Nietzsche calls 'a blissful, peaceful state of motion', and which for Nietzsche 'is the artist's and philosopher's vision of happiness' (1995, p. 254). This idea of blissful, peaceful motion is encapsulated by Rat's famous proclamation that '"there is *nothing* – absolutely nothing – half so much worth doing as simply messing about in boats"':

> 'Simply messing,' [Rat] went on dreamily: 'messing – about – in – boats. . . . In or out of 'em, it doesn't matter. Nothing seems really to matter, that's the charm of it. Whether you get away, or whether you don't; whether you arrive at your destination or whether you reach somewhere else, or whether you never get anywhere at all, you're always busy, and you never do anything in particular; and when you've done it there's always something else to do, and you can do it if you like, but you'd much better not. . . .' The Mole waggled his toes from sheer happiness, spread his chest with a sigh of full contentment, and leaned back blissfully into the soft cushions. '*What* a day I'm having!' he said. 'Let us start at once!' (p. 12)

What Rat is holding up here as an ideal – a maximum possible standard for how to conduct one's life – is a variety of what the American avant-garde composer, John Cage, has called 'purposeful purposelessness'. For Cage, the appeal of such activity resides in the fact that it is 'in accord with nature in her manner of operation' (1966, p. 155). Busyness here is equated with happiness, indeed, a superlative happiness, as Rat's use of italics indicates. But crucially too, the bustle must be carried out as and for its own gain, not in order to achieve an end which lies beyond it. Purposeful purposefulness does not *begin* to produce the same pleasurable effect. Indeed, Rat holds up such earnest activity as contemptuous: '"Otters, kingfishers, dabchicks, moorhens, all of them about all day long and always wanting you to *do* something – as if a fellow had no business of his own to attend to!"' (p. 15). The kind of messing about in boats which the novel associates with 'sheer happiness' involves a particular approach to time; specifically, it involves thinking in terms of what Anton Zijderveld calls 'subjective time' as opposed to 'objective time' (or clock time). Subjective time, for Zijderveld, is 'an ongoing, pre-reflectively experienced duration'; put simply, we measure time according to how it *feels*. If we measure time according to 'objective time', however, which we typically do in a fully modernized society, then we become 'ruled by the many regulations of bureaucracy'; we allocate activity to slices of the day 'in a functional manner' (p. 75). Boredom ensues, Zijderveld suggests, 'when one does not know how to fill one's clock-time'; one runs out of activities to allocate to chunks of the day (1979, p. 76). To measure one's life in subjective time rather than clock time is therefore, for Zijderveld, an effective means of keeping boredom at bay.

Unlike Toad and the wayfarer, Rat and Mole evade boredom by doing precisely this. There is nothing functional about messing around in boats, and there are certainly no rules involved. The activity will by definition last only as long as does the interest in it, and so it will never outlive its value. The novel observes a qualitative difference, however, both morally and ontologically, between purpose*ful* purposelessness and purpose*less* purposelessness, and this is a difference to which Rat is keenly alert. To do *nothing* is viewed as unnatural, unsocial, and worse, immoral. For example, when the baby otter goes missing, Rat complains, '"I simply can't go and turn in, and go to sleep, and *do* nothing, even though there doesn't seem to be anything to be done . . . . We'll get the boat out . . . . [I]t will be better than going to bed and doing nothing"' (p. 129). The activity made possible by the boat evolves, as circumstances dictate, from one which produces individual gain (pleasure) to one which produces social gain (the retrieval of a lost animal). Importantly, then, the psychological gratification which Rat and Mole derive from their messing about in boats is not achieved at the expense of others' well-being; it is achieved only in the knowledge that the well-being of the other river dwellers has already been secured. The novel thus casts an activity which, if seen in a Stoical light, might seem like weak indolence, and in a Puritan light, wrongful self-indulgence, into something which is compatible with both individualism and altruism. Indeed, in its very sociability (for it is through messing about in boats that Mole is brought into the fold), it even engenders social cohesiveness, providing not merely personal gain but fostering friendship, even a form of political brotherhood. So how does the novel ostensibly validate the appeal of motion over inertia – and specifically of motion that is purposefully purposeless as opposed to roving and restless?

To begin with, there is the repetitive motion of the story itself. At least since Aristotle, activity – or what in Aristotelian terms is usually translated as 'action' – has been taken to be a central, even a definitive, ingredient of literature. Referring specifically to tragedy, Aristotle writes in *Poetics*,

> Tragedy is an imitation of an action that is complete, and whole, and of a certain magnitude . . . As therefore, in the other imitative arts, the imitation is one when the object imitated is one, so the plot, being an imitation of an action, must imitate one action and that a whole, the structural union of the parts being such that, if any one of them is displaced or removed, the whole will be disjointed and disturbed. For a thing whose presence or absence makes no visible difference, is not an organic part of the whole. (1970, ch. 8)

Although tragedy is not a genre which children's authors have traditionally exploited, Aristotle's comments on tragedy have frequently been taken out of context and used as ways of thinking about literature more generally. Interestingly, several of the Aristotelian precepts which govern tragedy appear very particularly to apply in the case of children's literature. For example, nowhere is it more true that 'it is deeds and the story that are the end' and that 'in all things the end is what matters most' (1970, ch. 6) than in writing for children, as has been well-documented by children's literature critics including Maria Nikolajeva (2005) and Perry Nodelman and Mavis Reimer (2003). Aristotle was highly prescriptive about how action should be organized into story. Specifically, he insisted that a play should follow one main action, and should introduce as few as possible, preferably no, subplots. The kind of story which Aristotle advocates, then, is one that is streamlined, forwards-moving, quick-paced (the action encompassing only twenty-four hours), and linear.

These are not adjectives which we could use to describe the story of *The Wind in the Willows*. What, indeed, *is* the story of *The Wind in the Willows*? Certainly, there are recognizable narrative threads which chart the beginning, middle and end of discrete dramas. There is the trip to the Wild Wood, for example, where Mole gets lost, is rescued by Rat, and they are both taken in by Badger. And there are the various antics of Toad, which together culminate in the siege of Toad Hall. And there is the plot in which Mole leaves his home and discovers a new life for himself. But there is nothing singular about the story of *The Wind in the Willows*. The various strands of the story at times intersect and at times run independently – and sometimes are hard to assimilate at all, as in the case of the Piper at Dawn chapter. The novel therefore strikingly fails to adhere to an Aristotelian model of action. Nor is the novel strictly episodic, in the way that Kenneth Grahame's earlier works, *The Golden Age* (1895) and *Dream Days* (1898) had been, where snippets of individual stories are strung together to create an impression of a connected sequence. Instead, the action of *The Wind in the Willows* can best be described as a purposeful purposelessness: the characters are constantly doing things, but the things they do have not been selected by virtue of the role they play in an overarching plot. The motion is repetitive, but not in a teleological way.

And yet the activity of *The Wind in the Willows* is not altogether directionless. It is anchored by certain thematic ballasts which provide shape to each of the excursions it narrates. In particular, there is a tendency throughout the novel for the characters to gravitate back towards home. The novel emphasizes the enduring appeal of home, most overtly in Badger's sentimental encomium to home: 'home sweet home'. And then there is Mole's nostalgic yearning for home, which, although he overrides it, tinges all the experiences he encounters during the novel: 'the upper world was all too strong, it called to him still, even down there, and he knew he must return to the larger stage. But it was good to think he had this to come back to, this place which was all his own, these things which were so glad to see him again and could always be counted upon for the same simple welcome' (p. 106). But despite Mole's readiness temporarily to surrender his own home, ultimately what brings all the narrative threads of the novel together is the characters' collective outrage at the invasion of Toad's home by woodland creatures. However much the politics of Rat and Mole differ from the aristocratic, entitled endorsement of plutocracy espoused by Toad, they are not prepared to stomach the overthrow of someone else's right to return to their place of origin. The celebration of home in all its various guises exerts a narrative pull within the novel back towards a point of origin, such that excursions into foreign parts always involve a homecoming at the end, and disconnected narrative strands all bring characters back to the same physical starting point. Thus, while not strictly circular, the action in *The Wind in the Willows* – its story – is a species of purposeful purposelessness: purposeful in its desire to weave an eventual path back home; purposeless in its lack of concern about what occurs on the way, so long as something happens to stave off the characters' (and the reader's) boredom.

But the feature which most urgently contributes to the novel's validation of motion is Grahame's voluptuous style. The style of *The Wind in the Willows* has sometimes been criticized for being too sophisticated for children. Arthur Ransome, for example, insisted that the book was written in the 'wrong language': in a complicated allusive style that only adults could appreciate (1909, p. 190). And Humphrey Carpenter made a similar observation when he insisted that the novel's 'language is consistently adult, full of verbal ornateness and wit. Few children are likely to understand more than a small proportion of Grahame's nuances' (1985, p. 229). Its language, then, has been used to justify claims that the novel is not primarily directed at a child reader, presumably on the grounds that a child would be frustrated, and eventually bored, by the experience of encountering perpetual challenge. The assumption that, as Nicholas Tucker has put it, 'the endless paragraphs of a Proust, the convoluted sentences of a Henry James, or the sophisticated, literary English of a Meredith will not get through to children' is widespread in children's literary criticism, on the basis that 'on the whole, children usually seem to prefer a style that does not present too many difficulties, using . . . a less complex vocabulary' (1981, pp. 12–13). But to accept at face value the assertion that Grahame's style is ornate is to overlook the fact that the sense of Grahame's prose is largely communicated through its sheer energy. Much of the novel is conducted in direct speech, where Grahame is less prone to using the kind of sophisticated vocabulary which his critics have suggested renders his novel inaccessible to children. Where he deploys third-person narrative, it is striking how fast-moving his prose is. Chapters frequently begin in medias res, instantly plunging the child into the drama of the scene. This kind of immersion in the activity at hand is also pursued at a more localized level. For example, when the narrator refers to the stories which Rat tells Mole, these are described thus:

> Very thrilling stories they were, too, to an earth-dwelling animal like Mole. Stories about weirs, and sudden floods, and leaping pike, and steamers that flung hard bottles – at least bottles were certainly flung, and *from* steamers, so presumably *by* them; and about herons, and how particular they were whom they spoke to; and about adventures down drains, and night-fishings with Otter, or excursions far afield with Badger. Supper was a most cheerful meal .... This day was only the first of many similar ones for the emancipated Mole, each of them longer and fuller of interest as the ripening summer moved onward. He learnt to swim and to row, and entered into the joy of running water; and with his ear to the reed-stems he caught, at intervals, something of what the wind went whispering so constantly among them. (pp. 25–6)

This is a kind of epic style which collapses together actions from distinct times and places to create an impression of a busy sequence of events piled unceasingly one on top of the other. The sheer range of activities yoked into the same sentence is dizzying. And yet, contrary to what one might expect from vivid writing such as this, this is an account which makes abundant use of nouns rather than verbs; the child reader – the critical child – must infer the nature of the activity from the nouns supplied ('weirs', 'floods', 'adventures down drains'). The critical child contributes the specific nature of the motion to the scene in order to make sense of what is being conveyed. Grahame's prose is thus doubly active: it is active in the sense that it moves quickly and efficiently; but it is also active in the sense that it requires the reader to undertake work in order to speed the process up further. The fact that the nature of the readerly work entailed is the supply of *verbs* to the scene renders the role played by the reader even more active in character, since in a short space of time, the reader must flit between different kinds of *doing*.

Grahame's treatment of time, then – stretches of it passing with rapidity – animates his prose. Martin Heidegger suggests that boredom 'swallows up, as it were, the flowing sequence of nows and becomes a *single stretched "now"* which itself does not flow, but stands' (1995, p. 124). Grahame's prose performs precisely the opposite process: it establishes 'flow' between the 'sequence of nows', such that the 'now' never 'stands' still. In the German, the relationship between time and boredom to which Heidegger alludes is encoded etymologically into the term *Langeweile*, which, as Fenichel observes, encapsulates the sense that when the 'external world bring[s] only monotonous stimuli, or [when] subjective conditions prevent their being experienced as tension-releasing, then the "while is long"' (p. 301). In *The Wind in the Willows*, the 'while' is forever short, owing largely to the economy with which Grahame organizes activity into perpetual motion. When Mole gets lost in the Wild Wood, even Mole's fear is turned into a series of actions: 'Then the faces began . . . Then the whistling began . . . Then the pattering began . . .' (pp. 50–1) Again, much of the communicative work of these sentences is carried out by the nouns, leaving the reader to infer what verbs these nouns enact. The repetition of the nondescript verb 'began' links these otherwise unconnected activities into a seeming sequence, which ramps up the reader's curiosity, mimicking the acceleration of Mole's nervously pumping heart. In fact, the story of this episode is in itself rather unexciting: Mole gets lost, Rat finds him, they both find Badger, they chat long into the night; it is not a story which generates intrinsic motion. But Grahame's telling of it – his demand that the reader participate by filling in the gaps left by unspecified verbs – establishes the kind of dramatic uncertainty, and hence excitement, which Toad so compulsively seeks:

> 'There you are!' cried the Toad, straddling and expanding himself. 'There's real life for you, embodied in that little cart. The open road, the dusty highway, the heath, the common, the hedgerows, the rolling downs! Camps, villages, towns, cities. Here to-day, up and off to somewhere else to-morrow! Travel, change, interest, excitement! The whole world before you, and a horizon that's always changing!' (p. 32)

Toad's speech not only comprises of a glamorization of speed, it performs one too. In his enthusiasm, his sentences eschew grammatical protocol and descend into breathy lists, initially a list of nouns which are prefaced by adjectives, and then, in his haste, merely a list of nouns. He takes the reader on an imaginative tour which is conducted at breakneck speed, moving from village to town to city in the space of a mere comma. 'Travel, chance, interest, excitement!' might stand as a slogan for all that Toad aspires to; and it might also stand as a characterization of his own speech. In short, jerky moves, it constantly flits between one idea and the next, frequent punctuation connoting the frequent changes in direction which his description seeks to evoke, repeated exclamation marks escalating the reader's levels of adrenaline in line with his own. Toad's prose operates not merely sonically and visually but on all the senses; it seeks to animate the entire body:

> The 'poop-poop' rang with a brazen shout in their ears, they had a moment's glimpse of an interior of glittering plate-glass and rich morocco, and the magnificent motor-car, immense, breath-snatching, passionate, with its pilot tense and hugging his wheel, possessed all earth and air for the fraction of a second, flung an enveloping cloud of dust that blinded and enwrapped them utterly, and then dwindled to a speck in the far distance, changed back into a droning bee once more .... 'Glorious, stirring sight!' murmured Toad, never offering to move. 'The poetry of motion! The *real* way to travel! The *only* way to travel! Here to-day – in next week to-morrow! Villages skipped, towns and cities humped – always somebody else's horizon! O bliss! O poop-poop! O my! O my!' (pp. 39–41)

Critics have noted the erotic energy of passages such as this, but it is a particular kind of erotic potential that is harnessed, one which derives from solipsistic *physical* gratification and not from a shared experience. In this way, the energy encapsulated by such a passage is onanistic. Interestingly, Otto Fenichel has suggested that 'there are many threads ... connecting boredom and compulsive masturbation' (p. 300), and we see in Toad a similar kind of compulsiveness. The speed with which he transfers his allegiance from the cart to the car; the necessity with which he imbues it ('the *only* way to travel', his italics investing the sentiment with the insistence of a spoiled child): Toad lets his desire to fulfil his unstoppable appetite for movement go unchecked. Grahame's prose, in its accumulation of momentum, allows the reader vicariously to enjoy the quickening of Toad's desire while also enabling us to view it as childish in its very excesses. The disproportionate, unself-conscious delight ('O bliss! O poop-poop!') that Toad expresses enables the child reader, by comparison, to feel unusually mature and restrained. Nothing, of course, gives the child more delight than feeling superior and more all-knowing that those who are ostensibly their seniors, and Toad, by virtue of his independent status as lord of the manor, functions in every other respect like an adult rather than a child. Through Toad's prose, then, Grahame stimulates the child reader's engagement by enabling her to take up the position of the staid (boring) sage who perceives the folly of Toad's out-of-control speed addiction. The excess movement of Toad's prose, while it drives forward the reader's interest, undermines the appeal of the idea of unceasing motion which it ostensibly idealizes. Grahame thus enables the child critically to evaluate the desirability of Toad's solution – 'poetry in motion' – to the problem of boredom.

In so doing, the child reader is steered towards the position adopted by Rat and Mole, who take it upon themselves to 'rescue' Toad from what they perceive to be his death wish: '"Right you are!" cried the Rat, starting up. "We'll rescue the poor unhappy animal! We'll convert him! He'll be the most converted Toad that ever was before we've done with him!"' (pp. 108–9). But despite the obvious prudence of Rat and Mole's common sense over Toad's folly, the novel nonetheless exerts a thematic pull towards the restless spirit of Toad. It is Toad's adventures which we want to follow; Toad's fate which we want to see to completion; Toad's happiness which we want to secure. Perhaps this is precisely what makes the novel a children's novel. Toad, with his extreme fidgetiness, manifests, as we saw earlier, a peculiarly childish kind of boredom: in his extreme state of bored restlessness, he cannot stay still, not even in conversation, the free flow of which he constantly interrupts with boasts which break the rules of polite interaction and disrupt others' calm. Thus the motor, physical restlessness which impels Toad to be constantly on the move might be seen to reflect a distinctively childish kind of boredom – one which child readers will intuitively recognize. It is almost as though Toad has internalized the aspiration voiced by the Victorian polymath, Thomas Carlyle: 'I've got a great ambition to die of exhaustion rather than boredom' – only Toad's exhaustion derives from manic play and not manic work. In this, Toad epitomizes Anton Zijderveld's observation that a 'bored individual will behave erratically' (1979, p. 79): 'it can be observed that speech becomes gross and hyperbolic, music loud and nervous, ideas giddy and fantastic, emotions limitless and shameless, actions bizarre and foolish, whenever boredom reigns. A bored individual needs these irritants of body, psyche and mind because he is not behaviourally stimulated in any other way' (p. 84). In his giddiness, he requires an external force operating on him – a counter force – to slow him down. Such force needs to come in the form of physical power; words alone are impotent: '"*That*'s no good!" said the Rat contemptuously. "*Talking* to Toad'll never cure him. He'll *say* anything"' (p. 112). As with a child's solemn vows, his promises are meaningless: 'he has undertaken to give up motor-cars entirely and for ever. I have his solemn promise to that effect.' (p. 113) His own good intentions, like the cunning wheedling of a child determined to get her own way, are a ploy; they keep things constantly in motion, deferring the inevitable, enabling him to keep going in the erratic ways he desires, seeking only his immediate gratification. Toohey suggests that boredom 'is an emotion usually associated with a nourished body: like satiety, it is not normally for the starving' (2011, p. 5). Toad, indeed, is far from starving; stuffed with the pleasures of his own gains, he is a fat emblem of greed. And yet, although Søren Kierkegaard has claimed that 'boredom is the root of all evil' (Kierkegaard, 1987), Toad is not presented as morally outrageous, and not even as an especially serious social irritant. Instead, he is presented as a naïve figure who has much to learn. In this, he renders himself highly empathetic for the child reader, who knows only too well how little she understands the world, and whose escape from the very same affliction of fidgetiness – paralysis of indecision in the face of all that it has to offer – has likely impelled her to turn to the novel in the first place.

But, while, by contrast to Toad, it is clear that Rat and Mole are not giddy with fidgetiness, neither are they immune from restlessness:

> Restlessly the Rat wandered off once more . . . . On this side of the hills was now the real blank, on the other lay the crowded and coloured panorama that his inner eye was seeing so clearly. What seas lay beyond, green, leaping, and crested! What sun-bathed coasts, along which the white villas glittered against the olive woods! What quiet harbours, thronged with gallant shipping bound for purple islands of wine and spice, islands set low in languorous waters! (p. 170)

The unplanned encounter with the wayfaring rat unleashes in Water Rat a sudden, crippling bout of *wanderlust*, whose effects are no less incapacitating for all their unlikeliness. Habitually reconciled to the settled, low-level bustle of the river bank, Rat is spontaneously gripped by the hitherto unconsidered appeal of the exotic, the foreign, the faraway, the non-familiar: stimulation by new experiences for its own sake. But ironically the appeal of the unknown strikes him not through sampling it, not through *doing*, but through talking and imagining. What he yearns for is a poet's fantasy, not a mariner's reality. In fact, the novel sets up the wayfarer's life as inadequate and inconsequential; the episode, in its lack of assimilation into the rest of the novel, is a frustrating interruption to the quotidian, domestic, familiar interest of life on the river bank. It is *there* that the reader wants us to return, for another picnic on the water. The sudden allure of the unfamiliar is not motivated by a characteristic unsettledness, but rather by the peculiar boredom experienced by the artistic. Nietzsche, for example, proposed that those with an artistic bent, which he refers to as a rare sensibility, 'do not fear boredom as much as work without pleasure; they actually require a lot of boredom if *their* work is to succeed. For thinkers and all sensitive spirits, boredom is that disagreeable "windless calm" of the soul that precedes a happy voyage and cheerful winds. They have to bear it and must wait for its effect on them. Precisely this is what lesser natures cannot achieve by any means' (1995, p. 108). The chronology outlined by Nietzsche exactly maps onto what occurs in *The Wind in the Willows*: Rat's 'windless calm' precipitates a happy flurry of creative endeavour in the form of poetry-writing. The sole rationale for the inclusion of this odd episode is that it serves to remind the reader of the precariousness of intrinsic motivation, of interest in what is front of you, of the energy and focus to apply oneself with purposefulness. And yet the episode does not merely function to set up a contrast; in itself, it triggers Rat's renewed, more creative burst of energy, albeit one stage-managed by Mole: 'Grappling with him strongly he dragged him inside, threw him down, and held him. . . . "It's quite a long time since you did any poetry," he remarked" ' (pp. 184–6). Prosaic Mole, not, one would suspect, a character whom Nietzsche would regard as 'higher', nonetheless has the percipience to foresee what Rat needs. His actions are in direct contrast to those of the wayfaring Rat; whereas the wandering Rat effuses lyrical whimsy, Mole's efficient and direct style brings Rat back down to earth. There is a delightful irony in the way in which Mole foists poetry on Rat in a curiously utilitarian, unromantic way: immune himself from its magical effects, Mole nonetheless appreciates its therapeutic properties for Rat and reduces its function to a clinical one – rightly so, as it happens. Rat's disappearance into poetry does not inure him to his old life of drudgery, making it possible for him to go on, but on the contrary, revivifies his interest in it, enabling him to experience it anew, through an artistic medium.

The difference, then, between Rat and Toad is not in their susceptibility to boredom, for the novel illustrates the ways in which boredom is always lurking just under the surface, a persistent blot on the horizon; it is instead in the kind of activity they undertake to assuage it – in their ways of being.

While Toad dashes unthinkingly from one form of activity to another, Rat finds his inner resources and channels his frustration at the non-presence of the things he desires into fantasy. He models for the critical child the skills that she needs to learn in order to cope with boredom in the adult world, and in so doing, he discovers what Joris-Karl Huysmans's character, Jean des Esseintes, discovers in *À Rebours (Against Nature)* (1884): that 'travel [is] a waste of time, since . . . the imagination could provide a more-than-adequate substitute for the vulgar reality of actual experience' (2003, p. 35). Daydreaming, then, in *The Wind in the Willows* is not merely romantic whimsy, it performs a vital, and in the case of Rat, redemptive, function, since it rescues him from that pernicious affliction of boredom. It provides an analogous, and more easily accessed, kind of purposeful purposeless activity to messing about in boats; if done purposefully, it will stave away the restlessness, but only if it is done with no ulterior purpose than that. As Fenichel writes, 'it is well known that people endowed with imagination are rarely bored,' for 'a rich imagination enables a person to unburden himself to a certain extent in daydreams' (1854, p. 299). This is perhaps why, as Ulrich Knoepflmacher has observed, while 'Grahame always treats Toad's escapism as buffoonish, he treats Water Rat's restlessness with empathy and respect' (2010, p. 12). But the novel never overtly commits to one particular animal's method of coping with boredom over another's; it is left to the critical child to decide for him- or herself which option to prefer. While it may well be the case that the novel idealizes Rat's imaginativeness – offers it up as redemptive – so it also presents the appeal of Toad's hyperactivity, Badger's inactivity ('No animal, according to the rules of animal-etiquette, is ever expected to do anything strenuous, or heroic, or even moderately active during the off-season of winter. All are sleepy – some are actually asleep' (p. 71)) and Mole's practical inquisitiveness ('the Mole had a good deal of spare time on his hands, and so one afternoon, when the Rat in his arm-chair before the blaze was alternately dozing and trying over rhymes that wouldn't fit, he formed the solution to go out by himself and explore' (p. 49)). The reader is entrusted to choose for herself.

The very indeterminacy of *The Wind in the Willows* has provoked critical debate. Sarah Gilead sees the novel recanting Grahame's 'joyous opening vision, now reconceiving it as morally and socially perilous' and promoting 'the reader's acceptance (whether child or adult) of necessity, self-denial, and moral responsibility' (1988, p. 144). However, as Marah Gubar rightly observes, the novel is in fact 'infused with a deep regard for the pleasures of civilized life, as well as a resigned though by no means despairing recognition of its drawbacks' (2009, p. 25). To read the novel as elegiac is to read against the philosophic and aesthetic grain of the novel, even if, formally, the pastoral mode – so often a variety of elegy – is dominant. The reformation of Toad at the end may ostensibly prioritize a philosophy which advocates purposeful purposelessness, but the strength of Toad's endorsement of this philosophy seems unlikely to outweigh the strength of his compulsion for speed. 'I've had enough of adventures,' he declares. 'I shall lead a quiet, steady, respectable life, pottering about my property, and improving it, and doing a little landscape gardening at times. There will always be a bit of dinner for my friends when they come to see me; and I shall keep a pony-chaise to joy about the country in, just as I used to in the good old days, before I got restless, and wanted to *do* things' (p. 214). But there is no sense of regret or thwarted desire here; instead, the bubbly, irrepressible prose, which packs layer upon layer of the child's most favoured things (dinner, horses, playing indoors, playing in the garden) makes this reformed life extremely appealing precisely because it fills it to the hilt with *activity*. It is impossible to believe that Toad will restrict himself to 'pottering' and 'a bit of dinner'; the difficulties of so doing are well known to any child. As ever, Toad's prose strains against its own confines, revealing the latent energy beneath the surface which will, as the laws of physics dictate, escape its bounds and find an outlet somewhere; it's only a matter of time.

Roderick McGillis has suggested that '*The Wind in the Willows* is a visionary book, a book that tells us we can travel much farther in our imaginations than we can on foot or by train or boat' (1984–5, p. 186). But the book *tells* the critical child nothing of the sort, for *telling* is precisely what the novel does *not* do. The fantasy world it evokes for us, and all the activities it contains, may well banish the reader's boredom, and, by providing them with pleasure in vicarious form, may well save them the trouble of heading off to a river to hire a boat. But the novel also provides a space in which the critical reader can contemplate the inevitability, the naturalness, even the desirability, of boredom. While it may not offer the kind of sustained and overt meditation on boredom which we see in Marcel Proust's *Remembrance of Things Past*, James Joyce's *Ulysses*, or Henry

James's *Portrait of a Lady*, it requires the child reader critically to analyze the subtlety, complexity and vulnerability of human consciousness. It may well be that any reader of *The Wind in the Willows* is already possessed of the resources to assuage boredom (reading) and already predisposed to favour such purposeful purposiveness over all else. But the narrative draw of Toad's vibrant prose will give such a child – a critical child – wistful pause for thought.

6

On talking: J. R. R. Tolkien's *The Hobbit*

If we start from the rudimentary position that *The Hobbit* is a work of children's literature since, at the point of composing and publishing the text, J. R. R. Tolkien understood himself to be writing for young people, then it is tempting to assume that its very language – what Tolkien termed its 'linguistic matter' (*Letters*, p. 219) – must somehow relate to children. After all, what is there to a text, to any text, if not language? What else, if not its linguistic matter, could make *The Hobbit* a children's novel? Or, put another way, what is it that makes this novel's ideal reader a child? Of course, there are the illustrations; but as one of Tolkien's early child critics, the ten-year-old Rayner Unwin, averred, 'This book, with the help of maps, does not need any illustrations it is good and should appeal to all children between the ages of 5 and 9' (quoted in Hammond and Scull, 2011, p. 7; punctuation his own). Tolkien, however, was vehement in his antipathy to the idea that literature must be morphologically altered to make it fit for children: 'Do not write down to Children or to anybody. Not even in language,' he enjoined in 1959, two decades after the publication of his children's masterpiece (*Letters*, p. 298). While by this point in time Tolkien had made his peace with the fact that *The Hobbit* and *The Lord of the Rings* did appeal to children, he was nonetheless insistent that if this was so, it was certainly not on account of anything he had consciously *done* to them: 'I am not specially interested in children,' he wrote, and 'certainly not in writing for them: i.e. in addressing directly and expressly those who cannot understand adult language' (*Letters*, p. 297). Two years later he elaborated on this: 'Children are not a class or kind, they are a heterogeneous collection of immature persons, varying, as persons do, in their reach, and in their ability to extend it when stimulated. As soon as you limit your vocabulary to what you suppose to be within their reach, you in fact simply cut off the gifted ones from the chance of extending it' (*Letters*, p. 310). Quite clearly, at least according to the author himself, if the 'linguistic matter' of *The Hobbit* makes any concessions to children, then it is not on account of the words of which it comprises.

Unsurprisingly, given his idiosyncratic – not to mention professional – fascination with languages and their origins, the words Tolkien uses have long fascinated critics, whose starting point is often Tolkien's own comment in relation to *The Lord of the Rings* that 'the invention of languages is the foundation. The "stories" were made rather to provide a world for the languages than the reverse' (*Letters*, p. 219). Studies of Tolkien's language have painstakingly uncovered the intricate systems of words in his fiction, explicating the etymologies of the words he borrowed and analyzing the significance of the words he coined.[1] Such studies have exhaustively shown how Tolkien's 'mythology' derives from, is animated by, or is an 'outgrowth of' (Anderson, 2003, p. 4) his invented languages. Elizabeth Kirk, for example, analyzes how Tolkien creates a 'model' for 'the relationship of language to action, to values and to civilization'; and Margaret Hiley interrogates the ways in which Tolkien's language has mythical signifying systems superimposed upon it (Kirk, 1971; Hiley, 2004). But suppose we begin from a different starting point. Suppose we take language not to mean the diction Tolkien uses or the systems within which his words function (*langue*) but instead as the forms in or methods by which words are uttered (*parole*) (Saussure). This would shift the emphasis away from Tolkien's vocabulary (about which there is anyway surely little more to be said) towards the ends to which Tolkien *uses* his vocabulary – his narrative techniques or his speech acts – a dimension of Tolkien's language which has received much less concerted critical attention. If it is not the words that Tolkien uses that make *The Hobbit*'s language suitable for – ideal for – a critical child, then it must be what he does with them.

Narrative theorists going back to Plato have tended to agree that there are two main ways in which literature uses language: *diegetically* (by telling) and *mimetically* (by showing). In a novel, these two narrative modes are epitomized by on the one hand what Gérard Genette calls 'narrative of events' ('a transcription of the (supposed) non-verbal into the verbal') and on the other what he terms 'narrative of words' ('the discourse of characters') (Genette, 1980, p. 167; p. 170). To put this more crudely, action can either be presented through the words of the narrator or it can be presented through the words of the characters themselves. Naturally, novels for children, like novels more generally, tend to make use of a combination of narrative of events with narrative of words. However, it has often been proposed that 'children's literature characteristically focuses on showing rather than telling' (Nodelman, 2008, p. 214) This means that children's novels tend to create an illusion that the reader is witnessing first-hand events as they unfold, rather than being presented with a version of events that has already been filtered through the eyes of a narrator. Maria Nikolajeva, who distinguishes between 'external representation' ('including description, comments, actions, and speech') and 'internal representation' (which 'allows us to penetrate the characters' minds, to take part in their innermost thoughts and mental states'), observes that there is 'a clear tendency in fiction for younger children toward external characterization, while young adult fiction frequently employs internal means' (Nikolajeva, 2005, pp. 161–3). On account of this propensity for children's novels to appear to present rather than *re*present the scene at hand, John Stephens has suggested that 'with children's fiction . . . more attention needs to be paid to direct speech dialogue . . . because it exists in a higher proportion' (Stephens in Hunt, 1999, p. 82). Certainly, a quick survey of influential children's texts written contemporaneously to *The Hobbit* indicates that by the mid-1930s direct speech had become a major ingredient of the children's novel. In novels such as Arthur Ransome's *Swallows and Amazons* (1930), John Masefield's *The Box of Delights* (1935) and Alison Uttley's *A Traveller in Time* (1939), a large portion of the narrative is presented via direct speech. Needless to say, children's novels do not have a monopoly on direct speech, in the 1930s or at any other point in literary history; but when one considers the comparatively minor role that direct speech plays in some of the notable examples of adult literature from the same decade, for example in works by Virginia Woolf, William Faulkner and George Orwell, we can see in sharper focus its importance as a factor which might determine, or at least influence, the ages included within a text's implied – or its ideal: the idea it fixes of its – audience.

The Hobbit almost exclusively uses external rather than internal character representation. This means that invariably Tolkien's reader does 'not know any more about [the characters] than other characters would', a position which, at least for Nikolajeva, befits 'the cognitive level of [the] implied readers' of children's literature (2005, pp. 161–2). Accordingly, direct speech is a fundamental element of the novel. This is not to say that most of the novel is conducted through dialogue – it is not; most of the novel is comprised of omniscient third-person narrative, often, though not always, focalized through Bilbo Baggins. But it is to observe that dialogue – of which there is plenty – occurs at seminal moments of the novel, not because Tolkien resorts to direct speech as a vehicle for the dramatization of sensational events, but because at such moments, language *is* the event. At the novel's many dramatic peaks, it is spoken language – talk – which makes things happen. In this way, Tolkien's language reconnects with what the anthropologist, Bronislaw Malinowski, in his influential essay, 'The Problem of Meaning in Primitive Languages' (1923), termed 'its primitive function and original form'. Such language, Malinowski wrote, is 'a mode of behaviour, an indispensable element of concerted human action' (p. 481). Interestingly, given that what I am concerned with in this chapter is the ways in which Tolkien's language might appeal to the child reader – an inexperienced yet interrogative critical thinker – Malinowski perceived the function of language among uncontacted peoples (his field work was conducted in Papua New Guinea) to share something vital in common with the function of language among children: 'When the child clamours for a person, it calls and he appears before it. When it wants food or an object . . . its only means of action is to clamour, and a very efficient means of action this proves to the child' (1923, p. 486). He concludes that both among what today we would call 'uncontacted people' and among children, words are therefore not only a means of expression but 'the word gives power, allows one to exercise an influence over an object or an action' (p. 490). In *The Hobbit* too, words, especially words as they are presented through direct speech, make things happen. Tolkien's use of direct speech in *The Hobbit*, then, secures the appeal of the novel among children not merely because a child reader might find external character representation less arduous than internal character representation; it also secures the appeal of the novel among children because, if we accept Malinowski's theory, children already recognize the potential for spoken language to change the environment. For a child critic, Tolkien's attribution of power to words does not require any leap of faith. At the same time, though, the use of such language does not make children the only appropriate audience for his fairy story, as Tolkien was keen to stress: fairy stories will always appeal to a de facto audience comprised of readers of any age who wish, as he put it, to 'open a door on Other Time', to 'stand outside our own time, outside Time itself, maybe' – or to pick up on Malinowski's term, to return to a more 'primitive' existence. The rest of this chapter seeks to chart *The Hobbit*'s childish, or 'primitive', use of 'verbal magic' wherein spoken language becomes precious artillery capable of transforming the world in which it is sounded, artfully – to recall Dewey's term – shaping that world according to the ideals of its user.

The Hobbit opens with a scene-setting narrative overview addressed directly to the reader. It is surely this awkward direct address, clumsily reminiscent of children's novels from several decades earlier by authors such as Beatrix Potter, E. Nesbit or J. M. Barrie, which Tolkien later had in mind when he criticized the 'whims[ical]' and even 'facetious' mode in which the novel begins (*Letters*, p. 298). Certainly, his discomfort with the use of second-person address ('you will see whether he gained anything in the end') (*The Hobbit*, p. 4) can be judged by the fact that he almost entirely abandons use of this technique after the first four pages, when the narrative moves into direct speech and the novel proper gets under way. But here we encounter something interesting. While, following the logic outlined above, the direct representation of talk might provide a point of entry for the child reader, in fact the novel's first dialogue – between Bilbo Baggins and Gandalf – reveals conversation to be a fundamentally adult (and hence regrettable) preoccupation:

> 'Good morning!' said Bilbo, and he meant it. . . .
>
> 'What do you mean?' [Gandalf] said. 'Do you wish me a good morning, or mean that it is a good morning whether I want it or not; or that you feel good this morning; or that it is a morning to be good on?'
>
> 'All of them at once,' said Bilbo. 'And a very fine morning for a pipe of tobacco out of doors, into the bargain. If you have a pipe about you, sit down and have a fill of mine! There's no hurry, we have all the day before us!' . . .
>
> 'Very pretty!' said Gandalf. 'But I have no time to blow smoke-rings this morning. I am looking for someone to share in an adventure that I am arranging, and it's very difficult to find anyone.'

> 'I should think so – in these parts! We are plain quiet folk and have no use for adventures. Nasty disturbing uncomfortable things! Make you late for dinner! I can't think what anybody sees in them,' said our Mr Baggins. . . . 'Good morning!' he said at last. 'We don't want any adventures here, thank you! You might try over The Hill or across The Water.' By this he meant that the conversation was at an end.
>
> 'What a lot of things you do use *Good morning* for!' said Gandalf. 'Now you mean that you want to get rid of me, and that it won't be good till I move off.'
>
> 'Not at all, not at all, my dear sir!' (pp. 5–6)

Scholars have often proposed that the hobbit provides a point of identification for the child reader on account of his diminutive stature, and there is perhaps some truth to this; but it is important to note that the hobbit's small talk has a pungent whiff of the old man about it. While Bilbo, navigating his way through the fraught business of shaking off an unwelcome visitor within the bounds of politeness, participates in a decidedly adult comedy of manners, Gandalf emerges as the more energetic, uninhibited, and hence childlike, figure, a figure at home in the child's adventure story. If, as Stephen Miller suggests, we can distinguish between *conversation*, which is 'purposeless', and *talk*, which is 'purposeful' (Miller, 2006, p. 14), we might see Bilbo as a master of conversation, frustrating Gandalf's desire to talk. But it is not quite the case that Bilbo's conversation is purposeless. He is using language to attempt to 'establish [a bond] of personal union between [two] people brought together' rather than to 'frame and express thoughts' (Malinowski, 1923, p. 479). And his efforts indicate that he has fully digested some of the basic rules of conversation: for example, he takes pains to avoid his interlocutor losing face by directing him off to The Hill and The Water (Traugott and Pratt, 1980); he avoids open disagreement, by never directly asking Gandalf to leave (Schneider); and, crucially, he ensures that there are no embarrassing silences, respectfully responding to all questions and volunteering comments in exchange. Bilbo emerges as a morally upright character, someone who takes seriously the view expressed by John Mahaffy that conversation is a *duty* (Mahaffay, 1888). But this encounter is not what Milton Wright would characterize as 'resultful,' since 'to be successful, a conversation must be interesting to the persons taking part in it. This means to *all* of the persons' (Wright, 1936, pp. 15, 31). And such interest is contingent, as Daniel Menaker points out, on 'the main part of a conversation, particularly with a new acquaintance, establish[ing] some kind of common ground' (Menaker, 2010, p. 18). Far from bringing the two characters together, this conversation has driven them apart, exposing the oppositional positions which they occupy. In part, the opposition Tolkien sets up here is an opposition between taking risks and playing it safe – or what the novel goes on to characterize as *Tookishness* versus *Bagginsishness*. At the same time, though, it is an opposition between using words to do things (e.g., convey meaning, like Gandalf) and using words to not do things (e.g., to obfuscate one's meaning, like Bilbo Baggins). In addition, it is implicitly an opposition between a modern way of life, rooted in the home, and a pre-modern way of life, let loose in the great outdoors; or, to reanimate Dewey's vocabulary, we are offered an opposition between a progressive and a traditional approach. So we have here a cluster of associations: on the one hand the Baggins, a grumpy, though polite, old man whose civility is epitomized by his capacity to use words to deflect meaning (every word in the phrase 'Not at all, not at all, my dear sir!' is a lie); and on the other, the Took, an upbeat, if uncivilized, childlike figure ('I am looking for someone to share in an adventure') whose primitive nature is epitomized by his desire for words to *mean* something. If dialogue is the narrative hook with which Tolkien ensnares his child reader, it is a hook he uses to expose the ridiculousness of conversation – or, more specifically, the ridiculousness of polite sociability in the modern, adult world. The child reader does not want to hang around blowing smoke rings outside the hobbit hole; the child wants to go on the trip. The function of this conversation, then, is to galvanize the reader's frustration – their critical resistance – precisely with conversation. What the reader wants from direct speech, Tolkien assumes, is *direct* speech – which is to say, speech that cuts to the chase or, moreover, speech that *is* the chase.

When Bilbo Baggins undertakes to go on Gandalf's adventure, he evolves (or perhaps regresses) from a figure who uses language in place of action into one who uses language *as* action. He changes from a character whose default utterances are moans about the lack of creature comforts ('I am dreadfully hungry') (p. 89) to one who can use language to materialize absent food and shelter ('you will take me along quick to a fire, where I can dry' (p. 242)). He acquires the capacity to use language in this way from the example of Gandalf, whose talk luxuriates in the possibility for words to alter the things to which they relate. Gandalf is liberal in his use of imperatives ('Be good, take care of yourselves – and DON'T LEAVE THE PATH!' (p. 127)), fully invoking the privileges accorded to him by virtue of his superior social position. This position also gives him licence to ask the questions, forcing his companions, the dwarves and the hobbit, into the subservient role of supplying answers. But it is in his interaction with their enemies that Gandalf's talk is most manifestly bewitching. He sets the precedent for how to use spoken language to make things happen when the voyagers encounter their first hurdle: the three trolls in the wood. Bilbo and the dwarves have already succumbed to the trolls' greater physical strength, but Gandalf, crucially, is invisible, and hence can – indeed must – rely on the power of the voice alone to get his way. When Gandalf intervenes, the trolls are preoccupied by an undirected conversation of the kind that Gandalf despises:

> 'Blimey, Bert, look what I've copped!' said William.
>
> 'What is it?' said the others coming up.
>
> 'Lumme, if I knows! What are yer?'. . . .
>
> It was just then that Gandalf came back. But no one saw him. The trolls had just decided to roast the dwarves now and eat them later – that was Bert's idea, and after a lot of argument they had all agreed to it.
>
> 'No good roasting 'em now, it'd take all night,' said a voice. Bert thought it was William's.
>
> . . . . [A]nd so the argument began all over again. (pp. 34–8)

The coarse speech of the trolls reflects an aggressive misuse of language; their colloquialisms ('copped') betray their immunity to the beauty of a well-turned phrase, their indifference to aesthetic beauty mirroring their indifference to moral virtue. When Gandalf enters the affray, he demonstrates his understanding that it is not what is said that is significant to these crude conversationalists, but that *something* is said. By weighing in with a remark which opens up an argument that is already finished, he wilfully misconstrues one form of conversational silence for another: effectively, he turns a 'lapse' (which occurs when talk has been discontinued) into a 'pause' (which occurs when one speaker hands over to another) (Schneider, 1988, p. 49). In so doing, he propels the interlocutors into conflict, violating the guiding maxim of conversation, which is precisely to avoid discord – and in so doing, saving the day, since the trolls squabble themselves into a death trap.

Among the many vitalizing effects of Gandalf's performative utterances (Austin, 1962) is their effect on Bilbo Baggins, who, in imitation, gradually begins to relinquish his comparatively unambitious desire for language simply to be constative – 'All the same, I should like it all plain and clear' (*The Hobbit*, p. 21). The hobbit is first called on to conjure words which do more than merely describe in his encounter with Gollum, where he is required to tread that ever-precarious line between providing witty banter and not causing offence. True to form, Baggins is initially conservative, intuitively adhering to the three golden rules of polite conversation: don't impose, give options and be friendly (Lakoff, 1973, pp. 292–305). But his interlocutor is a slippery operator, and it is not clear that politeness alone will secure the outcome that Bilbo seeks (being shown the way out). Gollum, it should be remembered, has not of late had much exposure to conversation, and what he seeks from the hobbit is the simple satisfaction of reciprocated talk. Bilbo, therefore, must deliver what Gollum requires, ensuring that the dialogue keeps moving forward through 'simple pairs of initiative and reaction moves' (Schneider, 1988, p. 34). But at the same time, Bilbo becomes aware that 'holding the floor is a position of power' (p. 48); he therefore cannot afford to fail to come up with something to say. Verbal gymnastics are not, at this early point in the novel, the hobbit's forte, and his conversational ineptitude is redeemed only by the fact that Gollum's is even worse: '[Bilbo's] tongue seemed to stick in his mouth; he wanted to shout out: "Give me more time! Give me time!" But all that came out with a sudden squeal was: "Time! Time!" Bilbo was saved by pure luck. For that of course was the answer' (*The Hobbit*, p. 73). Through his accidental verbal prowess, the hobbit quickly realizes that if he is to get what he needs out of the conversation, then he will have to start to dictate the terms on which it operates:

> 'What has it got in its pocketses? Tell us that. It must tell first.' . . .
>
> 'Answers were to be guessed not given,' [Bilbo] said.
>
> 'But it wasn't a fair questions,' said Gollum. 'Not a riddle, precious, no.'
>
> 'Oh well, if it's a matter of ordinary questions,' Bilbo replied, 'Then I asked one first. What have you lost? Tell me that?'
>
> 'What has it got in its pocketses?' . . .
>
> 'What have you lost?' Bilbo persisted. (pp. 76–7)

Disrupting the smooth sequence of initiative and reaction moves, the hobbit sneaks in a question of a completely different order (particular not abstract) which thrusts Gollum from a position in which he holds the trump card (knowledge of the way out) to one in which he lacks it (knowledge of what Bilbo has in mind). By taking the initiative in this way, Bilbo recalibrates the dynamism in operation between the two interlocutors, transforming the encounter from one in which Bilbo is subject to Gollum's whims to one in which Gollum is subject to his. Essentially, by substituting one kind of question for another, he has seized the critical advantage; by assuming the role of question-master, which enables him to dictate what kinds of questions can be asked, he relegates Gollum to a position in which he must provide reactive rather than initiative conversational moves. By enfeebling Gollum in this way, the hobbit makes it possible to get what he wants (his liberty) without surrendering in return what he cannot afford to give (the ring).

Although Bilbo does succeed in outwitting Gollum, it is more through good fortune than design, and he still has some way to go before he is able to wield words with the finesse displayed by Gandalf. This is because Gandalf has realized that in order to most effectively work their magic, words must give pleasure to their audience: we 'must have stories in any conversation in order to carry it forward. People cannot discuss abstractions for a considerable time without becoming wearied; they must have narratives, recitals of what people said or did' (Wright, 1936, p. 187). This is most vividly demonstrated by the elaborate and impeccably timed story he tells Beorn to seduce him into offering the travellers food and shelter. By telling a tale so captivating and so suspenseful, Gandalf places his listener in a position of such eagerness for the words to continue that he is prepared to offer whatever Gandalf desires in return. 'Oh let 'em all come! Hurry up! Come along, you two, and sit down! . . . But now please get on with the tale,' begs Beorn (*The Hobbit*, p. 112). In effect, Gandalf uses words as a kind of currency. In a variation on the childish use of words to clamour for what is wanted (usually food), in so doing materializing it, Gandalf offers words in exchange for what he wants (food again), arousing in his interlocutor a hunger to hear more which rivals his companions' hunger to eat: 'If all beggars could tell such a good [tale],' observes Beorn, 'they might find me kinder. You may be making it all up, of course, but you deserve a supper for the story all the same. Let's have something to eat!' (p. 114).

But equally important to the use of language to allure is its use to repel – using language not merely to exert power over the environment but also to *over*power it. The old adage might proclaim that 'sticks and stones will break my bones but words will never hurt me'. But of course, the very fact that a mantra is required to deny the potency of words suggests that the opposite is true: words *do* hurt. The capacity for words to cause injury rests, as Bilbo Baggins resolutely discovers, on the usurpation of control involved in naming. As Malinowski has noted, 'a name has the power over the person or thing which it signifies' (1923, p. 478), and to assume the role of endowing something with a name is to decide upon, and hence control the parameters of, its identity. When the hobbit is confronted by an enormous spiderlike creature in the wood, he fearlessly chants:

Old Tomnoddy, all big body,
Old Tomnoddy can't spy on me!
Attercop! Attercop!
Down you drop!
You'll never catch me up your tree! (p. 145)

By arrogating the right to name the creature, Bilbo subjects it to his rule, since the spider can do nothing to influence Bilbo's choice of words. In addition, by employing inane monikers which domesticate and hence enervate the creature ('Old Tomnoddy', 'Attercop'), he de-escalates the threat, transforming it from something undefined, and hence unassailable, into something knowable and consequently surmountable. The solution, it transpires, is spellbindingly simple – the hurling of verbal abuse.

Bilbo's resort to offensive rhymes is a child's tactic, drawn straight from the repertoire of playground lore. Childish as the trick may be, though, it is devastatingly effective: 'they stopped advancing, and some went off in the direction of the voice. "Attercop" made them so angry that they lost their wits' (*The Hobbit*, p. 149). Bilbo drives his antagonists into a frenzy by assaulting them with words calculated to wound. This is a speech act in a forcible sense: his words stun the spiders, ambushing them by bending them to his will. In a book concerned with magic, it is tempting to see Bilbo's song as a kind of incantation which enchants those who hear it; but in fact, to use language to 'repuls[e] outer things' is 'an arrangement biologically essential to the human race', one which we find even in 'the early articulated words sent forth by children [to] produce the very effect which these words *mean*' (Malinowski, 1923, p. 587). Tolkien's protagonist has reconnected with his childish, primal instincts and rediscovered his capacity to use words to transfigure, potentially even to annihilate, the world he inhabits.

It is the hobbit's newfound linguistic ingenuity which ultimately proves to be his greatest contribution to the adventure, since it is this that enables them to vanquish the dragon whose crimes they have travelled so far to avenge. In a virtuoso solo performance, when Bilbo Baggins is brought face to face with Smaug, he steps up to the occasion, bringing into play his entire range of newly acquired (or recalled) strategies in a virtuoso performance of verbal pyrotechnics:

> 'No thank you, O Smaug the Tremendous! . . . I did not come for presents. I only wished to have a look at you and see if you were truly as great as tales say. I did not believe them.'
>
> 'Do you now?' said the dragon somewhat flattered, even though he did not believe a word of it. . . . 'Who are you and where do you come from, may I ask?'
>
> 'You may indeed! I come from under the hill, and under the hills and over the hills my paths led. And through the air. I am he that walks unseen.'
>
> 'So I can well believe,' said Smaug, 'but that is hardly your usual name.'
>
> 'I am the clue-finder, the web-cutter, the stinging fly. I was chosen for the lucky number.' (p. 200)

Keenly aware of the need to avoid aggravating the volatile dragon, the hobbit cajoles him with wheedling falsities. Not only is this essential for keeping him on side (a basic skill for a good conversationalist), in addition to biding valuable time while the hobbit calculates his next move, it moreover works performatively to debilitate the dragon. The hobbit's flattery serves to make the dragon forget that he is conversing with a probable enemy, ensnaring him into the fateful trap of exposing his unprotected breast: '"Dazzlingly marvellous! Perfect! Flawless! Staggering!" exclaimed Bilbo aloud, but what he thought inside was: "Old fool! Why there is a large patch in the hollow of his left breast as bare as a snail out of its shell!"' (pp. 203–4). By pandering to the dragon's ego, the hobbit's sycophantic words cause the dragon to reveal his weakness. Crucially, Bilbo Baggins succeeds in doing this because he has first piqued the dragon's interest through his witty repartee. Gandalf has taught the hobbit well; Bilbo recognizes that the most effective means of harnessing the outcome he wants is to prove an entertaining interlocutor, hence his recourse to riddles – the form which served him so well with (against) Gollum. By this late point in the novel, though, the hobbit has gained the confidence to compose his own riddles and not merely to rely on other people's. The hobbit's creative flair elicits the grudging admiration of his antagonist, seemingly reversing the power dynamics between them. Thus the tiny hobbit, the burglar, whose only credible tools are his words, steals the dragon's thunder – setting in motion a trajectory of events that will result in the fearful creature's eventual demise and the accomplishment of the task that the adventurers had set out to complete.

If *The Hobbit* dramatizes the appeal of Tookishness over Bagginsishness, then in Deweyan terms, it also testifies to the appeal of *active* language over *static* language; of talk as a vivid *idea* to be shaped in the moment versus conversation as a frozen *ideal*, already preordained by existing rules; of speaking out as a form of resistance; of the *freedom* enacted in and through *criticism*. While the performativity of Tolkien's direct speech nostalgically transports the adult reader back to an imagined collective past in which words do not merely refer to things, they actually *do* things, it also tantalizes the newly literate critical child with the liberty that is theirs for the taking through an imperious command of verbal ideas.

7

On loving: Malcolm Saville's *Lone Pine* series

We picture lovers face to face but Friends side by side; their eyes look ahead. (Lewis, 1960, p. 66)

Little remembered today, and almost entirely ignored by the academic community since his death in 1982, in his heyday Malcolm Saville was one of Britain's most popular and critically acclaimed children's novelists. The early books in his *Lone Pine* series, the first of which was *Mystery at Witchend* (1943), sold in their millions and were credited by their followers with instilling in children a lifelong love of reading.[1] By the time he came to finish the series, however, its readership had largely ebbed away and Saville had to fight increasingly bitter battles to keep his work in print as he struggled to convince his publishers of the appeal to 1970s readers of the *Lone Pine* adventures' formulaic narratives and their adolescent characters' by-now implausible commitment to being 'true to each other whatever happens always' (*Mystery at Witchend*, p. 81). While these reassuringly familiar elements had appealed to children scattered and battered by the brutal years of the Second World War, by the time Saville had completed the twentieth, and final, novel of the series, *Home to Witchend* (1978), he was writing for a savvy audience with ready access to Paul Zindel and Judy Blume. As Kimberley Reynolds has shown, in this 'epoch of sexual liberation that occurred in the years after the contraceptive pill and before AIDS', for the first time 'pubescent and adolescent readers could find books about people of their own age, with feelings they recognised doing things with their bodies that they wanted to do – or indeed were succeeding in doing' (Reynolds, 2007, p. 115). This generation of readers had been reared to believe that sexuality was a vital and legitimate component of adolescent experience, and as such, they expected to find it voiced on the page.

In fact, Saville had from the start been alert to the young reader's requirement for literature to recognize the peculiar *Sturm und Drang* of adolescent desire. However, as Victor Watson observes in *Reading Series Fiction* (one of the few scholarly accounts to give any sustained critical attention to Saville's works), British printing conditions in this pre-*Lady Chatterley* trial era hardly encouraged the overt representation of sexuality in children's literature. Moreover, Saville had placed himself in a curious bind. The characters in his novels – at least, the most frequently focalized ones – were significantly older than the children of comparable mid-century Robinsonnade-esque series, notably Arthur Ransome's *Swallows and Amazons* (1930–47) and Enid Blyton's *Famous Five* (1942–62). As in these near-equivalent adventure-story series by Ransome and Blyton, the *Lone Pine* adventures typically take their young characters outdoors, away from adult interference, where they must rely on cooperation, stamina, nous and courage to survive the extreme conditions in which they find themselves. As in the *Swallows and Amazons* and the *Famous Five* series, Saville's characters comprise a mixed-age and mixed-sex gaggle in which the eldest male characters take on leadership roles and the eldest female characters take on maternal roles, while the younger characters must assert their usefulness to the group by acquiring skills and knowledge which elude the other characters. But where the characters in Ransome's and Blyton's novels are clearly prepubescent, Saville's eldest character, David Morton, is fifteen at the beginning of the series and eighteen by its end – and apart from his siblings, the twins, Richard and Mary, who are twelve by the end, the rest of the Lone Piners are also adolescent from the start. That is to say, the main characters are at an age when 'most . . . people will have outgrown the need to be with the "in-crowd." They will be spending more and more time in couple relationships which are also sexual in nature' (Roffey, Tarrant and Majors, 1994, p. 7). By introducing characters who are older than those habitually seen in mid-century adventure series fiction, Saville jeopardizes that key ingredient of children's series fiction which so successfully draws its readers back for more – communal friendship – since his adolescent characters, to be plausible as such, will be left unsatisfied both by platonic relationships and by belonging to a group.

In addition, quite apart from being older than the characters of books in similar series, Saville's characters were significantly older than the real readers[2] to which his novels were originally marketed. The real-life Lone Pine club, a promotional device set up in the 1950s by Saville's publishers, George Newnes Ltd, to capitalize on and further stimulate enthusiasm for his novels, ostensibly reached out to pre-teens. Membership of the club provided a free badge, a sheet of adhesive Lone Pine stamps and a membership card, and it invited fans of Saville's books to seek out (or convert) four fellow enthusiasts of the series and together form a Lone Pine club of their own.[3] Such a scheme was unlikely to appeal to real readers – or what Mavis Reimer terms 'actual readers' (Reimer, 2010, p. 5) – of a similar age to Saville's characters. Children are, of course, and always have been, accustomed to reading about characters older than they. But, as numerous commentators have pointed out, the pervasiveness well into the twentieth century of the Victorian denial of child sexuality – or the cultural dominance of what Freud referred to as 'infantile amnesia' (Freud, 2002, p. 173) – meant that British children of the middle decades of the twentieth century were not accustomed to seeing explored in print the physicality, actualized or imagined, of adolescent desire.[4] The real child audience to which Saville's novels sought to appeal thus lacked, or at least supposedly lacked, the linguistic and conceptual vocabulary with which to comprehend this category of experience of which adults deemed them – or, to reappropriate Jacqueline Rose's rhetoric, *desired* them – to be ignorant (Rose, 1984, p. xii).[5]

Representation of the romantic relationships forged by the adolescent fictional Lone Piners thus involved a precarious balancing act. On the one hand, acknowledgement of the physical component of their attraction to one another was necessary to ensure psychological verisimilitude, thereby tempering the boy's own adventure trappings of the stories with a quieter attentiveness to emotional nuance and securing a mixed-gender readership. But, on the other hand, ensuring the novels' commercial viability required *not* explicitly identifying or naming this sexual desire as such to Saville's implied pre adolescent audience. It has often been suggested that the aesthetics of children's literature are 'explicitly literal' – that children's literature prioritizes 'basic communicat[ion]', a premise which Maria Nikolajeva interrogates in *Aesthetic Approaches to Children's Literature* (2005, p. xv).[6] Saville's style in particular, where it has attracted the notice of critics at all (and this is infrequently), has been seen to exemplify this kind of 'basic' aesthetic mode. His narrative style has been dismissed, often in the same breath as Enid

Blyton's, as lacking any 'hardening, . . . ironic or even whimsical detachment to provide an alternative viewpoint for the author's derivative sequence of events' (Cadogan and Craig, 1976, p. 348). Whether literary aesthetics – even those intended for children – can ever remain explicitly literal is a thorny theoretical question. This discussion seeks to show, though, that in the case of Malcolm Saville, the apparently basic mode of communication which his novels appear to epitomize is a façade. Saville's narrative voice does indeed purport to promise transparency; but this illusion – idyll – of transparency is negated by the ways in which the textual signifiers carry with them the potential to lead a critical reader towards conclusions that directly undermine the avowals of the narrator. In fact, in his representation of the affective lives of his characters, Saville's approach is fundamentally gestural. To detect the operation of *eros* in the novels, Saville's readers must deploy sophisticated critical thought to infer from what Dewey terms the 'evidence' of grammar, syntax, figuration, mood (the whole gamut of literary devices) the sexual character of the relationships depicted. That is to say, Saville's novels, despite – indeed, in the very operation of – their apparently explicit aesthetics court a critical child reader whose readerly activity will not, indeed, *cannot*, passively accept the premises ostensibly offered, but instead, seizing the initiative and thinking laterally, actively pursues the *un*said.

At an explicit level, then, Saville treats the emergence of a distinctive form of intimacy between the three teenage couples (David and Petronella, alias Peter; Tom and Jenny; Jon and Penny) as a self-evident and uncontroversial fact, informing the implied reader via the authorial voice, the narrator, and through direct speech that certain characters are 'special friend[s]' with one another (*Seven White Gates*, p. 44). And yet any interrogation or explanation of what is entailed in being a 'special friend', a label repeated throughout the series, occurs only at an implicit level. The implied reader is thus required independently to establish the apparently clear meaning of this linguistic marker which purports to signal one variety of love (*philia*) while in fact signalling an altogether different form (*eros*). As Donald McCormick observes, the erotic anyway always communicates through 'code' (1992, p. 62); but the necessity for communicating in code is made uniquely urgent by the presumed naivety of the audience – certainly of the imagined audience – of mid-century children's literature. This discussion will consider the effect on the implied child reader[7] of Saville's multifaceted, even duplicitous, and certainly (to borrow Laura Mulvey's term) 'illusionistic' (1988, p. 67) mode of representation whereby the erotic potential of the novels' central relationships is officially denied and yet nonetheless implicitly conveyed. It will propose that, in requiring the implied reader to become literate in covert codes of sexuality, Saville generates in the implied reader a form of *scopophilia* – a 'desire to see and make sure of the private and the forbidden' (Mulvey, 1988, p. 59). It is this erotic desire which fuels the reader's (both actual and implied) craving for each next title in the series. However, in eventually surrendering to mounting readerly pressure to satisfy the series' accumulating erotic tension, Saville ultimately precipitates the end of his *Lone Pine* series. It transpires that the success of Saville's children's adventure series – like the success of popular romance novels – had relied on the suppression, or at the very least the non-satisfaction, of his characters', and as a consequence, his implied reader's, scopophilia.

The series' three central romantic relationships are identified as 'special friendships' even in what Gérard Genette would term the novels' 'peritexts.' From the fourth novel, *The Secret of Grey Walls* (1947), through to the last in the series, Saville prefixed brief descriptions of the main characters to the text proper, the potted character biographies appearing either after or as part of the author's prefaces. By making it possible for the novels to be read out of chronological order, they enable a reader unfamiliar with the earlier novels to pick up the series midway through. Through them, Saville ostensibly addresses the implied reader in his own voice – or, to be more exacting, the voice of what Wayne Booth proposed we call the 'implied author' (1973, p. 73). The presence of this voice draws our attention to the existence of an embodied creator located outside the world of the text: 'I first knew Romney Marsh and Oxney as a boy. . . . Soon after I came back to live in Sussex where I was born, I went again to Oxney and . . . determined to write a story of today linked with a part of our history. This is it' (*Treasure at Amorys*, p. 6). By passing off peritextual authorial interpretations *of* the text (such as those offered in the prefatory character synopses) as incontrovertible facts *from* it, Saville covertly reminds his implied audience, indeed insists, that ultimate control over the characters lies in the hands of their original creator. In so doing, he reclaims for the authorial voice (the implied author) any authority over the characters that might be threatened by their popularity among a possessive fan base of real readers in whose imaginations these characters have taken on lives of their own. When the character synopses, then, characterize David as Peter's 'special friend' (*Grey Walls*, p. 30, and in all synopses thereafter), a label which packages the relationship as one borne of *philia* and not of *eros*, the nature of the relationship as such appears irrefutable, defying the implied reader to place any alternative spin on the relationship; this, after all, is the say-so of the implied author himself. The relationship between David and Peter, while it is the relationship on which this discussion will focus, is not the only one which is identified from the outset as something beyond a run-of-the-mill friendship; similar authorial references to the two other central adolescent couplings in the series (Jenny and Tom, Penny and Jon) also alert us to an understanding of exclusivity which is quietly at play between the six older characters. In the case of these two other adolescent pairings, Saville avoids labels altogether. Instead, in his character synopses, he resorts to synecdoche, homing in on a quintessential attribute of the relationship as a means of gesturing towards, but never spelling out, how it might operate more generally. The entry for Jenny, therefore, states that 'although David sometimes loses patience with her, Tom never does' (p. 31), implying through this observation of Tom's tolerance of her idiosyncrasy the extent and durability of his affection. Penny's entry records that 'for as long as she can remember the most important person in her short life has been her cousin Jon, whom she teases and infuriates, but would follow to the end of the world' (p. 32).[8] Here, the invocation of romantic cliché enables Penny's loyalty to function metonymically to suggest a relationship predicated on unconditional commitment – a relationship that is unmistakeably a variety of romantic love (*eros*).

It is perhaps unsurprising, given the propensity in mid-century children's literature for the cognitive and physical to be gendered masculine in contradistinction to the feminized affective, that Saville's peritextual references to these adolescent relationships always tether them to the female characters; the boys' character descriptions make no mention of them. By rooting romantic intimacy in the female domain, Saville implies that it is brought into being by the girls – or at least that it is produced for them, inflicted on the passive boys, who have neither initiated nor consented to it, and who are perhaps not even conscious of its existence. Though each of the female characters is conscious that a peculiar form of intimacy binds her to her chosen male partner, the language with which she identifies this intimacy mimics, and hence reinforces, the denial of *eros* which Saville's peritextual material effects. Repeatedly, Peter refers to David as her 'special friend', duplicating (or pre-empting) the terminology that the implied author subsequently uses in the prefatory character descriptions, such that this phrase becomes the conventional, approved means of describing these adolescent relationships. In *Seven White Gates*, Peter reports,

> Last summer the nicest people I've ever met came to live at Witchend, because they'd been bombed in London. Their name is Morton. Their father was in the R.A.F. and that left Mrs. Morton, their mother, who is a darling; David my special friend, and the twins, Dickie and Mary. David is fifteen like me, and the twins are nine. You can't imagine anything like these two. They're awfully alike of course, but they are the grandest couple because they always stick up for each other, always do everything together and often seem to know exactly what the other is thinking without either of them saying a word. (*Seven White Gates*, p. 44)

This is the first explicit acknowledgement in the series that there is anything distinctive about the relationship between David and Peter. The significance of the revelation, however, is downplayed by its submerged position within the paragraph. Diverted by a flurry of extraneous information, the implied reader is unlikely to dwell on the passing mention of Peter's relationship with David, which, sandwiched between her explanations of the other members of the Morton household, is dismissed as an unremarkable, incidental detail. Consistent with the terminology used to identify it ('friend'), the relationship's assimilation into the familial context via its syntactical positioning legitimizes it, affirming its sanction by parental endorsement and corroborating its compatibility with homely values. By calling it a 'friendship', Saville presents the relationship as a species of a genus with which the implied reader is already familiar. Since by implication it is therefore unmysterious, then the implied reader need not further interrogate what such a relationship might involve. And yet, despite the ready and untroubled deployment of this label by the author, character and, later, narrator, the characters themselves – particularly the female characters – recognize that what being a special friend might involve is changeable at best, indeterminable at worst. Peter in particular is frequently represented as in a state of worry over it, and her attempts to grapple with the uncertainty it engenders provide the narrative tension of several novels, notably *The Neglected Mountain* (1953), *Not Scarlet But Gold* (1962) and *Home to Witchend* (1978). In *Not Scarlet But Gold*, free indirect discourse registers that the category of special friendship is not as clear-cut as the implied reader has been led to believe: 'David was the trouble. . . . No letter had come and, what was even worse, he had written to Jenny giving her a message to pass on – just as if she was a casual acquaintance rather than the best friend he was ever likely to have!' (p. 28) If David and Peter can so differently (fail to) perceive where the boundaries of 'best friend[ship]' lie, then where is the reader to draw them?

Mid-century readers of series fiction were practised in the art of deciphering the semiotics of friendship. Friendship, as commentators have often observed, is one of the keystones of such literature. Murray Knowles and Kirsten Malmkjaer identify it alongside family, gender, home, race and religion as one of the prominent 'institutions' traditionally represented in children's literature (1996, p. 32). Certain genres of series fiction that were highly popular during the middle of the twentieth century – the school story, for example – serve as a vehicle for an in-depth and often nuanced study of this form of sociability, as Sheena Wilkinson has discussed in *Friends in the Fourth* (2007). Friendship plays an especially important role in children's series fiction since not merely is it a key subject addressed in such books, but it also provides an apt analogy for the kind of relationship which the implied reader enters into with the characters. Victor Watson, for example, likens reading series fiction to 'going into a room full of friends' (2000, p. 6), suggesting that the implied reader of such works (albeit mistakenly) considers himself to stand in a comparable relationship to the characters in the texts as they stand to one another. So what sort of relationship does this entail? In popular series such as the *Swallows and Amazons*, the *Famous Five* and the *Chalet School* books, all written contemporaneously with Saville's *Lone Pine* series, friendships are invariably founded on the enjoyment derived from the sharing of common activities. This is the kind of friendship (*philia*) which for Aristotle 'exists because of the pleasant' (p. 212). Such friendship, he suggests, is typical among children, since 'the young . . . pursue what is pleasant for them and what is there in front of them' (p. 211). Aristotelian *philia* is the dominant variety of friendship depicted in mid-twentieth-century popular series fiction and implied child readers of this period were routinely called upon to unravel its textual trappings. According to the logic of such depictions of friendship, intimacy is conveyed via the evocation of *badinage* in direct speech; equality, by the focalization of no one character above another; cooperation, by the dramatization of action over the analysis of interiority; loyalty, by the demonstration of readiness to endanger one's own life to rescue another; and durability, by the repetition – hypothetically *ad infinitum* – of familiar rituals (camping; feasting; rule-breaking). But when the adjective 'special' is prefixed to 'friendship', how does it alter the sense of the noun? Does it serve merely to suggest an exemplary form of the same species? Or does it indicate a change in genus altogether – a change that introduces new signs for the implied reader to interpret? What, essentially, is a special friendship?

Aristotle's theorization of *philia* in fact makes room for a consummate form of friendship founded on shared activity – a type of *philia* that might well translate as something approximate to 'special' or 'perfect' friendship. For Aristotle, perfect friendship carries with it a commitment to the pursuit of virtue. Such friendship, he posits, represents a culmination of human possibility. It is 'the friendship between good people, those resembling each other in excellence,' he asserts, 'that is complete; for each of these wishes good things for the other in so far as he is good, and he is good in himself' (p. 211). In many ways, the characters who together comprise the relationship which lies at the heart of the *Lone Pine* series, David and Peter, who both exhibit exemplary morality, and who find in each other reflections of their own probity, epitomize precisely this kind of idealized friendship. And yet, it is not quite sufficient to suggest that what makes the friendship between these two characters different to the friendships between the other characters in the novels is a heightened degree of altruism. Take, for example, the moment when David and Peter are first reunited in the second novel, a moment which is delayed until nearly halfway through the book, despite – or no doubt because of – its anticipation by the implied reader. The very imbalance in focalization that its deferral produces (whereby Peter's perspective shapes the entire first half of the novel, after which the perspective alternates between the remaining characters) itself disrupts the narrative equilibrium typical of the depiction of friendship in literature of this genre, and hence signals a shift in the type of relationship (and indeed genre) with which we are being presented:

David half dozed for a minute or two and was roused by the peewit call. At the same time Sally whinnied. David jumped awake and called in return and a clear, cheerful voice cried,

> 'Where are you, David?'
>
> It was Peter! And suddenly there she was on the track just below him, and he realised that she had come from the other side of the rocks.
>
> Good old Peter! Just the same in her bright blue shirt and grubby shorts, and with her brown face and fair plaits and jolly grin. . . . They shook hands rather shyly and then, before David could answer, Macbeth whimpered and the storm broke with a shattering crash of thunder. . . . The shock was so great that Peter put her hands over her ears and crowded back against David. . . . Then the rain came in solid sheets. Peter's shirt turned dark blue as David watched her stupidly and helplessly, and the water poured down her neck from the rocks against which he was leaning. (*Seven White Gates*, p. 139)

What David seeks here is not to enrich Peter but to be enriched by her. He doesn't look *with* her; he could hardly more blatantly look *at* her. His might initially appear to be the open-mouthed 'determining male gaze' that for Laura Mulvey 'projects its phantasy onto the female figure which is styled accordingly' (1988, p. 837). And far from being united through participation in a common interest, David and Peter are held apart by their acute awareness of one another's physical presence. Saville's contemporary, C. S. Lewis, who resuscitated for his mid-twentieth-century audience the ancient world's more variegated understanding of love (a variegation typically elided by modern English vocabulary), insists that 'friendship, unlike Eros, ignores . . . our physical bodies' (Lewis, 1960, p. 70). Here David's pleasure in this scene (his scopophilia) stems precisely from an appreciation of Peter's appearance – her legs, her skin, her hair. Likewise, Peter's breathiness, her series of hasty questions, her trailing away into ellipsis all belie the jangled nervousness that his tangible presence provokes. This, then, is not a form of friendship as Lewis understands the term; and nor is it strictly a form of special or perfect friendship, at least in as far as Aristotle conceives it. The additional ingredient of physical or emotional longing, however muted, which marks precisely the characters' separateness, even if this separateness brings them together in what Bracha Ettinger, revising Mulvey, terms a 'matrixial gaze' in which Peter is 'fully active' – in which she is a 'co-emerging self' who 'inform[s]'

David's 'knowledge', and not an 'Other' (Ettinger, 2006, p. 218) – makes this an altogether altered form of love. It makes it what Lewis, following Aristotle, identifies as *eros*. As Lewis recognizes, 'Nothing is less like a Friendship than a love-affair. Lovers are always talking to one another about their love; Friends hardly ever about their Friendship. Lovers are normally face to face, absorbed in each other; Friends, side by side, absorbed in some common interest' (Lewis, 1960, p. 61). Despite what the implied author's remarks might tell us, and despite what the characters themselves may say, the relationship between David and Peter, even as early as the second novel, is not a friendship at all – special or otherwise.

To ascertain what is meant by the 'special friendship' that exists between David and Peter – or, more accurately, to establish that it has been misleadingly branded as such in the first place – the critical reader, then, must dare to ignore, or even to reject, its characterization by both the implied author and the narrator. That is to say, the critical child must refuse to occupy the role of implied reader that the text proffers. Instead, the critical child must learn to trust not merely that he or she might possess information that is equal to or greater than that possessed by the characters embedded within the scene, but moreover that his or her capacity to read that scene might surpass that of any of its characters – and even the narrator. This relegation of the characters to positions of comparative unconsciousness is played out in the above encounter. David's drowsiness at the beginning of the scene figuratively denotes his inability consciously to interpret the ways in which Peter's physical presence troubles and delights him. Her arrival while he is asleep creates the impression that she has appeared as if in a dream – that her emergence acts out a private fantasy. The arousal of his desire is tacitly communicated in free indirect discourse via the repetition of the exclamation mark, heralding his excited state. The disarray of his emotions is registered by the abrupt compression of time ('And suddenly'); the moment is running away with itself, beyond his control, and impulse has taken over. These textual signifiers endow the implied reader with insight into the temporarily debilitating nature of his attraction to Peter, insight which the character himself appears to lack. The alert implied reader will thus be aware that a 'shy' handshake makes for something of a lame culmination to the mounting sexual tension, and that when Peter 'crowd[s] back against David', though it is passed off by the narrator as a blunder caused by the sudden onset of the storm, *this* is the real climax of the sequence, registering as it does the characters' palpable yearning for full bodily contact – a yearning so acute that it momentarily paralyzes David as he is captivated by her wet T-shirt.

In shifting the responsibility for the exposure of sexual desire away from the narrator and the characters and onto the implied reader, Saville sidesteps the problem of seeming to address subject matter too mature for his young audience. Ironically, though, obscuring the representation of sexuality in this way fuels its scope for titillation. In their very attempt to conceal the erotic, the novels serve to inflame it.[9] By virtue of the proactive role that the critical child must take in scrutinizing the characters' body language to establish the state of play between them, the characters, in particular the female characters, assume the capacity to function as erotic objects. Small wonder, then, that the novels' treatment of adolescent desire, for all it is downplayed by the implied author, proves to be one of the series' most potent elements. Even a reader who encounters the text without the aid of Bertram Prance's vivid illustrations, which accompanied the first editions, can hardly avoid noticing what Peter looks like, since her appearance is described in seductively precise detail throughout. Even the character synopses repeatedly conjure her chiefly in terms of her physical attributes:

> Imagine Peter with two fair plaits, fearless blue eyes and a clear brown skin. She looks her best in jodhpurs and a blue shirt. She . . . loves birds, animals and everything in the open air, and can swim faster than most boys of her age and ride a hundred times better. . . . Her life was changed when the Mortons came to Witchend, for then she realized how lonely she had been. . . . David is her special friend. (*Lone Pine Five*, pp. 29–30)

This mode of characterization places the critical child in a compromising position. On the one hand, the allusion to Peter's passions (her 'love' of the countryside as well as her 'lonel[iness]') solicits readerly empathy; it invites the reader to take on Peter's emotions as his or her own, equipping them with the means to view the world from Peter's perspective. At the same time, though, the emphasis on Peter's outward form requires us not solely to imagine *being* Peter but to imagine *watching* her. Potentially, this too might open up the possibility for empathy – empathy with Peter's capacity for self-reflexivity, or more probably with David's desire for her – but it is equally likely to provoke a form of readerly jealousy, whereby the reader desires Peter not on David's behalf but on their own. The characterization of David, which remains oddly restrained throughout the series (despite the impression created by the passage quoted earlier, he is rarely focalized, and we emerge with only a vague sense of what he looks like or gets up to beyond the confines of the stories), perhaps tacitly registers the threat that David poses to the reader and modulates his presence accordingly. The comparative accentuation of Peter's physicality, then, opens up a spatial gap between the reader and character; it situates the reader at a remove and invites him or her to occupy a position from which to enjoy the imagined tactility of her skin and voluptuousness of figure. However, the legitimacy of the erotic male gaze enabled by this position is safeguarded by Peter's trademark 'fair plaits'. These plaits, which are referenced with such frequency in the series that they become emblematic, encapsulate the tension at play in Saville's treatment of his adolescent characters' sexuality. On the one hand, the length and blondeness of her hair inserts Peter into a well-known tradition of literary seductresses (Helen of Troy; Rapunzel; Milton's Eve); and yet on the other, her arrangement of this hair into tidy plaits roots her firmly in the realm of childhood, underscoring her acceptance, even her espousal, of an adult convention designed to ensure the child's uniformity and functionality over her individuality and aesthetic allure. The fact that even for the 1940s, Peter's wholesome look is jarringly anachronistic (particularly for a sixteen-year-old) further complicates the picture; it makes her appropriation of a hairstyle that symbolizes non-awareness of sexuality a deliberate, and hence knowing, decision. Until she shears off her plaits towards the end of the series, signalling her consent to being viewed as an erotic object, or as Mulvey formulates it, her consent 'to hol[d] the look, and pla[y] to and signif[y] male desire', it is therefore unclear to what extent the reader – like David – is permitted to indulge the scopophilia stimulated by the narrative insistence on the delectability of her appearance (Mulvey, 1988, p. 837).

To continue to view Peter as an erotic object involves the critical child striking out on her own, trusting her own sceptical faculties in the face of the characters' purported ignorance and the narrator's obdurate reticence. It thus implicates the reader if not in a direct refutation of narratorial authority, then at least in a confrontation, however unconscious, of the limitations of third-person (supposedly omniscient) narrative. It requires acknowledgement that one can rely on the narrator only up to a point to keep the reader in the picture. For a child reader conceived along the lines which Rose proposed – one who acquires definition in a 'world in which the adult comes first (author, maker, giver) and the child comes after (reader, product, receiver)' (1984, pp. 1–2) – such a realization is at once liberating and bewildering. Licensed to unearth knowledge deemed unsuitable for the characters, the critical child is given – or grants herself – access to that which is presumably unsuitable for her too. Perry Nodelman has suggested that such 'supposedly adult material present as the shadow of texts of children's literature . . . is possibly even *intentionally* available to [child readers], as a requisite part of the process by which adults use non-childlike knowledge in their efforts to teach children how to be childlike' (2008, p. 209). But in the case of Malcolm Saville's *Lone Pine* series, the guilty thrill of superiority that the detection of this 'shadow' kindles is made doubly intoxicating by the fact that the implied reader – and in all probability the real reader too – is younger than the books' characters. The critical reader's intellectual maturity is thus flattered. Far from reaffirming her childlikeness, the narrative allows the reader to feel confident that her powers of insight exceed those not merely of the characters but moreover of the implied reader – to feel that she has been entrusted with sensitive information that is usually withheld from mere children. Even as they adhere to a seemingly basic mode of communication wherein an implied adult author addresses an implied child reader, Saville's novels therefore refuse to construct the child reader along the ignorant and disenfranchized lines envisaged by Rose and, in a more modulated way, Nodelman. On the contrary, the reader of Saville's fiction is – indeed, must be – a sceptical, knowing and critically independent figure.

Suppose, though, that the critical child has misread the signs. The illicit knowledge that the reader *thinks* that she has gleaned might transpire not to be knowledge at all. Even the most painstaking of readers might turn out to have been picking up the wrong clues, or wrongly piecing them together, all along. With a narrator who refuses to corroborate the reader's findings – indeed, a narrator whose interventions expressly negate the reader's findings – how is the reader to verify what he or she believes, but cannot prove, to be the case? All this uncertainty works to galvanize the critical child reader's desire to be presented with further signs: to continue to scrutinize the interaction between Peter and David to establish more convincingly what the characters' special friendship involves. This readerly desire, however, carries with it a lethal sting. In willing the characters to express their feelings less ambiguously, the critical child essentially wills the characters to grow up. This poses something of a conundrum. To affirm the reader's own understanding of sexuality, the characters must become conscious of, essentially reveal, their erotic interests in one another. But the erotic, as is well known, is by its nature contingent on only partial exposure of the love object.[10] Nothing is more likely to destroy the erotic than unrestricted access to the object of desire. To reveal what lies behind the erotic – to remove the veil – is therefore to do away with it. Moreover, no longer to keep the reader guessing, to confirm that the reader's inklings were right all along, eliminates the need for the reader to read on; no longer ignorant, the reader has found what she was looking for.[11] The extinction of readerly desire spells the end of the series, since if there is no curiosity left to satisfy, there is no longer a role for the narrative to carry out. Management of the erotic is thus a hazardous business for the children's series fiction writer – and for the children's writer more generally. Saville must attempt to satisfy the reader's desire for the characters to evolve and to confront the sexual underpinnings of their relationships while still keeping her guessing.

The incompatibility of these twin impulses dogs Saville's *Lone Pine* series, and, perhaps inevitably, it is what eventually kills the series off. By acknowledging and giving in to readerly desire – by letting the characters acknowledge and give into their desires – Saville ties up the overarching narrative threads, but in so doing he makes the implied reader, and then the critical child reader, and, of course, in turn, the real reader, redundant, since eventually there is no more guessing to be done. Perspicaciously, Saville defers the problem as long as he can by adopting the tried-and-tested strategy successfully accomplished by so many series-fiction writers before him: by refusing to let the characters age, however many school holidays might pass. At the same time, he also ensures that where the characters do show glimmers that they might be on the brink of grasping the implications of their feelings for one another, their insights are temporally displaced. In the seventh novel of the series, *The Neglected Mountain* (1953), for example, consciousness of their sexual interest in one another momentarily flickers through David and Peter before it is quickly batted away again. This consciousness, though, is attributed not to the present but to the future:

> Nobody would have described David as good-looking, but Peter was quite sure that no other boy could possibly look as friendly and nice, while David, not usually shy, suddenly realized that one day, and very soon now perhaps, other people would look at Peter and see that she was a very beautiful girl. (*The Neglected Mountain*, p. 59)

Such a depiction places David in a nonsensical, indeed an impossible, position: he is represented as pre-empting his own future consciousness even during his current state of unconsciousness (or at least semi-consciousness). By projecting the characters' awareness of the sexual implications of their exclusive friendship into the future in this way, Saville underscores the supposedly adult qualities of such awareness, steering the implied child reader's attention back to the world of childhood friendships. Moreover, he reinforces the undesirability of premature entry into the adult world by showing the characters themselves attempting to stall the process: '"It's odd to think we're getting old so quickly. I don't think I like it," Peter reflects in the same novel; and David concurs: "I don't either. On a morning like this I want to stay this age"' (*Neglected*, p. 120). The characters' resistance to that which the critical child is eager to accelerate buys Saville extra time, but it cannot avert the inevitable. This is because from the very start, by introducing thematic trappings which belong to the romance genre (however much the plots might be structured according to the logic of the adventure story), Saville provides the series with a teleology that inexorably propels the overarching narrative towards marriage. Even in the first novels, there are clues that the intermingling of the families will one day be formally ratified; and certainly by the fourth novel, it is clear that marriage with David is the expected, albeit unstated, outcome for Peter: Mr Sterling 'told her once again how glad he was that she had made such good friends as the Mortons and how he wished her to see as much of them as she could. . . . [He] twinkled at her over the top of his glasses. "You don't think you're always going to live with your old father, do you, my dear?"' (*Grey Walls*, p. 103). As ever, the character does not know what to make of her father's 'twinkle' – 'Peter was very thoughtful as she lit a hurricane lamp and went out to saddle Sally' (p. 103) – while the critical child, conversant with the fairy-tale romance tradition in which countless aged fathers have bequeathed their beautiful daughters to suitors who prove themselves worthy, knows full well the fate that lies in store for Peter.[12] Via these clues about the future, the reader is invited to project onto the present an element of fairy-tale romance that is not overtly represented or admitted by either the characters or narrator, but which is embedded in the very mingling of the genres that comprise the series.

Clearly, however, a position wherein the reader's consciousness substantially outstrips that of the characters cannot be sustained indefinitely. During the middle novels of the series – in those novels written during the late 1950s and early 1960s – the shadow of this dilemma begins to loom larger over the series. In the twelfth novel, *Mystery Mine* (1959), Saville acknowledges the difficulty it poses by announcing, somewhat defensively, in the novel's Preface that real readers 'who have known the members for some time have asked that they should not grow up from book to book, and so they continue to have adventures at their present ages' (pp. 9–10). The very fact that he perceives a need to speak to the issue testifies to the trouble it is causing him. By drawing attention to the deliberateness of his attempts to curtail the erotic, though, Saville merely exacerbates yet further the difference between the consciousness accorded to the characters and that of the implied reader; his characters' plausibility as adolescents begins to hang in the balance. As the 1950s folded into the 1960s, and as the momentum of the overarching romance mounted, it became untenable for Saville to continue to evade his characters' adolescent desires. Evidently, too, real readers had been contacting Saville requesting that the characters' emotional maturity begin to match their supposed ages. Thus, in the fourteenth novel, *Not Scarlet But Gold* (1962), Saville finally confronts the unavoidable:

> Over the years some readers have asked me never to let the Lone Piners get any older and others have felt, quite rightly I'm sure, that it is now time for the David and Peter of the first story, published nearly twenty years ago, to behave as if they are sixteen today. So now, at last, you older, faithful friends of the Lone Piners may notice that these characters are facing their adventures – and indeed each other – as if they were living in the 1960's. (p. 6)

Tellingly, the tone in which Saville makes this announcement is one of defeat. The repetition of phrases that emphasize the present moment ('now'; 'at last') invests the occasion with a sense of finality. His unconvincing, unnecessary aside, 'quite rightly I'm sure', betrays the reluctance of his capitulation to the demands of his real audience, an audience whom he casts in the role of 'faithful friends', discreetly petitioning for continued loyalty from those existing readers on whom he will come to rely with increasing desperation, since the axe he is about to blow will remove the reason for all but the most determined fans to persevere with the rest of the series. Saville thus paves the way for a shift in rhetoric – a retreat from the rhetoric of *philia* and an embracing for the first time of the rhetoric of *eros* – culminating in the moment for which the critical child has been waiting:

> 'I know now that I've loved you from the day, up on the Mynd, when I first met you.' . . .
>
> Suddenly she was being kissed and when she recovered her breath and said, 'David! You've never done that before,' he kissed her again.
>
> 'That's a pity,' he laughed. 'I grew up yesterday, Peter. There's never been any girl but you but I've been a fool not to tell you –' (p. 250)

As is consistent with the characters' earlier pre-emption of what they might later feel, here their recognition of their mutual desire is retroactive, projected back in time so that it appears to have been there all along (confirming, of course, what the critical reader always knew). But the narrative climax at this point in the series – merely the fourteenth out of a total twenty titles – is premature; for, as has already been discussed, the series, through the generic conventions on which it draws, has effectively promised the reader a conclusion in marriage, and what this moment gives us is an acknowledgement of love, not an engagement. Following suit, the brewing romance between Jon and Penny is clinched in the next book of the series, *Treasure at Amorys* (1964), and Tom and Jenny swear their undying affection in the book after that, *Man with Three Fingers* (1966). As the younger characters, Dickie and Mary, embarrassed by the disclosure of yet 'another love affair', resentfully observe in the closing words of *Treasure at Amorys*: 'I s'pose we've had this one [on our hands] nearly as long as David and Peter. We shall get used to it I s'pose' (p. 191). By bringing the hitherto-concealed erotic vein into the open, not just once, but three times over, and by bringing the narrative tension to a peak just three-quarters of the way through the series, Saville thus replaces one set of problems with another: if the series is to continue (and, contrary to the express views of his publisher and despite its dwindling popularity, Saville was adamant that it would), and if generic conventions dictate that it is eventually to result in marriage, then how is it to maintain the critical reader's interest in the meantime?

Saville had trained his reader to look out for the signs: to delight in the thrill of picking up on what the characters themselves had missed. But in an abrupt reversal, from this point in the series onwards, the characters are for the first time in possession of knowledge which exceeds that of the implied reader. Furthermore, it is a form of knowledge which cannot be shared with the implied reader, both on aesthetic grounds (prolonged analysis of the sweet nothings transacted between lovers has no place in the fast-paced adventure story) and on ideological grounds (graphic depiction of adolescent intimacy was not what the parents of real child readers had come to expect from the children's wing of respectable publishing house George Newnes). The critical child is thus in danger of being bored by the repetition involved in continual reiteration of the characters' love for one another, and at the same time alienated by the narrator's refusal to elaborate further on what this love might entail. As the characters serially couple off and retreat into the privacy of their relationships, the result is a kind of narrative stagnancy as the same moment of romantic epiphany is presented, as if for the first time, again and again:

> The firelight glinted on her beautiful golden hair as she looked down at her folded hands, thinking carefully as she always did before she spoke.
>
> David, with a sudden lump in his throat, thought, 'She's my girl. Ever since I first saw her riding her pony at Witchend it's been like this.'
>
> And Jon, with a quick glance down at Penny's copper head thought, 'Penny for me and David for Peter. That's how the world goes round. May the four of us always be the same to each other.' (*Rye Royal*, p. 124)

As soon as Saville explicitly identifies as such the *eros* encoded in his novels, they begin to lose their grip on the critical child. The decline in popularity of Saville's fiction among real readers from the 1970s onwards can in part be attributed to the changing tastes of the age. However, children are not usually put off by a novel's saturation in the values of a bygone era, as is demonstrated by the enduring success of series written by Enid Blyton and

Arthur Ransome – series in which, if the protagonists age at all, it is only imperceptibly. Instead, I would propose that Saville's *Lone Pine* series lost its audience because it attempted to satisfy the demands of the erotic within a form (children's adventure-story series fiction) which cannot accommodate the gratification of desire – or at least, can accommodate it only as a finale. In so doing, it made redundant the critical child reader whom the early novels had so successfully cultivated, since Saville had trained that reader to read with sexual curiosity, a scopophilia which is stymied by the static reiteration of the characters' unchanging love for one another. What began as a strategy to avoid directly confronting the sexual to ensure the appropriateness of his subject matter for a young audience turned out to be a highly successful formula for stimulating the critical child reader's thirst to read on – an approach from which the children's author departs at his cost.

Coda

got to pop?
pop where?
pop what?

(Michael Rosen, 'A Busy Day')

'Who's there?' Shakespeare's endlessly enigmatic play compels us to ask; and, for good measure, 'To be or not to be? (*Hamlet*, I.i.1; III.i.56).' Few works of literature – few questions – have inspired quite so much critical activity. This activity, packaged in the familiar forms of essays and lectures, articles and monographs, seems such especially *adult* activity. But what of the questions that the child asks in and of her reading matter? 'Got to pop? pop where? pop what?' Are these questions so very different in kind? What kind of activity is entailed in the asking and answering of the imagined child reader's wonderings?

In the Introduction to this book, I outlined John Dewey's concept of critical thinking in an attempt to highlight its usefulness for literary scholars. In true Deweyan spirit, this book is a thought experiment, motivated by an attempt to solve a problem. It has tested out a hypothesis (an idea which, as Dewey anticipates, I now realize that I had already been busy testing unconsciously, long before consciously embarking on the book, without knowing that this was the case). The proposition lying at the heart of this book is that when children read literary texts, they carry out a form of sceptical, investigative, dynamic, practical reading that can best be characterized as *critical activity*. To test out this idea, I have, as Dewey recommends, collected first-hand evidence by closely reading the signs available in a range of literary texts; I have scrutinized this evidence, and I have subjected it to the back-and-forth processes of induction and deduction. The course of study has been deliberate and purposeful, and orderly, systematic steps have been taken in restricted conditions. The author of this study has perhaps not always succeeded in demonstrating the disciplined habits which Dewey so prized (further training may be necessary), but she has allowed herself room to be creative and playful, and she has taken the odd risk. She has most certainly taken her time.

Literature's Children, as Dewey aspired for all experiments in critical thinking to be, has been motivated by distinct personal interest – by an obdurate fascination with the routine capacity of children to ask the unanswerable and cut to the quick, coupled with, I confess, an equally obdurate fascination with the apparently sophisticated critical practices which we institutionalize in adulthood and, for all their cleverness, their all-too-routine failure to hit that same spot. Inasmuch as the reasoning carried out over the course of this book has arrived at a judgement, it is that the imagined child reader, restless seeker of answers to endless supplies of question, can fruitfully be understood as a kind of critic; and that, by extension, criticism can fruitfully be understood as an activity of which the child is not only capable, but for which they turn out to be peculiarly well suited. It would be every bit as ludicrous, however, to propose that child readers are somehow *more* critical than any other readers than it would be to assume, as has so often been the case, that they are necessarily *less* critical than other readers. The purpose of this book has not been to carve out a special status for the critical child – to idealize her; to romanticize her; to turn her into art. It has rather been to carve out a space in which to observe the idea: to analyze it, to experiment with it, and in so doing, to attempt better to understand something of the complicated aesthetic and didactic exchanges that take place in and through children's literature.

There can be no conclusion, of course, for the point all along was not to uncover the answer, or to learn a lesson, but to gain from the hands-on experience of *doing*. It seems fitting, though, to end with the Deweyan sentiment that spurred me on to the finishing line: 'Strictly speaking, not the target but *hitting* the target is the end in view' (*DE*, p. 112). How right he is – as the critical child knew all along.

Notes

Introduction

1 See also Roberta Trites's excellent account of the workings of power in adolescent literature (2000).

2 See, for example, Marion Lochhead (1977). The term 'golden age' had passed into popular use by children's authors at least as early as 1888, when Ismay Thorn found the phrase apt to entitle one of her (now little-remembered) children's books, *The Golden Age: A Story of Four Merry Children* (1888).

3 For example, John Rowe Townsend (1967), Peter Hunt (1994a), Matthew Grenby (2008), Karen Coats (2017).

4 See Kimberley Reynolds (2011).

5 See Perry Nodelman (1988).

6 This is a term coined by Morag Styles in *From the Garden to the Street* (1998).

7 The term has acquired particular prominence in children's literature criticism. See, for example, Deborah O'Keefe (2003) and Jackie Wullschlager (1995).

8 See Introduction to Wakely-Mulroney and Joy (2018, pp. 11–23).

9 For a useful account of Dewey's influence, see Richard Stanley Peters (1977).

10 For a fuller account of Dewey's ideas about education, see Raymond D. Boisvert (1998) and Michael Bonnett (1994).

11 Other key figures associated with progressive education include Friedrich Froebel, Helen Parkhurst, Rudolf Steiner and Maria Montessori.

12 Take, for example, Natasha Glaisyer and Sara Pennell (2003).

13 This is starting to change. See, for example, Lisa Sainsbury (2017).

14 For a brilliant account of this problem, see Clémentine Beauvais (2013).

15 For more on the influence of Dewey's ideas about critical thinking on the philosophy of education, see, for example, Kwame Glevey (2006) and James Scott Johnson (2006) and (2008).

16 See Philip Sidney, 'Defence of Poesy' (1973); John Dryden, 'Of Dramatick Poetry' (1939); William Wordsworth, *'Preface' to Lyrical Ballads* (1974); Percy Bysshe Shelley, 'Defence of Poetry' (1977); Oscar Wilde, 'The Critic as Artist' (1909); T. S. Eliot, 'The Function of Criticism' (1951). See also, for example, Margalit Fox's *New York Times* obituary to Heaney (2013).

17 See Thomas De Quincey (1863) and Hartley Coleridge (1851).

18 See, for example, Algernon Charles Swinburne's 'A Child's Future' (1905) and James Joyce's A *Portrait of the Artist as a Young Man* (1960).

19 This idea is attributed to Pablo Picasso in a *Time* magazine article from 4 October 1976 (Davidson, 1976). See Francis Bacon's *Novum Organum* (1905) and John Stuart Mill's *System of Logic* (1973).

20 One scholar who has acknowledged the nimble ways in which children absorb narrative is Andrew Stibbs, whose *Reading Narrative as Literature* (1991) explores the practical implications in the classroom of the inquisitive ways in which children read.

21 This is a view perpetuated by many oft-cited works of literary theory including T. S. Eliot's 'Tradition and the Individual Talent' (1951); Jacques Derrida's *Acts of Literature* (1992) and Paul de Man's 'The Resistance to Theory' (1982), which are each underpinned – albeit in substantially different ways – by the idea that reading critically is a hard-won skill borne of effort and honed through purposeful exposure to a wide range of literary works.

22 See Matthew Arnold's 'The Function of Criticism at the Present Time' in Arnold (1960–77).

23 See Jean-Jacques Rousseau's *The Social Contract* (1973).

24 See Roland Barthes's 'Death of the Author' in Barthes (1977); Michel Foucault, 'What Is an Author?' in Foucault (1991); Wolfgang Iser, *The Act of Reading* (1978); Derek Attridge, *The Singularity of Literature* (2004).

25 For a fuller account of Dewey's influence on progressive education, see, for example, Jerome A. Popp (1998), Philip W. Jackson (2002) and James Scott Johnston (2006, 2008).

26 For a fuller account of discovery or experiential learning, see, for example, David A. Kolb (1983) and Lee A. Shulman and Evan R. Keislar (1966).

27 It is for this reason that progressivist educators facilitate physical movement in, around, and beyond the classroom, perceiving the process of discovery necessarily to entail motion.

28 For a useful, if now rather dated, overview of philosophical idealism, particularly in the nineteenth-century German tradition, see E. C. Ewing (1934). For a more recent account, see Robert Pippin (1997). My own use of the term is confined to the more narrow understanding that it acquires in Dewey's account of education, outlined above.

29 See Gérard Genette (1980).

30 Dewey does not directly refer to Freud in this work, but it is worth noting the temporal overlap between the lives of the two men, who were both born in 1859, Sigmund Freud dying in 1939 and John Dewey dying in 1952.

31 See Harry C. Boyte (2003). See also Daniel W. Stuckart (2012).

32 See Paulo Freire (1973) and bell hooks (2010). For commentary on critical pegagogy, see César Augusto Rossato, Ricky Lee Allen, Marc Pruyn (eds) (2006) and Joe L. Kincheloe (2004).

33 This was a belief largely shared by Dewey's contemporary, Bertrand Russell, who also wrote extensively on the philosophy of education but nonetheless disagreed with Dewey on one significant point: 'I should wish to agree completely,' Russell wrote, 'but to my regret I am compelled to dissent from his most distinctive philosophical doctrine, namely the substitution of "inquiry" for "truth" as the fundamental concept of logic and theory of knowledge' (1945, p. 819). See also Russell (1926).

34 See Nigel Blake, Paul Smeyers, Richard Smith and Paul Standish (2002); Amélie Oksenberg Rorty (1998); and Nel Noddings (1995).

35 Michael Rosen (2000, p. 62).

36 Peter Hollindale (1997).

37 See, for example, Judith Plotz (2001), Alan Richardson (1994) and Ann Wierda Rowland (2012).

38 See, for example, Paulo Freire, who advocates the need for education to cultivate a questioning consciousness in the child (1973).

39 Peter Hollindale observes this same problem in *Signs of Childness*.

40 See, for example, Paul Alpers (1996) and Terry Gifford (1999).

41 Hollindale (1997).

42 For a compelling account of the importance of hope in the formation of culture, see Ernst Bloch (1995).

43 Scholars who have theorized this term in illuminating ways include George Boas (1966), Neil Postman (1982), James Kincaid (1994) and Ann Higonnet (1998).

1 Eighteenth-century children's poetry and the complexity of the child's mind

1 For more on the ballad tradition in this period, see Robin Ganev (2009).

2 For a recent account of how children's poetry of the later eighteenth and early nineteenth century (the romantic period) takes up this invitation, see Donelle Ruwe (2014).

2 Laughter and the permission to critique

1 See David Nokes (1988) and Martin C. Battestin (1974).

2 For an efficient account of the Puritan antipathy to laughter, see Anca Parvulescu (2010).

3 For example, see John Newbery, *A Little Pretty Pocket-Book* (1744).

3 On seeing: Kate Greenaway's *Under the Window*

1 See Anya Krugovoy Silver (2000).

2 See Anne Lundin (1993), M. H. Spielmann and G. S. Layard (1905) and A. K. Silver (2000).

3 Notable exceptions include Morag Styles's *From the Garden to the Street* (1998); the collection *Poetry and Childhood*, edited by Morag Styles, David Whitley and Louise Joy (2010); Catherine Robson's *Heart Beats: Everyday Life and the Memorized Poem* (2012); Debbie Pullinger's *From Tongue to Text: A New Reading of Children's Poetry* (2017); and Katherine Wakely-Mulroney and Louise Joy (eds), *The Aesthetics of Children's Poetry* (2018).

4 James Kincaid (1994); Jacqueline Rose (1984).

5 For a powerful critique of this view, see Marah Gubar (2011).

6 In fact, no words – whether in prose or versified – could ever fulfil a merely descriptive function to image, since the very form of the picture book derives from the interrelatedness of word and image, whether consonantly or dissonantly so. See Perry Nodelman, *Words about Pictures* (1988); Maria Nikolajeva and Carole Scott, *How Picturebooks Work* (2003).

7 See Lawrence Klein (1994).

8 See, for example, 'Hey Diddle' or 'Sing a Song of Six Pence' in *Mother Goose: Nursery Rhymes* (1965).

4 On crying: E. Nesbit's *The Railway Children*

1 See, for example, John Rowe Townsend (1967) and Seth Lerer (2008).

2 See Chamutal Moimann (2005).

3 See Louise Joy (2013) for an earlier discussion of this question.

5 On being (bored): Kenneth Grahame's *The Wind in the Willows*

1 Svendsen suggests that the 'word "boring" is bound up with the word "interesting"; the words become widespread at roughly the same time and they increase in frequency at roughly the same rate' (2005, p. 28).

6 On talking: J. R. R. Tolkien's *The Hobbit*

1 Prominent studies of Tolkien's language include: Verlyn Flieger (1983); Tom Shippey (1982); William Provost (1990); Alan McComas (1993); Mary Zimmer (1995); C. W. Sullivan III, in Perry Nodelman and Jill May (1985); and Michael Livingstone (2012).

7 On loving: Malcolm Saville's *Lone Pine* series

1 In an interview with Malcolm Saville for *Books for Keeps*, Pat Triggs estimated that over two million *Lone Pine* books had been sold by 1980. As evidence of his influence on children, she cites a thirteen-year-old fan who enthuses, 'If there were many writers like you, many more people would read out of school time' (1980, n. pag.).

2 I am here following the distinctions between 'characterized', 'implied' and 'actual' readers laid out by Mavis Reimer (2010).

3 For a discussion of Saville's audience, including excerpts from his prolific correspondence with his real child readers and facsimiles of the membership invitation and application forms for the real Lone Pine Club, see Mark O'Hanlon (2001). Information about Saville's readership is also documented in O'Hanlon (1996). Saville himself published a compilation of extracts from his correspondence with children in an article entitled 'What Children Write to Me' (*Books for Your Children*). For an in-depth memoir of one particular Saville fanatic, see Viv Turner (2010).

4 For a detailed account of nineteenth- and early twentieth-century discourses of child sexuality, see Shuttleworth (2010, pp. 207–20).

5 This chapter, along with James Kincaid, takes the perceived sexual innocence of children to be an adult projection predicated on a discursive binary wherein 'the child is that species which is free of sexual feeling or response' and 'the adult is that species which has crossed over into sexuality' (1994, pp. 6–7). For an interesting challenge of Kincaid's analysis, see Gubar (2009).

6 Victor Watson suggests that Saville shared with Enid Blyton 'the same fundamental aesthetic . . . based on [the] assumptions . . . that children's fiction should be direct and open in structure and style; that readers' imaginations could be quickened by clarity of description; and that fictional richness could be made available in the explicitly literal' (2000, p. 112). Perry Nodelman in *The Hidden Adult* extensively debates children's literature's purported 'simplicity of style and focus on action' (2008, p. 8).

7 I use the descriptor 'child' here not in a fixed binary way to designate that which is supposedly non-adult, but, following Peggy Whalen-Levitt, to designate that which 'a given text calls upon [its] reader to know and to do: to know, in terms of experience of both life and literature; to do, in terms of producing a meaning for this particular text, in time, from start to finish' (1983, p. 159).

8 That Jon and Penny are cousins did not appear to concern Saville until later in the series, when, according to Viv Turner, he began to worry about the wisdom of pairing them off in marriage. He wrote in a letter to Viv Turner, 'I've got myself into rather a mess with J and P because they are cousins and "are not supposed to marry"' (2010, p. 113).

9 For a sustained exploration of the relationship between the erotic and the forbidden (the taboo), see Bataille (1986). For an argument about the reliance of the erotic on 'invention, constant variation,' see Paz (1995, p. 8).

10 See, for example, Flugel (1930).

11 This is based on the Lacanian principle that 'desire is neither the appetite for satisfaction nor the demand for love, but the difference that results from the subtraction of the first from the second' (Lacan, 1977, p. 287).

12 Another manifestation of the romance genre which recurs repeatedly in the series is that of the rescue plot. The boys rescue their respective girls in several stories; see, for example, *Mystery Mine* and *Where's My Girl?* The plot is also reversed, with the girls rescuing the boys, in more than one novel; see, for example, *The Secret of Grey Walls* and *Man with Three Fingers*.

Works Cited

Abbott, E. H. (1908), *On the Training of Parents*. London: Pilgrim Press.

Addison, J. (1711), 'Laughter', *Spectator*, 249, 15 December.

Adorno, T. W. (1986), *Aesthetic Theory*. Trans. Lenhardt. London: Routledge & Kegan Paul.

Alpers, P. (1996), *What Is Pastoral?* Chicago, IL: University of Chicago Press.

Anderson, D. A. (2003), *The Annotated Hobbit*. Rev. edn. London: HarperCollins.

Anderson, S. (2007), 'Time, Subjectivity, and Modernism in E. Nesbit's Children's Fiction'. *Children's Literature Association Quarterly*, 32:4 (Winter), pp. 308–22.

Anon (1709), *A Guide for the Child and Youth*. In two parts. London: M. and J. Roberts.

Anon (1716), *Advice to a Son, Directing Him How to Demean Himself in the Most Important Passages of Life*. 4th edn. London.

Anon (1762), *The Art of Poetry on a New Plan, Illustrated with a Great Variety of Examples from the Best English Poets; and of Translations from the Ancients: Together with Such Reflections and Critical Remarks as May Tend to Form in Our Youth an Elegant Taste, and Render the Study of this Part of the Belles Lettres More Rational and Pleasing*. 2 vols. London: John Newbery.

Anon (1766), *The History of Little Goody Two-Shoes*. London: J. Newbery.

Anon (1767), *Little Master's Miscellany. Consisting of Divine and Moral Essays. In Prose and Verse*. Birmingham: T. Warren.

Anon (1769), *An Essay on Laughter*. London: T. Davies.

Anon (1880), *The Mothers' Home-Book: A Book for Her own and Her Children's Management with Hints and Helps for Every-Day Emergencies*. London: Ward, Lock.

Anon (1965), *Mother Goose: Nursery Rhymes*. London: Oxford University Press.

Anon (n.d.), *The Polite Academy; or, School of Behaviour for Young Gentlemen and Ladies. Intended as a Foundation for Good Manners and Polite Address, in Masters and Misses*. 10th edn. London: Darton and Harvey, B. Crosby, and B. S. Collins.

Applebee, A. N. (1978), *The Child's Concept of Story: Ages Two to Seventeen*. Chicago, IL: University of Chicago Press.

Appleyard, J. A. (1991), *Becoming a Reader: The Experience of Fiction from Childhood to Adulthood*. Cambridge: Cambridge University Press.

Aristotle (1970). *Poetics*. Trans. Gerald F. Else. Ann Arbor: University of Michigan Press.

Aristotle (2002), *Nicomachean Ethics*. Trans. Christopher Rowe. Oxford: Oxford University Press.

Arizpe, E., and Styles, M. (2003), *Children Reading Picturebooks: Interpreting Visual Texts*. London: RoutledgeFalmer.

Arnold, M. (1960–77), *The Complete Prose Works of Matthew Arnold in Eleven Volumes*. Ed. R. H. Super. Ann Arbor: University of Michigan Press.

Attridge, D. (2004), *The Singularity of Literature*. London: Routledge.

Attridge, D. (2015), *The Work of Literature*. Oxford: Oxford University Press.

Austin, J. L. (1962), *How to Do Things with Words*. Oxford: Clarendon Press.

Avery, G. and Briggs, J. (eds) (1989), *Children and Their Books: A Celebration of Iona and Peter Opie*. Oxford: Clarendon Press.

Bacon, F. (1905), *Novum Organum*. London: Routledge.

Barbauld, A. L. (1781), *Hymns in Prose for Children. By the Author of Lessons for Children*. London: J. Johnson.

Barney, R. A. (1999), *Plots of Enlightenment: Education and the Novel in Eighteenth-Century England*. Stanford: Stanford University Press.

Barrie, J. M. (2009), *Peter Pan*. London: Vintage.

Barthes, R. (1977), *Image, Music, Text*. Ed. S. Heath. London: Fontana.

Bataille, G. (1986), *Erotism: Death and Sensuality*. Trans. M. Dalwood. San Francisco: City Lights Books.

Battestin, M. C. (1974), *The Providence of Wit: Aspects of Form in Augustan Literature and the Arts*. Oxford: Oxford University Press.

Beauvais, C. (2013), 'The Problem of Power: Metacritical Implications of Aetonormativity for Children's Literature Research'. *Children's Literature in Education*. 44:1, 74–86.

Beauvais, C. (2015), *The Mighty Child: Time and Power in Children's Literature*. Amsterdam: John Benjamins.

Beauvais, C., and Nikolajeva, M. (eds), (2017), *The Edinburgh Companion to Children's Literature*. Edinburgh: Edinburgh University Press.

Bell, M. (2007), *Open Secrets: Literature, Education, and Authority from J-J. Rousseau to J.M. Coetzee*. Oxford: Oxford University Press.

Benjamin, W. (2008), *The Work of Art in the Age of Mechanical Reproduction*. Trans. J. A. Underwood. London: Penguin.

Bennett, A. J. (2009), *Ignorance: Literature and Agnoiology*. Manchester: Manchester University Press.

Bernardin de Saint-Pierre, J-H. (1796), *Studies of Nature*. Vol. 4. London: Printed for C. Dilly.

Bettelheim, B. (1976), *The Uses of Enchantment*. New York: Alfred A. Knopf.

Birch, D. (2007), *Our Victorian Education*. Oxford: Blackwell.

Blake, N., Smeyers, P., Smith, R., and Standish, P. (eds) (2002), *Blackwell Guide to Philosophy of Education*. Boston: Blackwell.

Blake, W. (1979), *Blake's Poetry and Designs*, ed. M. L. Johnson and J. E. Grant. New York: W. W. Norton.

Blake, W. (1982), *The Complete Poetry and Prose of William Blake*, ed. D. V. Erdman. Rev. edn. Berkeley: University of California Press.

Blekinsop, A. (n.d.), *A Shilling'sWorth of Advice, on Manners, Behaviour and Dress; Shewing How "Gents" May Become Gentlemen; Young Ladies More Attractive; Servants Practically Refined; School-Boys Manly and Humane; Mr. Jones's Young Men Really Pokite; and Any One a "Gentleman", or "Gentlewoman": With a Word to Those Out of Their Teens; and a Few Hints to Papas and Mamas*. London: Printed for the author.

Bloch, E. (1995), *The Principle of Hope*. Trans. N. Plaice, S. Plaice and P. Knight. Cambridge, MA: MIT Press.

Blyton, E. (2017), *The Famous Five Collection*. London: Hodder Children's Books.

Boas, G. (1966), *The Cult of Childhood*. London: Warburg Institute.

Bode, K. (2017), 'The Equivalence of "Close" and "Distant" Reading; or, Toward a New Object for Data-Rich Literary History'. *Modern Language Quarterly*, 78:1, 77–106.

Boisvert, R. D. (1998), *John Dewey: Rethinking Our Time*. Albany: State University of New York Press.

Bonnett, M. (1994), *Children's Thinking: Promoting Understanding in the Primary School*. London: Cassell.

Booth, W. C. (1973), *The Rhetoric of Fiction*. 2nd edn. Chicago, IL: University of Chicago Press.

Bourdieu, P. (1986), 'The Forms of Capital', in *Handbook of Theory and Research for the Sociology of Education*, ed. J. G. Richardson. New York; London: Greenwood Press, pp. 46–58.

Boyte, H. C. (2003), 'A Different Kind of Politics: John Dewey and the Meaning of Citizenship in the 21st Century'. *The Good Society*, 12:2, 1–15.

Bratton, J. S. (1981), *The Impact of Victorian Children's Fiction*. London: Croom Helm.

Brent-Dyer, E. M. (1988), *The School at the Chalet*. London: Chambers.

Brewer, D. A. (2011–12), 'Counting, Resonance, and Form: A Speculative Manifesto (with Notes)'. *Eighteenth-Century Fiction*, 24:2, 161–70.

Briggs, J., Butts, D., and Grenby, M. (eds) (2008), *Popular Children's Literature in Britain*. Aldershot: Ashgate.

Brinkmann, K. (ed.) (2007), *German Idealism: Critical Concepts in Philosophy*, 4 vols. London: Routledge.

Buell, L. (1995), *The Environmental Imagination: Thoreau, Nature Writing and the Formation of American Culture*. Cambridge: Harvard University Press.

Bunyan, J. (1686), *A Book for Boys and Girls, or Country Rhymes for Children*. London: Printed for N. P.

Cadogan, M., and Craig, P. (1976), *You're a Brick, Angela! A New Look at Girls' Fiction from 1839 to 1975*. London: Victor Gollancz.

Cage, J. (1966), *Silence: Lectures and Writings*. Cambridge: Massachusetts Institute of Technology.

Cameron, L. L. (1820), *The Polite Little Children*. Wellington, Salop: F. Houlston.

Carpenter, H. (ed.) (1981), *Letters of J. R. R. Tolkien*. Boston, MA: Houghton Mifflin.

Carpenter, H. (1985), *Secret Gardens: A Study of the Golden Age of Children's Literature*. London: Unwin Hyman.

Carroll, L. (1981), *Alice's Adventures in Wonderland and Through the Looking Glass*. New York: Bantam.

Case, A., and Shaw, H. E. (2008), *Reading the Nineteenth-Century Novel: Austen to Eliot*. Oxford: Blackwell.

Chambers, A. (1978), 'The Reader in the Book: Notes from Work in Progress'. *Children's Literature Association Quarterly*, 1, 1–19.

Chavasse, P. H. (1886), *Advice to a Mother on the Management of Her Children and on the Treatment on the Moment of Some of Their More Pressing Illnesses and Accidents*. London: J&A Churchill.

Clapp-Itnyre, A. (2016), *British Hymn Books for Children, 1800–1900: Re-Tuning the History of Childhood*. Farnham: Ashgate.

Coats, K. (2004), *Looking Glasses and Neverlands: Lacan, Desire, and Subjectivity in Children's Literature*. Iowa City: University of Iowa Press.

Coats, K. (2017), *The Bloomsbury Introduction to Children's and Young Adult Literature*. London: Bloomsbury.

Coleridge, H. (1851), *Sonnets and Other Poems Referring to the Period of Childhood in Poems by Hartley Coleridge*, Vol. 2. London: Edward Moxon.

Coleridge, S. T. (1907), *Biographia Literaria*, ed. J. Shawcross, 2 vols. London: Oxford University Press.

Coleridge, S. T. (1957–73), *The Notebooks of Samuel Taylor Coleridge*, Vol. 3. Ed. K. C. London: Routledge & Kegan Paul.

Coltman, J. (1781), *Every Man's Monitor; or The Universal Counsellor, in Prose and Verse*. London: J. Buckland.

Cooper, A. A. (1711), *Characteristicks of Men, Manners, Opinions, Times*, 3 vols. London: John Darby.

Costello, P. R. (ed.) (2012), *Philosophy in Children's Literature*. Plymouth: Lexingham Books.

Cotton, J. (1646), *Milk for Babes, Drawn Out of the Breasts of Both Testaments*. London: Henry Overton.

Creasey, M. (2013), 'Does Violence Have a Place in Children's Literature?' *Oneota Reading Journal*. 2010. Web. 6 April 2013.

Darton, F. J. H., and Alderson, B. (1982), *Children's Books in England*. 3rd edn., rev. Cambridge: Cambridge University Press.

Davidson, H. C. (gen ed.) (1901), *The Book of the Home: A Practical Guide to Household Management*, 8 vols. London: Gresham.

Davidson, R. P. (1976), 'Modern Living: Ozmosis in Central Park', *Time Magazine*, 4 October, 72.

De Bolla, P. (2003), *Art Matters*: Harvard: Harvard University Press.

De Man, P. (1982), 'The Resistance to Theory'. *Yale French Studies* (63): 3–20.

De Quincey, T. (1863), *The Works of Thomas de Quincey, Vol. IX, Autobiographical Sketches 1790–1803*. Edinburgh: Adam and Charles Black.

Demers, P. (ed.) (1983), *A Garland from the Golden Age: An Anthology of Children's Literature from 1850–1900*. Toronto: Oxford University Press.

Demers, P. (ed.) (2015), *From Instruction to Delight: An Anthology of Children's Literature to 1850*. Don Mills, Ontario: Oxford University Press.

Denison, W. (1871), *Advice to Children*. London: William Hunt.

Dennis, J. (1701), *The Advancement and Reformation of Modern Poetry. A Critical Discourse. In Two Parts*. London: Richard Parker.

Derrida, J. (1992), *Acts of Literature*. Ed. Derek Attridge. London: Routledge.

Dewey, J. (1910), *How We Think*. London: D. S. Heath.

Dewey, J. (1949), *Knowing and the Known*. Boston, Mass.: Beacon Press.

Dewey, J. (1985), *Democracy and Education, 1916: The Middle Works of John Dewey 1899–1924*, Vol. 9, ed. J. A. Boydston. Carbondale and Edwardsville: Southern Illionois University Press.

Dewey, J. (1981–90), *John Dewey: The Later Works: 1925–1953*, ed. J. A. Boydson, 17 vols. Carbondale and Edwardsville: Southern Illinois University Press.

Dewey, J. (1990), *The School and Society and the Child and the Curriculum*. Chicago, IL: University of Chicago Press.

Dewey, J. (1998), *Experience and Education*: West Lafayette, Ind.: Kappa Delta Pi.

Dewey, J. (2005), *Art as Experience*. London: Penguin.

Dryden, J. (1939), *Of Dramatic Poetry and Other Essays*. London: J. M. Dent.

Dryden, J. (1975), *All for Love*, ed. N. J. Andrew. London: Ernest Benn.

Dusinberre, J. (1999), *Alice to the Lighthouse: Children's Books and Radical Experiments in Art*. Houndmills, Basingstoke: Palgrave Macmillan.

E. C. (1874), *Our Children, How to Rear and Train Them: A Manual for Parents, in the Physical, Educational, Religious, and Moral Training of their Children*. London: Cassell, Petter, & Galpin.

Edgeworth, M., and Edgeworth, R. L. (1798), *Practical Education*. 2 vols. London: J. Johnson.

Edgeworth, M. (1800), *The Parent's Assistant; or, Stories for Children*. London: J. Johnson.

Eisenberg, N. (2000), 'Empathy and Sympathy'. *Handbook of Emotions*. 2nd edn, ed. M. Lewis and J. M. Haviland-Jones. New York: Guildford Press, pp. 677–91.

Eliot, T. S. (1951), *Selected Essays 1917–1932*. 3rd edn. London: Faber and Faber.

Empson, W. (1935), *Some Versions of Pastoral*. London: Chatto and Windus.

Empson, W. (1991), *Seven Types of Ambiguity*. 3rd edn. London: Hogarth.

Ettinger, B. (2006), 'Matrixial Trans-subjectivity', in *Theory, Culture & Society*, 23:2–3 (May), 218–22.

Everard, G. (1886), *Human Tears and Their Antidote*. London: S. W. Partridge.

Ewing, A. C. (1934), *Idealism: A Critical Survey*. London: Methuen.

Feaver, W. (1977), *When We Were Young*. New York: Holt, Rinehart and Winston.

Fenichel, O. (1854), 'On the Psychology of Boredom', in *Collected Papers, First Series*, ed. H. Fenichel and D. Rapaport. London: Routledge & Kegan Paul.

Fenn, E. (n.d.), *Rational Sports. In Dialogues Passing among the Children of a Family*. London: John Marshall.

Fenn, E. (n.d.), *School Occurrences: Supposed to Have Arisen among a Set of Young Ladies, under the Tuition of Mrs. Teachwell. And to Be Recorded by One of them*. 3rd edn. London: John Marshall.

Ferguson, F. (2003), 'The Afterlife of the Romantic Child: Rousseau and Kant Meet Deleuze and Guattari'. *South Atlantic Quarterly*, 102:1, 215–34.

Flieger, V. (1983), *Splintered Light: Logos and Language in Tolkien's World*. Grand Rapids: Eerdmans.

Flugel, J. C. (1930), *The Psychology of Clothes*. London: Hogarth Press.

Foucault, M. (1991), *The Foucault Reader*, ed. P. Rabinow. London: Penguin.

Fox, M. (2013), 'Obituary to Seamus Heaney'. *New York Times*, 30 August 2013.

Freire, P. (1973), *Education for Critical Consciousness*. New York: Seabury Press.

Freud, S. (2001), *The Standard Edition of the Complete Psychological Works. Vol. 7: A Case of Hysteria, Three Essays on Sexuality; and Other Works*, ed. J. Strachey. London: Hogarth Press.

Froebel, F. (2001), *The Education of Man*. London: Routledge.

Fromm, E. (1963), *The Dogma of Christ and Other Essays on Religion, Psychology and Culture*. London: Routledge & Kegan Paul.

Ganev, R. (2009), *Songs of Protest, Songs of Love: Popular Ballads in Eighteenth-Century Britain*. Manchester: Manchester University Press.

Genette, G. (1980), *Narrative Discourse: An Essay in Method*. Trans. J. E. Lewin. Ithaca: Cornell University Press.

Genette, G. (1997), *Paratexts: Thresholds of Interpretation*. Trans. J. E. Lewin. Cambridge: Cambridge University Press.

Giddens, E. (2017), 'Children's Literature and Distant Reading', in *The Edinburgh Companion to Children's Literature*, ed. C. Beauvais and M. Nikolajeva. Edinburgh: Edinburgh University Press.

Gifford, T. (1999), *Pastoral*. London: Routledge.

Gilead, S. (1988), 'The Undoing of Idyll in, in *The Wind in the Willows*'. *Children's Literature*, Vol. 16: 145–58.

Glaisyer, N., and Pennell, S. (2003), *Didactic Literature in England, 1500–1800: Expertise Constructed*. Aldershot: Ashgate.

Glevey, K. E. (2006), *Thinking and Education*. Leicester: Troubador.

Gorham, D. (1982), *The Victorian Girl and the Feminine Ideal*. London: Croom Helm.

Gould, F. J. (1899), *The Children's Book of Moral Lessons. First Series: 'Self-Control' and 'Truthfulness'*. London: Watts.

Graham, K. V. (1998), 'Of School and the River: *The Wind in the Willows* and its Immediate Audience'. *Children's Literature Association Quarterly*, 23:4 (Winter), 181–6.

Grahame, K. (1979), *Dream Days*. London: Bodley Head.

Grahame, K. (1995), *The Golden Age*. Herfordshire: Wordsworth Editions.

Grahame, K. (1961), *The Wind in the Willows*. London: Methuen & Co.

Green, P. (1959), *Kenneth Grahame, 1859–1932: A Study of His Life, Work, and Times*. London: John Murray.

Green, R. L. (1962), 'The Golden Age of Children's Books', *Essays and Studies* n.s. XV, pp. 59–73.

Gregory, R., and Kohlmann, B. (2012), *Utopian Spaces of Modernism: British Literature and Culture, 1885–1945*. Houndmills: Basingstoke.

Grenby, M. O. (2008), *Children's Literature*. Edinburgh: Edinburgh University Press.

Grenby, M. O. (2011), *The Child Reader: 1700–1840*. Cambridge: Cambridge University Press.

Griffin, M. J., and Moylan, T. (eds). (2007), *Exploring the Utopian Impulse*. Oxford: Peter Lang.

Griswold, J. (2006), *Feeling Like a Kid: Childhood and Children's Literature*. Baltimore, MD: Johns Hopkins University Press.

Gubar, M. (2001), 'Partners in Crime: E. Nesbit and the Art of Thieving'. *Style*, 35:3 (Fall), 410–29.

Gubar, M. (2009), *Artful Dodgers: Reconceiving the Golden Age of Children's Literature*. Oxford: Oxford University Press.

Gubar, M. (2011), 'On Not Defining Children's Literature'. *PMLA*, 126:1 (January), 209–16.

Hammond, W. G., and Scull, C. (2011), *The Art of the Hobbit by J. R.R. Tolkien*. London: HarperCollins.

Hardie, M. (1906), *English Coloured Books*. London: Methuen.

Hartley, D. (1749), *Observations on Man, His Frame, His Duty, and His Expectations. In Two Parts*. London: S. Richardson.

Healy, S. (1984), *Boredom, Self, and Culture*. Rutherford: Fairleigh Dickinson University Press.

Heidegger, M. (1995), *Fundamental Concepts of Metaphysics: World, Finitude, Solitude*. Trans. W.C. Neill and N. Walker. Bloomington: Indiana University Press.

Herder, J. G. (2002), *Philosophical Writings*. Trans. and ed. M. N. Forster. Cambridge: Cambridge University Press.

Higonnet, A. (1998), *Pictures of Innocence: The History and Crisis of Ideal Childhood*. London: Thames and Hudson.

Hiley, M. (2004), 'Stolen Language, Cosmic Models: Myth and Mythology in Tolkien'. *Modern Fiction Studies*, 50:4, 838–60.

Hobbes, T. (1839), *The English Works of Thomas Hobbes of Malmesbury*, Vol. IV, ed. Sir William Molesworth. London: John Bohn.

Hobbes, T. (1997). *Leviathan*, ed. R. E. Flatman and D. Johnston. New York: W. W. Norton.

Hodgson Burnett, F. (1991), *The Secret Garden*. London: Heinemann.

Holland, N. N. (1985), 'Reading Readers Reading', in *Researching Response to Literature and the Teaching of Literature: Points of Departure*, ed. C. R. Cooper. Norwood, NJ: Ablex.

Hollindale, P. (1988), *Ideology and the Children's Book*. Stroud: Thimble Press.

Hollindale, P. (1997), *Signs of Childness in Children's Books*. Stroud: Thimble Press.

Home, H. (1781), *Loose Hints Upon Education, Chiefly Concerning the Culture of the Heart*. Edinburgh: John Bell.

hooks, b. (2010), *Teaching Critical Thinking: Practical Wisdom*. New York: Routledge.

How, F. (1907), *The Book of the Child: An Attempt to Set Down What Is in the Mind of Children*. Bath: Sir Isaac Pitman.

Hunt, P. (1988), 'Degrees of Control: Stylistics and the Discourse of Children's Literature', in *Styles of Discourse*, ed. N. Coupland. London: Croom Helm, pp. 163–82.

Hunt, P. (1994a), *An Introduction to Children's Literature*. Oxford: Oxford University Press.

Hunt, P. (1994b), *The Wind in the Willows: A Fragmented Arcadia*. New York: Twayne.

Hunt, P. (ed.) (1990), *Children's Literature: The Development of Criticism*. London: Routledge.

Hunt, P. (ed.) (1999), *Understanding Children's Literature*. London: Routledge.

Hutcheson, F. (1750), *Reflections upon Laughter: And Remarks upon the Fable of the Bees*. Glasgow: Printed by R. Urie, for D. Baxter.

Huysmans, J-K. (2003), *Against Nature*. Trans. Robert Baldick. Harmondsworth: Penguin Classics.

Immel, A. (2009), 'The Didacticism That Laughs: John Newbery's Entertaining Little Books and William Hogarth's Pictured Morals'. *Lion and the Unicorn*, 33:2, 146–66.

Immel, A., and Witmore, M. (eds) (2006), *Childhood and Children's Books in Early Modern Europe, 1550–1800*. New York: Routledge.

Inglis, F. (1981), *The Promise of Happiness: Value and Meaning in Children's Fiction*. Cambridge: Cambridge University Press.

Iser, W. (1974), *The Implied Reader: Patterns of Communication in Prose Fiction from Bunyan to Beckett*. Baltimore, MD: Johns Hopkins University Press.

Iser, W. (1978), *The Act of Reading: A Theory of Aesthetic Response*. Baltimore, MD: Johns Hopkins University Press.

Jackson, P. W. (2002), *John Dewey and the Philosopher's Task*. New York; London: Teachers College Press.

James, H. (1981), *The Portrait of a Lady*. Oxford: Oxford University Press.

James, H. (1972), *Theory of Fiction: Henry James*, ed. James E. Miller Jr. Nebraska: University of Nebraska Press.

Janeway, J. (1676), *A Token for Children: Being an Exact Account of the Conversion, Holy and Exemplary Lives and Joyful Deaths of Several Young Children*. London: Dorman Newman.

Johnston, J. S. (2006), *Inquiry and Education: John Dewey and the Quest for Democracy*. Albany, NY: SUNY Press.

Johnston, J. S. (2008), *Deweyan Inquiry: From Education Theory to Practice*. Albany, NY: SUNY Press.

Joy, L. (2012). '"Snivelling like a kid": Edith Nesbit and the child's tears', in *Towards a Lachrymology: Tears in Literature & Cultural History*, ed. Tim Webb, *Litteraria Pragenzia: Studies in Literature and Culture*, 22:43, 128–143.

Joyce, J. (1960), *A Portrait of the Artist as a Young Man*. Harmondsworth: Penguin.

Joyce, J. (1937), *Ulysses*. London: Bodley Head.

Kant, I. (1956), *Critique of Pure Reason*. Trans. L. W. Beck. Indianapolis: Bobbs-Merril.

Keats, J. (1990), *A Critical Edition of the Major Works*, ed. E. Cook. Oxford: Oxford University Press.

Key, E. (1909), *The Century of the Child*. New York: G. P. Putnam's.

Kidd, K. (2011), *Freud in Oz: At the Intersections of Psychoanalysis and Children's Literature*. Minneapolis: University of Minnesota Press.

Kierkegaard, S. (1987), *Either-Or, Part I*. Trans. H. V. Hong and E. H. Hong. Princeton, NJ: Princeton University Press.

Kilner, M. A. (1790), *The Adventures of a Pincushion: Designed Chiefly for the Use of Young Ladies: in Two Volumes*. London.

Kincaid, J. (1994), *Child-Loving: The Erotic Child and Victorian Literature*. 2nd edn. London: Routledge.

Kincheloe, J. L. (2004), *Critical Pedagogy*. Oxford: Peter Lang.

Kirk, E. D. (1971), 'I Would Rather Have Written in Elvish': Language, Fiction and *The Lord of the Rings*'. *NOVEL: A Forum on Fiction*, 5:1, 5–18.

Klein, L. (1994), *Shaftesbury and the Culture of Politeness: Moral Discourse and Cultural Politics in Early Eighteenth-Century England*. Cambridge: Cambridge University Press.

Knoepflmacher, U. C. (1998), *Ventures into Childland: Victorians, Fairy Tales, and Femininity*. Chicago, IL: University of Chicago Press.

Knoepflmacher, U. C. (2010), 'Oscar Wilde at Toad Hall: Kenneth Grahame's Drainings and Draggings'. *The Lion and the Unicorn*, 34:1 (January), 1–16.

Knowles, M., and Malmkjaer, K. (1996), *Language and Control in Children's Literature*. London: Routledge.

Kolb, D. A. (1984), *Experiential Learning: Experience as the Source of Learning and Development*. Englewood Cliffs, NJ: Prentice Hall.

Krupp, A. (2009), *Reason's Children: Childhood in Early Modern Philosophy*. Lewisburg: Bucknell University Press.

Lacan, J. (1977), *Ecrits: A Selection*. Trans. Alan Sheridan. London: Tavistock.

Lakoff, R. (1973), 'The Logic of Politeness; Or, Minding Your p's and q's', in *Papers from the Ninth Regional Meeting of the Chicago Linguistic Society*. Chicago, IL: University of Chicago Press, pp. 292–305.

Langley, E. (n.d.), *The Path to Pleasure for Good and Dutiful Children*. [No pub details.]

Lawrence, D. H. (1932), *Lady Chatterley's Lover*. London: William Heinemann.

Le Guin, U. (1992), *The Language of the Night*. New York: HarperCollins.

Leavis, F. R. (1962), *The Great Tradition: George Eliot, Henry James, Joseph Conrad. Harmondsworth*, Middlesex: Penguin Books in association with Chatto and Windus.

Lerer, S. (2008), *Children's Literature: A Reader's History, From Aesop to Harry Potter*. Chicago, IL: University of Chicago Press.

Lerer, S. (2009), 'Style and the Mole: Domestic Aesthetics in *The Wind in the Willows*'. *Journal of Aesthetic Education*, 43:2 (Summer), 51–63.

Lesnik-Obserstein, K. (1994), *Children's Literature: Criticism and the Fictional Child*. Oxford: Clarendon Press.

Lewis, C. S. (1960), *The Four Loves*. New York: Harcourt, Brace.

Lipman, M. (2003), *Thinking in Education*. Cambridge: Cambridge University Press.

Livingstone, M. (2012), 'The Myths of the Author: Tolkien and the Medieval Origins of the Word Hobbit'. *Mythlore: A Journal of J. R. R. Tolkien, C.S. Lewis, Charles Williams, and the Genres of Myth and Fantasy Studies*, 30:117/118, 129–46.

Lochhead, M. (1977), *The Renaissance of Wonder in Children's Literature*. Edinburgh: Canongate.

Locke, J. (2007), *Some Thoughts Concerning Education*, ed. J. W. Adamson. Mineola, NY: Dover.

Lodge, O. (1910), *Parent and Child: A Treatise on the Moral and Religious Education of Children*. New York: Funk and Wagnalls.

Lundin, A. (1993), '*Under the Window* and *Afternoon Tea:* "Twirling the Same Blade of Grass"'. *The Lion and the Unicorn*, 17:1, 45–56.

Lundin, A. (2004), *Beyond Library Walls and Ivory Towers: Constructing the Canon of Children's Literature*. New York: Routledge.

Lutz, T. (1999), *Crying: The Natural and Cultural History of Tears*. New York: W. W. Norton.

Macaulay, C. G. (1798), *Letters on Education. With observations on religious and metaphysical subjects*. London: Printed for C. Dilly.

Mahaffy, J. P. (1888). *The Principles of the Art of Conversation*. New York: J. P. Putnam.

Malinowski, B. (1923), 'The Problem of Meaning in Primitive Languages', in *The Meaning of Meaning: A Study of the Influence of Language upon Thought and of the Science of Symbolism*. London: Kegan Paul, Trench, Trübner.

Masefield, J. (2008), *The Box of Delights*. London: Egmont.

Matthews, G. B. (1980), *Philosophy and the Young Child*. Cambridge, MA: Harvard University Press.

Mauss, M. (1954), *The Gift: Forms and Functions of Exchange in Archaic Societies*. Trans. I. Cunnison. London: Cohen & West.

May, J. (1995), *Children's Literature and Critical Theory: Reading and Writing for Understanding.* New York: Oxford University Press.

Mayfield, J. S., (ed.) (1944), *A Letter by Algernon Charles Swinburne on Learning that Kate Greenaway had Died.* [No publication details.]

McComas, A. (1993), 'Negating and Affirming Spirit through Language: The Integration of Character, Magic, and Story in *The Lord of the Rings*'. *Mythlore: A Journal of J. R. R. Tolkien, C. S. Lewis, Charles Williams, and the Genres of Myth and Fantasy Studies*, 19:2/72, 4–14.

McCormick, D. (1992), *Erotic Literature: A Connoisseur's Guide.* New York: Continuum.

McGann, J. (2004), 'A Note on the Current State of Humanities Scholarship'. *Critical Inquiry* 30:2 (Winter), 409–13.

McGavran, J. H. (1999), *Literature and the Child: Romantic Continuations, Postmodern Contestations.* Iowa City: University of Iowa Press.

McGavran, J. H. (ed.) (1991), *Romanticism and Children's Literature in Nineteenth-Century England.* Athens: University of Georgia Press.

McGillis, R. (1984–5), 'Utopian Hopes: Criticism Beyond Itself'. *Children's Literature Association Quarterly*, 9:4 (Winter), 184–6.

McGillis, R. (ed.) (2003), *Children's Literature and the Fin de Siècle.* London: Praeger.

Margaret, M. (1988), *How Texts Teach What Readers Learn.* Stroud: Thimble Press.

Maybin, J., and Watson, M. (2009), *Children's Literature: Approaches and Territories.* Basingstoke: Palgrave Macmillan.

Menaker, D. (2010), *A Good Talk: The Story and Skill of Conversation.* New York: Hachette.

Michals, T. (2014), *Books for Children, Books for Adults: Age and the Novel from Defoe to James.* Cambridge: Cambridge University Press.

Mill, J. S. (1973), *A System of Logic, Ratiocinative and Inductive*, ed. J. M. Robson. Toronto: University of Toronto Press; London: Routledge & Kegan Paul.

Miller, J. R. (1888), *The Perfect Home.* London: Swan Sonnenschein, Lowrey.

Miller, S. (2006), *Conversation: A History of a Declining Art.* New Haven: Yale University Press.

Milton, J. (1966), *Milton's Sonnets*, ed. E. A. G. Honigmann. London: Macmillan.

Moimann, C. (2005), '"Poke Your Finger into the Soft Round Dough": The Absent Father and Political Reform in Edith Nesbit's *The Railway Children*'. *Children's Literature Association Quarterly*, 30:4 (Winter), 368–86.

Montagu, B. (1830), *Thoughts on Laughter by a Chancery Barrister.* London: W. Pickering.

Montessori, M. (1989), *Education for a New World.* Oxford: Clio Press.

Moretti, F. (2013), *Distant Reading.* London: Verso.

Mulvey, L. (1988), 'Visual Pleasure and Narrative Cinema', in *Feminism and Film Theory*, ed. C. Penley. New York: Routledge.

Myers, B. (1909), *The Care of Children from Babyhood to Adolescence for the Use of Mothers and Nurses*. London: Henry Kimpton.

Myers, M. (1987), 'Wise Child, Wise Peason: Geoffrey Summerfield's Case Against the Eighteenth Century'. *Children's Literature Association Quarterly*, 12, 108–9.

Natov, R. (2003), *The Poetics of Childhood*. London: Routledge.

Nel, P., and Paul, L. (eds) (2011), *Keywords for Children's Literature*. New York: New York University Press.

Nesbit, E. (1960), *The Railway Children*. Harmondsworth: Penguin.

Nesbit, E. (1987), *Long Ago When I Was Young*. London: Beehive.

Nesbit, E. (1994), *The Story of the Treasure Seekers*. London: Penguin.

Nesbit, E. (2008), *Wings and the Child, or the Building of Magic Cities*. London: Hodder and Stoughton.

Nesbit, E. (2014), *Five Children and It*. London: Scholastic.

Newbery, J. (1776), *Poetry Made Familiar and Easy*. Vol. 4, *The Circle of the Sciences*. 4th edn. London: T. Carnan and F. Newbery.

Newbery, J. (1966), *A Little Pretty Pocket-Book*. Introduction by M. F. Thwaite. London: Oxford University Press.

Newell, P. (ed.) (1972), *A Last Resort? Corporal Punishment in Schools*. Penguin: London.

Nietzche, F. (1995), *Human, All Too Human*. Stanford, CA: Stanford University Press.

Nikolajeva, M. (2000), *From Mythic to Linear: Time in Children's Literature*. Lanham, MD: Scarecrow Press.

Nikolajeva, M. (2005), *Aesthetic Approaches to Children's Literature: An Introduction*. Oxford: Scarecrow Press.

Nikolajeva, M. (2009), 'Theory, Post-Theory, and Aetonormative Theory'. *Neohelicon* 36:1, 13–24.

Nikolajeva, M. (2010), *Power, Voice and Subjectivity in Literature for Young Readers*. New York: Routledge.

Nikolajeva, M. (2014), *Reading for Learning: Cognitive Approaches to Children's Literature*. Amsterdam/Philadelphia: John Benjamins.

Nikolajeva, M., and Scott, C. (2003), *How Picturebooks Work*. New York: Garland.

Noddings, N. (1995), *Philosophy of Education*. Boulder, CO: Westview.

Nodelman, P. (1980), 'Progressive Utopia, or How to Grow Up without Growing Up', in *Proceedings of the 6th Annual Converend of ChLA*, ed. P. A. Ord. Villanova: Villanova University Press, pp. 146–54.

Nodelman, P. (1988), *Words about Pictures: The Narrative Art of Children's Picture Books*. Athens, GA: University of Georgia Press.

Nodelman, P. (2008), *The Hidden Adult: Defining Children's Literature*. Baltimore, MD: Johns Hopkins University Press.

Nodelman, P. (ed.) (1988), *Touchstones: Reflections on the Best in Children's Literature*, 2 vols, ed. P. Nodelman. West Lafayette, IN: Children's Literature Association.

Nodelman, P., and Reimer, M. (2003), *The Pleasures of Children's Literature*. 3rd edn. Boston, MA: Allyn and Bacon.

Nokes, D. (1988), *Raillery and Rage: A Study of Eighteenth Century Satire*. Brighton: Harvester.

O'Hanlon, M. (1996), *The Complete Lone Pine: The 'Lone Pine' Books of Malcolm Saville*. Worcester: Mark O'Hanlon.

O'Hanlon, M. (2001), *Beyond the Lone Pine: A Biography of Malcolm Saville*. Worcester: Mark O'Hanlon.

O'Keefe, D. (2003), *Readers in Wonderland: The Liberating Worlds of Fantasy Fiction. From Dorothy to Harry Potter*. New York: Continuum.

O'Malley, A. (2003), *The Making of the Modern Child: Children's Literature and Childhood in the Late Eighteenth Century*. New York: Routledge.

O'Malley, A. (2012), *Children's Literature, Popular Culture and Robinson Crusoe*. Basingstoke: Palgrave Macmillan.

Osborne, S. G. (1865), 'Letter', *The Times*, 5 January.

Panton, J. E. (1896), *The Way They Should Go: Hints to Young Parents*. London: Downey.

Parkhurst, H. (1922). *Education on the Dalton Plan*. Introduction by T. P. Nunn. London: G. Bell.

Parvulescu, A. (2010), *Laughter: Notes on a Passion*. London: MIT Press.

Paz, O. (1995), *The Double Flame: Essays on Love and Eroticism*. Trans. Helen Lane. London: Harvill Press.

Peters, R. S. (1977), *John Dewey Reconsidered*. London: Routledge & Kegan Paul.

Pfister, M. (2002), *A History of English Laughter: Laughter from Beowulf to Beckett and Beyond*. Amsterdam: Rodopi.

Phillips, A. (1993), *On Kissing, Tickling and Being Bored: Psychoanalytic Essays on the Unexamined Life*. London: Faber and Faber.

Piaget, J. (1959), *The Language and Thought of the Child*, 3rd. edn. Trans. M. Gabain and R. Gabain. London: Routledge & Kegan Paul.

Pippin, R. B. (1997), *Idealism as Modernism: Hegelian Variations*. Cambridge: Cambridge University Press.

Plotz, J. (2001), *Romanticism and the Vocation of Childhood*. New York: Palgrave.

Pope, A. (1720), *Miscellaneous Poems and Translations by Several Hands*. Vol. 1. 3rd edn. London: Bernard Lintot.

Pope, A. (1978), *Pope: Poetical Works*, ed. H. Davis. Introduction by P. Rogers. Oxford: Oxford University Press.

Popp, J. A. (1998), *Naturalizing Philosophy of Education: John Dewey in the Postanalytic Period*. Carbondale, IL: Southern Illinois University Press.

Poss, G. D. (1975), 'An Epic in Arcadia: The Pastoral World of *The Wind in the Willows*'. *Children's Literature*, 4, 80–90.

Postman, N. (1982), *The Disappearance of Childhood*. London: W. H. Allen.

Proust, M. (2006), *Remembrance of Things Past*. Trans. C. K. Scott-Moncrieff. Ware, Herts: Wordsworth Editions.

Pullinger, D. (2017), *From Tongue to Text: A New Reading of Children's Poetry*. London: Bloomsbury Academic.

Ransome, A. (1909), 'Betwixt and Between', *Bookman* (UK) January: 190–1.

Ransome, A. (2014), *Swallows and Amazons*. London: Red Fox.

Reimer, M. (2010), 'Readers: Characterized, Implied, Actual', in *Jeunesse: Young People, Texts, Cultures*, 2:2, 1–12.

Reynolds, K. (1994), *Children's Literature in the 1890s and the 1990s*. Plymouth: Northcote House.

Reynolds, K. (2007), *Radical Children's Literature: Future Visions and Aesthetic Transformations in Juvenile Fiction*. Basingstoke: Palgrave Macmillan.

Reynolds, K. (2011), *A Very Short Introduction to Children's Literature*. Oxford: Oxford University Press.

Richards, I. A. (2001), *Practical Criticism: A Study of Literary Judgement*, ed. J. Constable. London: Routledge.

Richardson, A. (1994), *Literature, Education, and Romanticism: Reading as Social Practice 1780–1832*. Cambridge: Cambridge University Press.

Robson, C. (2012), *Heart Beats: Everyday Life and the Memorized Poem*. Princeton, NJ: Princeton University Press.

Roffey, S, Tarrant, T., and Majors, K. (1994), *Young Friends: Schools and Friendship*. London: Cassell.

Ronell, A. (2012), *Loser Sons: Politics and Authority*. Champaign: University of Illinois Press.

Rorty, A. O. (ed.) (1998), *Philosophers on Education: New Historical Perspectives*. New York: Routledge.

Rose, J. (1984), *The Case of Peter Pan, or the Impossibility of Children's Fiction*. Philadelphia: University of Pennsylvania Press.

Rosen, M. (2000), *The Oxford Book of Children's Poetry*, ed M. Harrison and C. Stuart-Clark. Oxford: Oxford University Press.

Rosen, M. (2002), *No Breathing in Class*. Illus. K. Paul. London: Puffin Books.

Rosenberg-Orsini, J. G. (1785), *Moral and Sentimental Essays, on Miscellaneous Subjects*. 2 vols. Vol. 1. London: Printed for J. Robson.

Rosenblatt, L. M. (1978), *The Reader, the Text, the Poem: The Transactional Theory of the Literary Work*. Carbondale: Southern Illinois University Press.

Rossato, C. A., Allen, R. K., Pruyn, M. (eds) (2006), *Reinventing Critical Pedagogy: Widening the Circle of Anti-Oppression Education*. Plymouth: Rowman & Littlefield.

Rousseau, J-J. (1973), *The Social Contract and Discourses*. Trans. G. D. H. Cole. London: Dent.

Rousseau, J-J. (1991), *Emile, or, On Education*. Trans. A. Bloom. Harmondsworth: Penguin.

Rowland, A. W. (2012), *Romanticism and Childhood: The Infantilization of British Literary Culture*. Cambridge: Cambridge University Press.

Rudd, D. (2000), *Enid Blyton and the Mystery of Children's Literature*. Houndmills: Palgrave Macmillan.

Rudd, D. (2013), *Reading the Child in Children's Literature: An Heretical Approach*. Houndmills, Basingstoke: Palgrave Macmillan

Ruskin, J. (1884), *The Art of England*. Orpington: George Allen.

Russell, B. (1926), *On Education, Especially in Early Childhood*. London: George Allen & Unwin.

Russell, B. (1945), *A History of Western Philosophy*. New York: Simon and Schuster.

Ruwe, D. (2014), *British Children's Poetry in the Romantic Era: Verse, Riddle, and Rhyme*. Basingstoke: Palgrave Macmillan.

Ryle, J. C. (1859), *No More Crying: An Address to Children*. London: Wetheim, Macintosh, and Hunt.

Sainsbury, L. (2013), *Ethics in British Children's Literature: Unexamined Life*. London: Bloomsbury.

Sainsbury, L. (2017), '"But The Soldier's Remains Were Gone": Thought Experiments in Children's Literature'. *Children's Literature in Education*, 48:2 (June), 152–68.

Sales, R. (1983), *English Literature in History, 1780–1830: Pastoral and Politics*. New York: St Martin's Press.

Salzmann, C. G. (1799), *Elements of Morality, for the Use of Children; with an Introductory Address to Parents*. Vol. 1. Trans. M. Wollstonecraft, 4th edn. London: J. Johnson.

Saussure, F. (2013), *Course in General Linguistics*. Trans. R. Harris. London: Bloomsbury.

Saville, M. (1943), *Mystery at Witchend*. London: George Newnes.

Saville, M. (1944), *Seven White Gates*. London: George Newnes.

Saville, M. (1947), *The Secret of Grey Walls*. London: George Newnes.

Saville, M. (1949), *Lone Pine Five*. London: George Newnes.

Saville, M. (1953), *The Neglected Mountain*. London: George Newnes.

Saville, M. (1959), *Mystery Mine*. London: George Newnes.

Saville, M. (1962), *Not Scarlet but Gold*. London: George Newnes.

Saville, M. (1964), *Treasure at Amorys*. London: George Newnes.

Saville, M. (1966), *Man with Three Fingers*. London: George Newnes.

Saville, M. (1972), *Where's My Girl?* London: Armada.

Saville, M. (1973a), *Rye Royal*. London: Armada.

Saville, M. (1973b), 'What Children Write to Me.' *Books for Your Children*. October, 1973.

Saville, M. (1978), *Home to Witchend*. London: Armada.

Schiller, F. (1985), 'On Naïve and Sentimental Poetry', in *German Aesthetic and Literary Criticism: Winckelmann, Lessing, Hamann, Herder, Schiller, Goethe*, ed. H. B. Nisbet. Cambridge: Cambridge University Press.

Schneider, K. P. (1988), *Small Talk: Analysing Phatic Discourse*. Hitzeroth: Marburg.

Schopenhauer, A. (1976), *Essays and Aphorisms*. Trans. R. K. Hollingdale. Harmondsworth: Penguin.

Shakespeare, W. (1982), *Hamlet*. Ed. H. Jenkins. London: Arden Shakespeare.

Shakespeare, W. (1998). *Troilus and Cressida*. Ed. D. Bevington. London: Arden Shakespeare.

Shelley, P. B. (1977), *Shelley's Poetry and Prose*, ed. D. H. Reiman and S. B. Powers. New York: W. W. Norton.

Shelley, P. B. (2003), *The Major Works*, ed. Z. Leader and M. O'Neill. Oxford: Oxford University Press.

Shine Thompson, M., and Keenan, C. (eds) (2006), *Treasure Islands: Studies in Children's Literature*. Dublin: Four Courts Press.

Shippey, T. (1982), *The Road to Middle-Earth*. London: Allen and Unwin.

Shulman, L. S., and Keislar, E. R. (eds) (1966), *Learning by Discovery: A Critical Appraisal*. Chicago, IL: Rand McNally.

Shuttleworth, S. (2010), *The Mind of the Child. Child Development in Literature, Science, and Medicine, 1840–1900*. Oxford: Oxford University Press.

Sidney, P. (1973), *Miscellaneous Prose of Sir Philip Sidney*. Eds. K. Duncan-Jones, K. and van J. A. Dorsten Oxford: Clarendon Press.

Silver, A. K. (2000), '"A Caught Dream": John Ruskin, Kate Greenaway, and the Erotic Innocent Girl'. *Children's Literature Association Quarterly*, 25:1, 37–44.

Simpson, D. J., Jackson, M. J. B, and Aycock, J. C. (2005), *John Dewey and the Art of Teaching: Toward Reflective and Imaginative Practice*. Thousand Oaks, London: Sage.

Smart, C. (1771), *Hymns for the Amusement of Children*. London: T. Carnan.

Spacks, P. M. (1995), *Boredom: The Literary History of a State of Mind*. Chicago, IL: University of Chicago Press.

Spielmann, M. H., and Layard, G. S. (1905), *The Life and Work of Kate Greenaway*. London: Bracken Books.

Stals, J. L. (1995), 'Childhood, Path of Escape', *Utopias*, special issue *Public* 12. Trans. A. Benzaquén. Toronto: Public Access, pp. 74–82.

Stearns, F. P. (1896), *The Real and Ideal in Literature*. London: G. P. Putnam's Sons.

Stein, G. (1968), *Geography and Plays*. New York: Something Else Press.

Steiner, R. (1996), *The Education of the Child and Early Lectures on Education*. Hudson, NY: Anthroposophic Press.

Stephens, J. (1992), *Language and Ideology in Children's Fiction*. New York: Longman.

Stephens, J. (1999), 'Analysing Texts: Linguistics and Stylistics', in *Understanding Children's Literature*, ed. P. Hunt. London: Routledge, pp. 73–85.

Stibbs, A. (1991), *Reading Literature as Narrative: Signs of Life*. Milton Keynes: Open University Press.

Stuckart, D. W. (2012), 'Dewey and Citizenship Education'. *Theory & Research in Social Education*, 37:2, 284–92.

Studholme, J. (1777), *An Essay on Human Nature*. Carlisle: J. Harrison.

Styles, M. (1998), *From the Garden to the Street: An Introduction to 300 Years of Poetry for Children*. London: Cassell.

Styles, M., Whitley, D., and Joy, L. (2010), *Poetry and Childhood*. Stoke-on-Trent: Trentham Press.

Sullivan, C. W., III (1985), 'J. R. R. Tolkien's *The Hobbit*: The Magic of Words', in *Touchstones: Reflections on the Best in Children's Literature*, vol. 1, ed. P. Nodelman and J. May. West Lafayette: Children's Literature Association, pp. 253–61.

Summerfield, G. (1985), *Fantasy and Reason: Children's Literature in the Eighteenth Century*. Athens: University of Georgia Press.

Svendsen, L. (2005), *A Philosophy of Boredom*. London: Reaktion.

Swinburne, A. C. (1905). *The Poems of Algernon Charles Swinburne, in Six Volumes*. London: Chatto & Windus.

Taylor, I. (1991), *The Art of Kate Greenaway: A Nostalgic Portrait of Childhood*. Exeter: Webb and Bower.

Tennyson, A. (1971), *Complete Poems and Plays*. Oxford: Oxford University Press.

Thacker, D. C., and Webb, J. (2002), *Introducing Children's Literature: from Romanticism to Postmodernism*. London: Routledge.

Thiel, E. (2008), *The Fantasy of Family: Nineteenth-Century Children's Literature and the Myth of the Domestic Ideal.* New York: Routledge.

Thorn, I. (1888), *A Golden Age: A Story of Four Merry Children.* London: Blackie.

Tolkien, J. R. R. (1996), *The Hobbit.* London: HarperCollins.

Tolkien, J. R. R. (2014). *The Lord of the Rings.* London: HarperCollins.

Tompkins, J. (1985), *Sensational Designs: The Cultural Work of American Fiction, 1790-1860.* Oxford: Oxford University Press.

Toohey, P. (2011), *Boredom: A Lively History.* New Haven, CT: Yale University Press.

Townsend, J. R. (1967), *Written for Children: An Outline of English-Language Children's Literature.* Lanham: Scarecrow Press.

Townsend, J. R. (1994), *Trade and Plumb-Cake Forever, Huzza! The Life and Work of John Newbery, 1713–1767.* Cambridge: Colt Books.

Trapp, J. (1742). *Lectures on Poetry Read in the Schools of Natural Philosophy at Oxford.* London: C. Hitch and C. Davis.

Traugott, E., and Pratt, M. (1980), *Linguistics for Students of Literature.* New York: Harcourt Brace Jovanovich.

Triggs, P. (1980), 'Authorgraph No. 3 – Malcolm Saville', *Books for Keeps.* No. 3, July. Web. 6 September. 2011. http://booksforkeeps.co.uk/issue/3/childrens-books/articles/authorgraph/anthorgraph-no3-%E2%80%93-malcolm-saville.

Trimmer, S. (1786), *Fabulous Histories. Designed for the Instruction of Children, Respecting Their Treatment of Animals.* London: J. Johnson.

Trites, R. S. (2000), *Disturbing the Universe: Power and Repression in Adolescent Literature.* Iowa City: University of Iowa Press.

Trites, R. S. (2014), *Literary Conceptualizations of Growth: Metaphors and Cognition in Adolescent Literature.* Amsterdam: John Benjamins.

Tucker, N. (1981), *The Child and the Book: A Psychological and Literary Exploration.* Cambridge: Cambridge University Press.

Turner, V. (2010), *Malcolm Saville: A Friendship Remembered.* Somerset: Girls Gone By Publishers.

Urban, F. (1856), *The First Book of Manners: Or, Introduction to Polite Behaviour. For the Use of Private Families, and Schools.* London: Hamilton, Adams.

Uttley, A. (1977), *A Traveller in Time.* Harmondsworth: Puffin Books.

Wakely-Mulroney, K. (2016), 'Isaac Watts and the Dimensions of Child Interiority'. *Journal for Eighteenth-Century Studies,* 39:1, 103–19.

Wakely-Mulroney, K., and Joy, L. (eds) (2018), *The Aesthetics of Children's Poetry: A Study of Children's Verse in English.* London: Routledge.

Wall, B. (1991), *The Narrator's Voice: The Dilemma of Children's Fiction.* Basingstoke: MacMillan.

Wartenberg, T. E. (2013), *A Sneetch Is a Sneetch and Other Philosophical Discoveries: Finding Wisdom in Children's Literature*. Chichester: Wiley-Blackwell.

Watson, V. (2000), *Reading Series Fiction: From Arthur Ransome to Gene Kemp*. London: Routledge.

Watson, V. (2001), *The Cambridge Guide to Children's Books in English*. Cambridge: Cambridge University Press.

Watts, I. (1716), *Divine Songs Attempted in Easy Language for the Use of Children*. 2nd edn. London: Printed for M. Lawrence.

Watts, I. (1971), *Divine Songs Attempted in Easy Language for the Use of Children*. Introduction by J. H. P. Pafford. London: Oxford University Press.

Wesley, C. (1763), *Hymns for Children*. Bristol: E. Farley.

Whalen-Levitt, P. (1983), 'Pursuing "The Reader in the Book"', in *Children and Their Literature: A Readings Book*, ed. J. P. May. West Lafayette: ChLA, 154–9.

Whalley, J. I. (1974), *Cobwebs to Catch Flies: Illustrated Books for the Nursery and Schoolroom 1700–1900*. London: Elek.

Whalley, J. I., and Chester, T. R. (1988), *A History of Children's Book Illustration*. London: John Murray, with the Victoria and Albert Museum.

White, G. (1897–98), *Children's Books and Their Illustrators*. London: Studio.

Wicksteed, J. H. (1936), *The Challenge of Childhood: An Essay on Nature and Education*. London: Chapman & Hall.

Wilde, O. (1909), 'The Critic as Artist', in *Intentions*. 4th edn. London: Methuen.

Wilkinson, S. (2007), *Friends in the Fourth: Girls' School and College Friendships in Twentieth-Century British Fiction*. London: Bettany Press.

William, P. (1990), 'Language and Myth in the Fantasy Writings of J. R.R. Tolkien'. *Modern Age: A Quarterly Review*, 33:1, 42–52.

Williams, R. (1973), *The Country and the City*. Frogmore, St Albans: Granada.

Wimsatt, W. K., and Beardsley, M. C. (1954), *The Verbal Icon: Studies in the Meaning of Poetry*. Lexington: University of Kentucky Press.

Wollstonecraft, M. (1787), *Thoughts on the Education of Daughters with Reflections on Female Conduct*. London: J. Johnson.

Woolf, V. (1976), *Mrs Dalloway*. London: Grafton Books.

Wordsworth, W. (1974), *Poetical Works*, ed. T. Hutchinson and E. de Sélincourt. London: Oxford University Press.

Wright, M. (1936), *The Art of Conversation, and How to Apply Its Technique*. London: Whittlesey House.

Wullschlager, J. (1995), *Inventing Wonderland: The Lives and Fantasies of Lewis Carroll, Edward Lear, J. M. Barrie, Kenneth Grahame and A. A. Milne*. Michigan: University of Michigan Press.

Yeoman, A. (1998), *Now or Neverland: Peter Pan and the Myth of Eternal Youth*. Toronto: Inner City Books.

Zijderveld, A. C. (1979), *On Clichés: The Supersedure of Meaning by Function in Modernity*. London: Routledge & Kegan Paul.

Zimmer, M. (1995), 'Creating and Re-Creating Worlds with Words: The Religion and the Magic of Language in *The Lord of the Rings*'. *Seven: An Anglo-American Literary Review*, 12, 65–78.

Zipes, J. (2001), *Sticks and Stones: The Troublesome Success of Children's Literature from Slovenly Peter to Harry Potter*. New York: Routledge.

Zipes, J. (2003), *Utopian and Dystopian Writing for Children and Young Adults*, ed. C. Hintz and E. Ostry. New York: Routledge.

Zipes, J. (2009), *Relentless Progress: The Reconfiguration of Children's Literature, Fairy Tales, and Storytelling*. London: Routledge.

Index